MW00533280

LAGOS

TIM COCKS

Lagos
Supernatural City

*Tales of Survival, Spirituality and the
Struggle for Power in Africa's Biggest Metropolis*

HURST & COMPANY, LONDON

First published in the United Kingdom in 2022 by
C. Hurst & Co. (Publishers) Ltd.,
New Wing, Somerset House, Strand,
London, WC2R 1LA
© Tim Cocks 2022
All rights reserved.
Printed in Great Britain by Bell and Bain Ltd, Glasgow

The right of Tim Cocks to be identified as the author of
this publication is asserted by him in accordance with the
Copyright, Designs and Patents Act, 1988.

Distributed in the United States, Canada and Latin America by
Oxford University Press, 198 Madison Avenue, New York, NY 10016,
United States of America.

A Cataloguing-in-Publication data record for this book
is available from the British Library.

ISBN: 9781787386945

Soyinka epigraph: © Conversations with Wole Soyinka, edited by
Biodun Jeyifo (University Press of Mississippi, 2001). Reprinted by
permission of Melanie Jackson Agency, LLC and Wole Soyinka.

This book is printed using paper from registered sustainable
and managed sources.

www.hurstpublishers.com

For my parents

*Yoruba metaphysics holds the view of there being three major areas of existence
... It's the world of the unborn, the world of the dead, and the world of the
living ... But I believe there is also a fourth. It is not made obviously concrete
by the rituals, by the philosophy that is articulated by the Ifa priests. This is the
fourth area—the area of transition. It is the chthonic realm, the area of the
really dark forces, the really dark spirits, and it also is the area of stress of the
human will.*

Wole Soyinka, discussion at Washington University, 1973

*In proportion as any man's course of life is governed by accident, we always find
that he increases in superstition ... All human life ... being subject to fortuitous
accidents, it is natural that superstition should prevail everywhere ... and put
men on the most earnest inquiry concerning those invisible powers who dispose
of their happiness or misery.*

David Hume, *The Natural History of Religion*

Eko o gba gbere (Lagos does not tolerate any form of sloth).

Yoruba proverb

CONTENTS

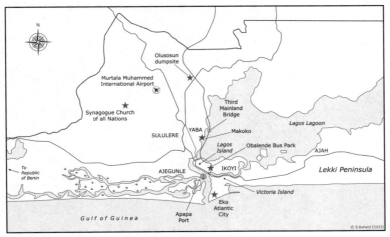

Lagos

PREFACE

I was the Reuters Nigeria bureau chief between the end of 2011 and 2015, and it was while I was living in Lagos that I met the characters featured in this book. I have since returned twice. The people in this book are all real and their stories are true.

This is not a book about my own experience of Lagos. When I do come into the story, it is only in a chapter at the end of each main character's story—usually because my interaction with them sheds so much light on this beguiling city that I couldn't resist putting it in. Besides that, I mostly let the extraordinary lives of Lagosians speak for themselves. If at times I appear to take the liberties of a Victorian novelist—the omniscient narrator knowing every intimate thought and whim of his characters—it is all based on detailed interviews stretching over months or years. I have tried as far as possible to corroborate everything I was told, checking it against reports from other witnesses or public, corporate and media archives, in the few cases where such things were available. Each main character was also shown a draft of relevant chapters prior to publication.

Some of the things the characters experience, like visions and dreams, they interpret in supernatural terms. It is obviously impossible for me to corroborate those. Like all mystical or religious feelings, they are personal. They are also, in my opinion, impossible to avoid in a book about Lagos. This is not—and let's be really clear about this—because Nigerians are somehow more given to religious or superstitious thinking than anyone else. The tendency to see conscious purpose beneath the chaos of life is deeply imbedded in the human psyche; you don't have to spend much time sifting through the plethora of conspiracy theories on the Internet to see that. Even supposedly 'scientific' ideologies, like the dogma of free-market economics that underpins the religion of capitalism, with its perfectly rational firms and consumers guided by an 'invisible hand', look more like articles of faith than science when you examine them closely. Yet nothing brings out faith in a transcendent realm like a crisis, and the crisis stalking Africa's biggest city has been a long time in the making. If, as the science writer Jared Diamond has suggested, religion and ritual help our species deal with anxiety in the face of danger and hardship, then no wonder the supernatural in Lagos is so all-embracing.

The people in this book mostly live on the extremes of Lagos, a city that has more of them than most (extremes and people). Predictably, that means there is violence. But I'd hate the reader to come away with the impression that Lagos is somehow an exceptionally violent place. Its homicide rate compares favourably with cities in the northern United States, and extremely well when set against the city in which I now live, Johannesburg. Armed robbery and kidnapping are everywhere, and local politicians (as you'll see) have an ugly habit of settling scores on the streets. But I doubt this is more so than in quite a number of 'developing' cities, and Lagos is safer than many. Despite its reputation for violent crime, most Lagosian criminals would rather use their brains to con money out of you (and they are very good at that) than resort to guns or knives. I also hope that the warmth and sense of humour I experienced from Lagosians comes through. In some ways, I have never lived as a foreigner in any place where I was made to feel so at home as in Lagos. I was welcomed as a fellow Lagosian, a badge I wore with pride.

There are two place names whose similarity is liable to cause confusion: Maroko, the slum that Lagos's military governor destroyed in the 1990s to make way for luxury apartments, is distinct from Makoko, the floating slum that is the focus of Part VI, which hasn't (yet) been demolished.

All of the main characters' names are real, with the exception of Kemi in Part VII. (Kemi is actually her middle name; she asked that I not use her first name for fear of retribution.) Occasionally, I refer to Yoruba words. In most cases, I've avoided using accents, unless leaving them out would be liable to cause confusion by signalling another word.

A word on population. No one knows how many people live in Lagos. Like so many other statistics in Nigeria, there is no reliable data on the country's population, especially in its main city, which swells with hundreds of new, undocumented arrivals every day. Estimates currently range between 15 and 25 million. I stuck with 20 million, which was a million under what the state government estimated it to be when I moved there a decade ago. If it was on the high side then, I doubt it still is after years of breakneck growth.

PROLOGUE

A PLACE OF ENDLESS IMPOSSIBILITY

A piece of gold that wants to shine must be passed through fire.

Yoruba proverb

The fundamental conundrum of Lagos is its continued existence in spite of a near-complete absence of those infrastructures, systems, organisations, and amenities that define the word 'city'. Lagos ... inverts every essential characteristic of the so-called modern city. Yet, it is still—for lack of a better word—a city; and one that works.

Rem Koolhaas, Harvard Project on the City

Awolowa Road, Ikoyi island, 2014

It all starts with a bump. A minibus that looks like it belongs in a scrapyard knocks into the rear of a shiny black Range Rover. It is mid-morning on Awolowo Road, an artery connecting two ends of leafy Ikoyi island beneath a cat's cradle of street wires that have long since stopped supplying regular power. The jeep driver gets out, taking care to park so he blocks both lanes of traffic. Through the car's lightly tinted windows it is clear the back seat is empty—anyone who can afford a car like this in Lagos has a chauffeur—which means this chauffer will have to explain that tiny dent to his oga (master) when he wheels back into his compound. On cue, he explodes into a rage fit to repel a charging rhino.

The minibus driver, whose eyes are bloodshot from lack of sleep or vitamins or both, spits out the toothpick he was chewing. Naturally, he blames the jeep driver for braking too quickly. He is backed by a conductor who, despite his urchin skinniness and torn shirt, radiates menace. Without warning, six or seven 'area boys'—Lagos gangs who make it their business to get involved in any scuffle that might end in money changing hands—join in. A chain reaction of furious shouting ignites, but everyone's words are drowned out by hooting from traffic behind. Chests are thumped, hands make angry gestures, overheated minibus passengers open windows. A man clutching a Bible gives up and grumpily exits the bus to complete his journey on foot. Anger builds.

Anger builds relentlessly in Lagos. For some, it starts with having to get up at 5 a.m. in an overcrowded 'face me, face you' apartment with no running water and too many squealing children. Then perhaps a two- or three-hour commute across Africa's most populous city, through foul-tempered traffic. Then back again, along potholed streets, to a home with no electricity other than from a generator rasping like half a dozen chainsaws—if it's working, that is. The landlord wants two years' rent up front and will change the locks if it's short by a month. The policeman at a checkpoint wants two days' wages up front for your violating a traffic law he just made up. Maddening obstacles will multiply; tempers will fray. Lagos turns you into a pressure cooker of frustration: 20 million pressure cookers waiting to erupt.

The traffic is now backed up all the way to Falomo roundabout, blocking the bridge over the Five Cowries Creek to the financial district of Victoria Island. A motorist attempts to

U-turn his vehicle by mounting the middle barrier, only to be stopped by a traffic cop with a glint in his eye. The pair erupt into their own squabble over the appropriate bribe, and the cop raises a whip to support his argument. Up ahead, more traffic has congealed next to a queue for a filling station—tell-tale sign of a fuel shortage. Pump attendants are trying to prevent more cars from squeezing in and making the jam even worse. A self-appointed traffic warden tries to instil order with cryptic hand signals (the real one is still demanding his bribe). All vehicles remain still, despite this furious commotion. Wind-borne rubbish drifts past stationary cars. And then I notice an old woman with ragged clothes and very few teeth walking past the scene. On the dirt sidewalk, she sets down a wicker basket with fishtails spiralling out of it and pauses to regard the mayhem. She turns to me, nodding in satisfaction and breathing out as she purses her winkled lips. It is one of those rare moments when it's better to be a pedestrian.

'This is Lagos,' she says, breaking into a gap-toothed grin. 'This is Lagos-o.'

* * *

Some weeks later, a wooden shack selling bootleg CDs in Ikeja is blasting out music by the late King of Afrobeat, Fela Kuti. Ikeja lies on the Lagos mainland, where most of the city's inhabitants live. The district was the birthplace of Fela's hip-shaking and strangely hypnotic Afro-jazz fusion. The song playing is called 'Go Slow', Nigerian slang for a traffic jam, almost as if it were a taunt to the cars and rickshaws crawling by in the liquefying heat. A street kid caked in red dust chuckles as he rotates his pelvis to the tune.

In the song, Fela coined a word for the hardships that people in Lagos put up with every day: 'impossibility-ism'. He meant it to refer to all the city's frustrations: the traffic, the endless noise, ubiquitous power cuts, fuel shortages, extortion at police road-blocks, the street gangs who mug you for unofficial fees, thieving landlords, armed robbery, kidnapping, widespread fraud ... The list goes on. This book is about all of these things; it is also about how faith enables Lagosians to cope with them.

Welcome to Lagos, the creaking engine of Nigeria, a raucous and utterly exhausting West African country of probably 200 million people (according to the latest best estimates, although no one knows for sure), about a sixth of the population of the continent. The largest of Africa's three megacities is a turbocharged microcosm of this beguiling country: overpopulated, rambunctious, split down the middle between Muslims and Christians; blighted by corruption, dysfunction and sporadic violence; yet redeemed by that charm, humour and friendliness, that strange magic, which make it so irresistible to those of us who've lived in it and loved it.

I wanted to capture the spirit of a haunted city—a city built and broken by centuries of slavery and colonialism, a recent past of oil-fuelled corruption and waste, a perhaps more optimistic present as Lagos finds its heyday, but a future overshadowed by some quite brutal demographics. All cities are haunted by past and future, but in Lagos the ghosts seem to leave a slime residue that is especially tangible, visceral even. I started with a simple question: how do Lagosians put up with this mayhem, and still remain so indefatigably upbeat? For if chaos is Lagos's most defining feature, its infectious optimism has to be a close second. It took me years to find the answer: faith. Here you will meet people who live off rubbish tips or squat over gutters to shit, and people who live in faux-baroque mansions and take helicopters to beat the traffic. If anything unites these disparate universes, it is that they face the city's chaos equipped with unshakable belief in an unseen, supernatural order.

There is something very human about that: all of us tend to turn to the sacred when faced with disorder and uncertainty, driven by instincts that sometimes guide us far better than reason. Psychology tells us that even when we think we're acting on 'rational' motives, there are darker forces at work pulling the levers behind Reason's curtain. Many an atheist has ended up praying through in-flight turbulence. Religion and superstition remain a powerful force in the world (look at the United States). Even in supposedly secular countries, a yearning for an occult dimension persists, especially in times of crisis: just visit any New Age shop selling tarot cards and 'healing crystals' or look at the blind faith the world's money men place in central bankers and neoclassical economists—the high priests of consumer capitalism—despite many of their prophecies being as reliable as those of a Nigerian televangelist.

Ever since the ancient Mesopotamian *Epic of Gilgamesh*, the story of the city has been one of spiritual struggle, of the human soul ripped from the forests and hills in which it spent tens of thousands of years among members of its own clan, thrust into an alienating world forged of stone and full of strangers. It is the world that greets millions of migrants all over the Third World as they step out of battered minibuses taking them from rural poverty to slums in the shadow of skyscrapers. Perhaps something about the spectacular apocalyptic-ness of Lagos—the faded corporate high-rises, ash-stained concrete housing blocks and warehouses criss-crossed by great hulking bridges, the frenzied shanties spilling into the lagoon—makes it natural to yearn for a non-material plane.

Head north up the Lagos–Ibadan expressway and the slums of the Lagos mainland give way to vast estates owned by preachers with names like 'Winners Chapel' and 'The Mountain of Fire and Miracles' while billboards feature sharp-suited Nigerian pastors advertising a 'Three-Day War to Kill the Witches'. Some venues fit as many as a quarter of a million people, and many of their pastors are multimillionaires. Five times a day, the muezzin call rings out from thousands of mosques across Lagos and its outskirts for the Muslim faithful, who make up roughly the other half of the city. And many more times a day, someone somewhere will discreetly offer kola nuts or the blood of a slaughtered goat to placate some ancient Yoruba god or ancestral spirit, in one of thousands of sacred shrines. Some will be favoured by these mysterious entities, others slighted by them, but in any case, it doesn't much matter which god or ghost they plump for: they will still need to hustle.

'You won't be welcomed here,' says Eric Obuh, a former rag-picker whose story appears in this book. 'We say "This is Lagos", not "Welcome to Lagos". It means: don't expect anyone to help you. You have to hustle if you want food before bedtime.'

Unwelcome they may be, but that doesn't stop more than a thousand migrants trundling into Lagos each day. From the dust bowls of the Sahara up north to the mangrove-fringed creeks of the Niger Delta down south, they just keep coming—keep being absorbed into this giant urban sponge menacingly encircled by the Atlantic and a vast, flood-prone lagoon. There are not enough houses for them, not enough roads, schools, power, clean water or jobs, just as there weren't for the people who came before them. Elites are worried. 'They wonder how many more people can be loaded onto the table before it collapses,' says Olumide Owoeye, a demographer at southwest Nigeria's Bowen University.

Across the globe, the tables are already collapsing. The world's population is on course to hit nearly 10 billion by 2050, and almost all of that growth will happen in (mostly developing) cities. Perhaps we'll look back fondly on the dark, satanic mills of early industrial Europe. London took the whole of the nine-teenth century to grow its population sevenfold; Lagos is now sixty-five times bigger than it was in 1950. Which is to say that, one way or another, our planet's future will be decided in places like Lagos.

PROLOGUE

'The cities of the future,' wrote Mike Davis in *Planet of Slums*, 'rather than being made out of glass and steel are largely constructed out of crude brick, straw, recycled plastic, cement blocks and scrap wood ... surrounded by pollution, excrement and decay.'

Perhaps that's too bleak? Perhaps, when celebrated Dutch architect Rem Koolhaas cheerfully describes Lagos as 'not a kind of backward situation but an announcement of the future', we needn't shudder. For in Lagos, improvements are being made that might just stop it from collapsing. They start small: a lick of paint on a crumbling building here, a row of hedges sprucing up a highway there. Then bigger: motorways are built, bridges erected and traffic rules enforced. Gradually, Lagos's rulers start trying to tame the monster it has become. They collect tax from people who'd never paid it, crush violent crime in places that were swarming with it, clean up trash from streets buried in it, and plant trees in landscapes that previously saw nothing but concrete and rusting metal.

Yet while there is a collective sigh of relief from the tiny middle class, the poorest on the margins start to see how precarious is their stake in the Supernatural City. The tiny spaces they have creatively adapted into market stalls, informal rental parking space and makeshift shelter are 'in the way'. They are detritus blocking a grand vision for an 'African Singapore' that has no room for them. Their homes will be bulldozed to widen highways, slums razed to clear space for luxury flats, street traders swept away for air-conditioned supermarkets. Each wave of destruction will leave tens of thousands of slum dwellers homeless. In the blink of an eye, the city's 'real estate' will be carved up between a dozen or so powerful oligarch families, many of them claiming rights to huge swathes of Lagos land on the basis of their ancestral gods.

1

MAN-OF-WAR

Atop NECOM House, Lagos Island, 2016

Whenever I look at a map of Lagos, the image that always springs to mind is of a beached Portuguese man-of-war. The relentless urban sprawl, with its shacks and town houses, is the beach. The polyp's distinctive sail-shaped bubble is the lagoon at the centre of the city. And its poisonous blue tentacles are the tangle of creeks that extend out of the lagoon, breaking up south Lagos's neighbourhoods into myriad islands before running into the Atlantic. Lagos is, always has been, a city defined—and menaced—by water.

Water is Lagos's biggest paradox. The city exists only because of its position between the Atlantic and a lagoon with a harbour big enough to park a whole naval fleet. Yet its expansion from a seaside trading settlement of 20,000 people in the 1800s to a megalopolis of some 20 million today has meant a battle against sea, swamp and storm that constantly threaten to swallow it. Thousands of newcomers every week erect houses on precarious wetlands, where many collapse. Land is often 'reclaimed' by developers, only for the waters to claim it back.

The city takes its name from the Portuguese word for 'lakes', and much of it is built around the various nooks of the lagoon, which covers more than six and a half thousand square kilometres. Lagos's wealthiest households face the lagoon, their flashy boats tethered to its shore. The southern parts of the city facing the Atlantic, over which millions of slaves were shipped to the New World, are saturated with canals and brooks connecting lagoon to sea. Drains are few and blocked. The briefest burst of rain turns roads into rivers. The rainy season, which lasts about half the year, spares neither slum nor luxury apartment—everybody gets submerged. The rich splatter jeeps through instant lakes; the poor hitch up robes to wade through puddles; the middle classes lose their battered saloon cars in hidden ditches. Down one street during a heavy downpour, I saw two enterprising fishermen paddling their canoes as if it were just another creek.

The highest view you can get over Lagos and its tentacled lagoon is from atop NECOM House. West Africa's tallest building, erected for a now defunct state telecoms firm, lies in the heart of what used to be the main commercial district, Lagos Island, before congestion and street gangs forced many businesses to move. From its rooftop, the view is a jambalaya of office blocks, town houses, hotels, churches, mosques and shops spaghettied by freeways. Flyovers slice it up, joining bridges stretched over the lagoon's different tentacles. Multi-coloured roofs jostle so close together that they give the impression of a wild stampede in every direction to the water's edge.

NECOM's thirty-two storeys were finished at the end of a 1970s oil boom, when Lagos was still capital of the 'Giant of Africa', as guidebooks called Nigeria. It eventually went bust, rotting from the inside under the military misrule that followed. In its last days, it was providing just half a million landlines to a country of 120 million (Nigerians of the pre-mobile age remember spending half a day trying to make a phone call). These days, the most useful thing NECOM House does is act as a lighthouse to the thousands of ships bringing goods into Lagos's congested ports of Apapa and Tin Can Island.

Their black shapes are visible for miles from up here. Right out to the gunmetal horizon, rows of container ships import the things—cars, plastics, milk, toothpicks—that Nigeria gave up producing when oil started flowing in the 1950s. To the east of those ports, across the wide channel stuffed with ships where the lagoon meets the Atlantic Ocean, lies Victoria Island (V.I.)—the newish financial district that is the locus of the insanely wealthy Nigerian elite. With its smart hotels and restaurants, it is home to one of the world's highest concentrations of millionaires.

Further south, poking out of V.I. like a lizard's tail, is the 'Eko Atlantic' city, a ten-square-kilometre stretch of reclaimed land set to be the hottest new development in Lagos. Millions of tonnes of sand have been poured into the sea for this planned Dubai-style gated community. Eko Atlantic is, or will be when it's finished, Lagos's answer to that most ominous of trends in extreme twenty-first-century capitalism: the private city. It is also a most revealing answer to the threat of climate change: a bubble of private luxury for a quarter of a million rich people protected by a concrete perimeter. The perimeter can, it is claimed, withstand storm surges and sea level rises of several feet, even while the sand dredged from the Lagos lagoon to build it erodes the coast and makes poor neighbourhoods in the vicinity more prone to flooding. The Eko Atlantic is a place of chrome skyscrapers with sea views, four-lane highways with wide pavements, business parks, restaurants, palm trees, and a luxury marina with ample space for luxury boats. It gets 24-hour power from a private grid, clean water from the tap—both unimaginable in other parts of Lagos—proper sewerage facilities. Oh, and not a single affordable room for the armies of cooks, cleaners, drivers, car washers and security guards that will be needed to attend to the whims of its hyper-affluent residents. The servers will instead sit in morale-melting traffic for hours to reach the gates of Elysium. Many of the flats in its residential towers were sold out before the first bricks were laid, some before they'd even finished filling in the sea.

On a clear day, you can also see the thin Five Cowries Creek separating the northern shore of V.I. from Lagos Island and neighbouring Ikoyi island. Ikoyi is the city's other exclusive residential district, home of rich Nigerians and expatriates, and the place I lived in for nearly four years. It's as wealthy as Victoria Island but lacks the bustle, being more residential: all coconut palms, tennis lawns and luxury apartments. It is still shabbily Lagos in its way: roads are cratered, drains blocked. But it retains the posh private clubs—golf, boat, polo—founded when Ikoyi was a ghetto for Lagos's white rulers.

Finally, off the western edge of the islands, the longest bridge in sub-Saharan Africa, Third Mainland Bridge, ribbons across the lagoon for 11.8 kilometres. The Third Mainland Bridge connects Lagos's three main islands—that is, Lagos Island, Victoria Island and Ikoyi—with the continent of Africa. It was completed under military ruler Ibrahim Babangida in the early 1990s to relieve traffic on the other two bridges to the burgeoning mainland neighbourhoods. From up here, it looks like a bicycle chain lying sideways in a murky puddle. As with the other bridges, it didn't take long for it to become throttled by traffic, every day except those mercifully peaceful Sundays, when half the city retreats to sing praise to Jesus, while the other, Muslim half simply rests their exhausted bones.

The bridges of Lagos are the city's spine. They hold its otherwise amorphous jellyfish-like shape together. They traverse salty lagoon to join islands, sandbanks and peninsulas. They are at once what unite Lagos and expose how glaringly divided it is—connecting mansions with tin-roof slums. Along them, 4x4s in shiny black carry the wealthy to seal their deals or play in their gilded playgrounds, while their specially hired AK-47-toting VIP police escorts force lesser cars off the road. They jostle for space with decrepit minibuses stuffed with weary humanity. Meanwhile, underneath the network of flyovers connecting the bridges, there is an entire undercity, where the homeless and down-and-outs sleep rough, play football, wash and hustle. Observe the bridges for long enough, and you will see all of Lagos.

* * *

From this high vantage point over the city—staring down at cars oozing over its suspended freeways—I wonder whether Lagos isn't the perfect microcosm of our increasingly urban and unequal planet: billionaires importing champagne and collecting sports cars while half the city's population live in slums with no running water or sanitation. A migrant a minute arriving with nothing but a change of clothes, hoping for a job that isn't there. Discordant buildings. Relentless cement. Too many cars and not enough roads. Too many roads and not enough houses. Too many houses and virtually no public green space between them, despite all the admirable efforts by the state government to address all of these things. Every waking hour consumed by hustle. In Lagos, I once saw a stretched Hummer whizzing past a beggar in rags, splashing a filthy puddle over the poor man for good measure.

In any city, money is what separates the man in the penthouse suite from the one sleeping on a concrete ledge under a bridge. The bigger the city, the more frantic that equation becomes, as space shrinks and the number of hands chasing the dollars multiplies. But in a country like Nigeria, where a predetermined quantity of oil wealth gushes out of the ground each day and overshadows other endeavours (the so-called oil curse), an idea naturally forms: *my success depends on how big a share I can grab.*

So, hustle or die. Hustle, hustle, hustle and do your best not to be hustled yourself: for that is how the winners and losers will be determined. The immigration official hustles you for money to let you into Lagos airport. The street kid hustles you for money to park your car in a public space. The policeman hustles you for money because it's the weekend and he wasn't paid on time (and, more persuasively, because he's holding a gun). While you boil with rage in a traffic jam stretching from here to the next ice age, the hawker selling pirated DVDs or fried plantains at your window will cheerfully breathe your fumes until his lungs are charcoal if it gets him enough money for a portion of yam. And don't expect a miracle from God without a hefty donation to your Pentecostal pastor.

Check your change, check your pockets, check the product you just bought isn't fake or poisonous, check a phoney estate agent hasn't sold your house to multiple buyers when you get back from holiday. Make sure you get paid up front, but never, if you can help it, pay up front. Pay off only those who need to be paid off, like the thugs and the cops—the ones capable of erecting roadblocks (literal and imaginary). But show no weakness. The Lagosian brain has a specially fitted device for detecting weakness. Weakness is a wallet-killer. Don't let anyone squeeze into your traffic space, on pain of death. Never mind the paintwork on your car: show even the slightest concern for your car's aesthetics and you'll be stuck at the same traffic light till dawn. Take a deep breath. Don't stop, never stop, not even for that dead body that will most likely fester for days on the roadside (you don't want to be tarred with blame if you attend to it). Let it be collected by the municipal authorities or, failing that, merge with the tarmac like a squashed rat. Keep moving. Stop and you'll be the next body in the street.

Stop and you'll starve.

PART I

THE IRON LADY

A squirrel that wants to climb the plantain tree must have sharp claws.

Yoruba proverb

Let us make no pretence about it, every human being loves power; power over his fellow men in the state, or in business enterprises; or, failing that, power over his wife and children, and over his brothers, sisters, and friends. Of these categories of power, the desire for power over one's fellow men is the strongest.

Obafemi Awolowo, statesman and former premier of the
Western Region in colonial times, in an address to a
students' parliament, 1975

2

TOYIN

Obalende, adjacent to Lagos Island, 2003

Blood was spattered all over the road. Some of it had already started to congeal in the Lagos heat into little black dots. It was coming from a bus driver being punched and kicked repeatedly by the touts outside Obalende Bus Terminus. Toyin relished the variety of sounds the victim was making: a whiny yelp, the guttural sound of his wind being knocked out, the faint crack of his ribs on impact. She pulled her boot back to get momentum, and swung it into his torso.

The driver deserved it, to be sure. The 'city bus' he was driving was an affront to the Obalende Boys, the gang that ran the busiest bus station on the three islands of Lagos. Most Lagosians used the old creaky yellow minibuses that plied much of the city, from which Toyin's gang extorted handsome sums of money. But these shinier, white buses owned by a businessman with links to the governor were supposed to be off limits to the touts. The gangs had been warned to leave them alone, and so their emboldened drivers were refusing to pay 'loading fees'. They had to be taught a lesson.

Other gang members were smashing the bus's windows with nail-studded clubs and letting the air out of its tyres. By now, the sun was just up, bathing Lagos in a mellow light ahead of the steamy harshness that kicks in around nine. Obalende is a typically apocalyptic Lagos cityscape: a post-modern jumble of flyovers, bridges, cloverleafs and motorways, with high-rises poking up between them, that forms the main valve in the city's clogged heart. Ramps rise and descend, carving up spaces stuffed with crumbling, half-abandoned high-rises, concrete shacks blackened with soot, sagging power lines and gable-roofed apartment blocks. Toyin knew almost every street and its regular inhabitants, down to the lowliest hawker.

Ever since she was a girl, she had loved what she called 'the rugged life'—fighting and hustling on the streets of Lagos. It was much more rewarding than sitting around looking pretty so that a boy would lavish money on her, as many Nigerian women were taught to do. With her slump-shouldered physique and round belly, Toyin would have stood out from the mostly wiry young men beating up the driver that day. But her bulging biceps were ample warning that she was as tough as any. Toyin had, by West African standards, pale skin—Nigerians call this much-sought-after shade 'yellow'. She never needed the dangerous, skin-burning peroxide tonics that many Nigerian women apply to lighten themselves. Her narrow eyes looked 'almost Chinese', she would say. She had a round face, a small jaw, teeth that stuck out, and a mouth that curled in a disconcerting way but could also smile warmly.

The official name of Toyin's gang was National Union of Road Transport Workers: Obalende Chapter. But that was just one of Nigeria's many misnomers for a massive extortion racket. As long as anyone can remember, Lagos has been full of such 'unions' and 'associations', labels that legitimise gangsterism. They are top-down affairs, with a national leader sitting atop a spider's web of extortion. There is the national association for market women, shoe hawkers, car washers, scrap scavengers, scrap dealers, even shea butter makers. There is the Nigeria Automobile Technicians Association, the Nigeria Association of Food Vendors, and the Witches and Wizards Association of Nigeria.

Yet none of them do extortion quite like the 'transport union'. For in Lagos, whether you reside in a shack-lined slum or a tree-lined avenue, if you are in the business of moving people or things around, you will pay a portion of your earnings to a tout. It might happen something like this ...

A skinny but wirily muscular boy leaps out of nowhere onto the side of a bus on Mobolaji Johnson Avenue, not far from the high-rises on the Lagos mainland that house the main state government offices. The traffic is stalled, so the driver has little chance to escape. The boy and three thugs backing him are chanting 'Owo mi da?'—'Where is my money?' in Yoruba, the main ethnic language of Lagos and southwest Nigeria. It is a common phrase, easily understood even by those who don't speak much Yoruba.

The bus driver knows that if he refuses to pay, they may smash his wing mirror or drag him out and beat him. His weary eyes fix a contemptuous stare on the boy, but he doesn't resist. He reaches into the pocket of his torn combat trousers and pulls out a filthy-looking 100-naira note. The boy snatches it, then vanishes into the crowd of female hawkers taking advantage of the stoppage to sell hot dough balls and sachets of Pure Water to passengers. The bus crawls away.

Thanks to its strategic location, Obalende was one of the biggest such transport rackets. It lies about four kilometres down a flyover joining the Third Mainland Bridge, that bleak structure connecting Lagos's three main islands with Africa. Every weekday, millions of Lagosians pour out of the continental Lagos mainland, where most of them live, and cross one of just three bridges to come and work on these islands, and then go back again. After reaching Obalende, some will travel east to work as cooks or drivers or guards in Ikoyi's leafy, residential streets, where Nigeria's rich rub shoulders with expatriates in mansions shaded by mango trees. Some will go south over Falomo Bridge across the Five Cowries Creek to their white-collar jobs in the corporate offices, banks and insurance companies of upmarket Victoria Island—or perhaps in the restaurants, bars and night-clubs that entertain its professional class. Others—an assortment of traders, state government civil servants, cyber-criminals, artists and con artists—will head immediately west to the queerly romantic dystopia that is Lagos Island. This is the oldest part of the city, with its government high-rise buildings, its gnarly sausage trees, grey old churches, peeling colonial offices and hyperactive markets. Most of these commuters can't afford a car, so they take the bus. To the gangs who run the bus stations, all those millions of journeys mean one thing: money.

Like the other 'chapters' of the 'transport union', the extortion racket run by the Obalende Boys was a more or less exclusively male affair. With a notable exception: Toyin. Somehow, in a world of men, where a woman's role tends to be cleaning up after them and cooking food to fill their ever-expanding stomachs, she was a gangster on a par with the meanest boys of the Obalende bus park.

* * *

Toyin had learned at an early age that there were two survival strategies for Nigerian girls. You bat your eyelids at the boys in the hope of courting their protection—or you beat them at their own game. She grew up in Lagos in the 1970s, just as a heady, oil-fuelled boom was taking off and Nigerians were getting into money in a big way.

Back then, Lagos had fewer than two million people, but her street in Offin, Lagos Island, was one of the most crowded in

Africa. Its Portuguese-style colonial villas and tropical modernist concrete box-blocks were crammed with families of eight living in single rooms nicknamed 'face me, face you'. They lived the island's life of endless noise and hustle, amid impatient drivers, blaring car horns, beggars, touts, chaotic motorcycle taxis, blocked drains brimming with raw sewage, and streets blanketed in trash. Toyin grew up to love it, even after visiting 'quieter' parts of Lagos. Whether you've been there for five minutes or a lifetime, there is something oddly addictive about the entropy of Lagos Island. It's the frenetic activity of its vast sea of market stalls; the way its cityscape comprises so many building styles stitched together with no rhyme or reason—a mock-Tudor house next to a corporate box-building glistening with unnecessary quantities of ill-proportioned windows, next to the deteriorating but still beautiful creations of nineteenth-century Brazilian freed slaves, like the Ilojo Bar, with its baroque floral decorations, its tiled roof, exquisite arches and wrought-iron balconies, next to a wood-and-metal-sheeting shack. Nowhere else did Toyin feel at home than among the bustle of these buildings.

Toyin's father, Bashir, was a door-to-door salesman across West Africa, though he seemed much better at picking up concubines on his long journeys than making money. Her mother, Latifat, was a market woman and the first of Bashir's four wives, the maximum number permitted by the Koran. The family was all Muslim, as are about half of Toyin's Yoruba ethnic group— Latifat was the daughter of a prominent imam upcountry—the other half being Christian.

As the senior wife, Latifat was the most powerful female in the household. What she'd lost being shuffled down the conjugal ladder as her husband took on younger and prettier models was more than compensated for by the authority she had. Latifat taught Toyin to be smart and business-like in a way only female Lagos market traders are—and never to rely on men for money. 'Make your own way,' she would tell her daughter, while pounding cassava in a great pestle or boiling water to make Nescafé for Bashir.

Latifat sold booze in one of the world's biggest open-air markets, Eko Idumota, also on Lagos Island, a place so crowded that just to walk down the street involved stepping over hawkers selling underwear, women cradling toddlers, or exhausted beggars sleeping on discarded plastic. A riot of people shaded by parasols sold clothes, phone credit, flat-screen TVs, Chinese medicines, fake Ralph Lauren polo shirts, crayfish for flavouring pungent stews. The collective din of pop music from roadside shops, car horns and thousands of generators was relentless, and it built to a climax at the splendidly kitsch bronze facades and gold turrets of the Lagos Central Mosque on Nnamdi Azikiwe Street. Like many Yoruba Muslims, Toyin's parents saw no contradiction between their mystical Sufi faith and Lagos's drinking culture. Both drank.

Toyin's first taste of sweet violence was at her Koranic school, where the pupils were reading passages in the Hadiths about peace and love. The school bully punched and winded her outside the gates, and she ran home in tears. She was eight.

'Why are you crying, girl?' Latifat asked her in the kitchen, her pot of pounded yam fizzing on the stove.

After her daughter had explained, Latifat said: 'Go back to the bully tomorrow and retaliate.'

So, the next day Toyin walked up to him, grabbed him by the hair, punched him in the face, and pulled him into the dirt road on which the school lay. After a few more blows to his head and a kick in the stomach, she stuffed his mouth with sand and left him gasping while a crowd cheered. She surprised herself with how fierce she could be.

By the time Toyin entered her late teens—by then the winner of multiple street fights and two inter-school boxing tournaments, one of them against a male opponent—nobody argued with her anymore. She also didn't suffer that other curse afflicting her female peers at the onset of adolescence: boys didn't hit on her. That suited her just fine.

When Toyin left home at the age of 20, it was, predictably, not in the arms of a suitor. She knew it was scandalous to move out as a single woman, but she had had enough of living with Bashir's fourth wife, Titilayo, who had a barbed-wire tongue and never missed the opportunity to disparage Toyin's lack of a husband. One night, carrying a satchel with a change of clothes, Toyin knelt down in prayer to Allah and, fingering each of her prayer beads, begged him to make a success of her life. Then she walked out of the door.

The only place where she knew she'd be welcomed was at her friend Ataru's. He was the head of a notorious gang around Lagos Island, although at the time they held hardly any territory. 'Ataru' was a shortening of his nickname, Atari Ajanaku, because he was so strong and brave—as the Yoruba saying goes: Atari Ajanaku kin séru omode ('the head of the elephant is not a load to be carried by a child'). He was a descendant of the Afro-Brazilian returnee slaves who had come back more than a century ago and made their mark on the city, infusing it with ornate Portuguese architecture—like the crumbling, moss-covered terraced house in which he was then living. Along with the stuffy British colonial buildings, they remain the most distinctive feature of Lagos, coolly nostalgic relics amid the endlessly drab concrete blocks that now clutter its skyline.

Toyin had met Ataru three years earlier at a lion masquerade in Bamgbose Street, Lagos Island—one of those Yoruba rituals when occult forces become personified in scary masks. Youths were beating drums and playing flutes around two people inside a kind of lion pantomime costume, and the lion was shaking itself into a frenzy. Ataru had just started dating Toyin's older sister, Kemi. From the outset, he and Toyin hit it off as friends. Days after moving into Ataru's place, Toyin had met most of the louts that made up the inner circle of his gang. There was Jaga the Troublemaker, the Ghanaian, Ogbo from Ondo state, Ozubio (otherwise known as the Tall and Slender One), Kaka, and a heavily tattooed, muscle-bound thug called Gasper.

Ataru's gang had some serious muscle, but what they lacked was real estate. And the most coveted piece of gang real estate on the islands belonged to the chapter of the transport union that ran the Obalende Bus Terminus, arguably the most important hub for buses between the islands and the mainland.

Now, this union, the Ajah Boys, had a fierce reputation, and they were resented because they were not 'indigenes', as Lagosians like to say, but outsiders, from Ajah, a sandy suburb along Lagos's east straddling the lagoon and the Atlantic coast. That made them natural enemies of Ataru's gang, the Obalende Boys. But Ataru had understood the importance of building alliances, even with potential enemies. The various rackets he was running—selling fake naira currency, stolen vehicle parts, small quantities of 'Indian hemp'—needed willing bus drivers to help courier them. And for that, access to one of the biggest bus stations in Lagos was an unparalleled advantage. He cut the Ajah Boys into a share of the profits he'd made from using the bus park.

Also among the people circulating through Ataru's bawdy household was a man called Gbolahan, a self-styled 'travelling businessman', like Toyin's father. Toyin had never had much interest in men, but she found herself strangely attracted to this tall, unassuming man, who always wore traditional robes instead of the T-shirts and jeans popular with Ataru's crew. He was somehow gentler, more polite than the rest of the rabble. None of the other guys had shown any signs of finding her attractive. They slapped her on the thighs and laughed boisterously as if she were a man. Her own behaviour, and even her physique, did much to encourage this. She was butch, with muscular arms and legs, but fat around the waist and with shoulders that were, if anything, the opposite of broad: she was almost pear-shaped.

But the more time she spent with Gbolahan, the more obvious it became that he saw her in a way other men didn't: he fancied her. It was so unusual that she couldn't help being flattered. The first time they had sex was in her tiny, hot room at Ataru's, while he and his various misfits were out on the streets up to some shady business or other. They sweated in a stuffy warmth made more cloying by the corrugated iron roof overhead. Toyin had had little interest in sex while growing up—despite it being the topic of astonishing amounts of gossip in the overheated streets of Lagos Island. Her first time was enough to convince her that she hadn't been missing out. What, she wondered, was all the fuss about? But she carried on seeing Gbolahan all the same.

If the truth be known, she was hardly besotted with him, but she liked him. He always treated her with a courtesy that bordered on formality, a refreshing change after the bawdiness of Ataru's gang. He never seemed to descend into that lazy sense of ownership as so many men do once they've fucked a woman. Toyin didn't doubt that he had other girls on the side: that was almost obligatory. But if he did, he kept them away from her— luckily for them, since she had a fierce temper and mean fists. Toyin was living in Gbolahan's apartment, with leather sofas and a TV; and with the money she got from him and the dressmaking she did on the side, she was living in more comfort than she'd ever known. And the ruggedness of the streets started to look decidedly less attractive.

She got pregnant. In much Nigerian folklore, a female remains a girl, not properly mature, until she has borne a child. And, indeed, Toyin would later look back on giving birth as the only time she ever really felt womanly. Femininity had always repelled her, but now she could vaguely see the attraction. At the naming ceremony for her new daughter—amid the traditional foods of locust beans, dried fish and smoked bush rat, surrounded by bowls of honey and palm oil—the women in Toyin's family seemed to be looking at her differently, with none of that hostility she sometimes detected. Even Titilayo, who had never said a kind word to her, smiled warmly. The elders gave Toyin's daughter the name Aramide, meaning 'my people have arrived'. In Yoruba tradition, the elders always choose the name—because much can go wrong in the baby's life if the name isn't expertly chosen to suit the inscrutable whims of the ancestors.

Two years later, Toyin gave birth to a boy, Tunde, and shortly afterwards to another girl, Daminola. She found herself curiously content being Gbolahan's housewife. She never wanted for anything—there was always food on the table and he treated her with total courtesy. When they argued, he never hit her, and, perhaps more surprisingly given her bad temper, she never hit him. The only source of some tension was the lack of any sign of a wedding offer, despite persistent nagging by her parents.

There was no warning on the night he abandoned her; no coming back reeking of other women's market-grade perfume after increasingly late nights; no mood change. One day, he told her he was going on a business trip, and could he please borrow some money? She emptied her purse, and he slipped out.

For months, Toyin's mind had cooked up all kinds of excuses for why he hadn't called. Then, one night, while smoke was wafting up onto her balcony from someone's paraffin fire, it struck her, cold as the heart of Olokun, god of the deep sea: he wasn't coming back. For what would be one of only a handful of times in her life, Toyin burst into tears. She knew then that she would have to raise the three children she bore for Gbolahan, alone. *Make your own way.*

* * *

Toyin had found a suitably cheap 'face me, face you' studio for herself and the children, amid the incessant noise of Eko Idumota. But she was desperate for money. Then, one evening, she was hanging out with Ataru's gang among the wrought-iron walls and metal statues of leaping horses that form Tafawa Balewa Square—a former racecourse in the British colonial days. They were all there: Ataru, Gasper, Jaga, the Ghanaian. The event had been sponsored by Benson & Hedges, and they'd received money via Ataru to hand out trays of free B&H cigarettes (this was the end of the 1990s).

A gunfight broke out between two feuding gangs (although neither of them had any quarrel with Ataru's), and suddenly the whole packed arena was filled with people screaming and fleeing. The police swiftly moved in to break it up and, after making some arrests, it wasn't long before they started making their way towards Toyin and her friends, suspecting they were part of the squabble—Ataru's gang was always in trouble for one thing or another. All of the gang members were armed, except Toyin, and the police were by now blocking all the main exits. This could mean jail. 'We're trapped,' Ataru said, looking around nervously.

But Toyin remembered a discreet exit, around the far side. 'This way,' she said to the others, calmly, and they scampered past women selling groundnuts and cold orange Fanta under the shade of parasols.

'Stop there,' the police were shouting. 'We are arresting you.' Toyin ran faster, leading the boys out of the exit and through a series of narrow alleyways threading through the island's odd mix of shacks, iron-roofed British colonial offices, tropical modernist blocks and endless human activity. The police split up into two groups and began running, firing warning shots into the air, but it was too late to turn back now. The gang passed under the noodled flyovers joining the ring road leading to the Third Mainland Bridge, while police gunshots still rang out and people scampered to get out of the way. Finally, they arrived at Obalende roundabout. The police were making their way towards them at the far side of the bridge. In desperation, they headed for the bus park.

Their reception by the Ajah Boys at the entrance was predictably hostile—the two gangs had long hated each other—but Ataru managed to persuade them to let his Obalende Boys in, on the basis of their loose business alliance. Once inside, they were safe: the mafia in the bus parks enjoyed a measure of protection from some high-up politicians who collected a cut of their earnings, and it was an unwritten rule that police never raided them on their turf. As the police left, they shot back mean glances. Toyin smiled: she had led Ataru's gang to safety.

A week later, she was in her apartment cooking cow-leg pepper soup and semolina for her children, when Ataru's voice called up to her window. He and Gasper were outside. 'Come up,' she said, and their flip-flops shuffled up the concrete steps past the bare walls of her block.

'That was quick thinking back there,' Ataru said, after she had brought them some Nescafé in plastic beakers. 'We could use you.' He thrust 2,500 naira ($22) into her hand. 'This is money to feed you. You'll get more when you need it. Just come to us.'

With that, Toyin was a gang member.

* * *

At first, this didn't seem to entail much, except for running a few errands and stashing the odd bit of cash from street rackets. Then, shortly after the new millennium was ushered in to fireworks and colossal church services by Nigerian televangelists, the gang spied an opportunity. Obalende Bus Terminus, still property of their rivals, the Ajah Boys, was ripe for the taking. Resentment of the Ajah Boys had been growing. People hated the way they shared their wealth with their own people in Ajah, instead of putting it into the local community.

It was one of the many conflicts in Lagos streets over who really belongs where. In a city so crowded that some sleep in gutters or in concrete pipes, every inch of space is claimed by someone: as somewhere to eat, to work, to defecate. In centuries past, the right to reside somewhere depended on lineage, the ghosts of long-dead ancestors cementing a person's spiritual ties to the earth. But as Lagos swelled with fortune seekers from all over West Africa, hoping to profit from the slaves and palm oil being shipped over the Atlantic in the early nineteenth century, the ties binding people to their ethnic homelands began to be torn asunder. The right to reside came to depend not on where your ancestors came from, but on where you had grown up. You were an 'indigene' if you were from the 'area': if you knew its streets and its people knew you. What would later be called the 'area boy' was born.

Like Toyin, Ataru and the gang were all from Lagos Island, but Ataru himself had grown up on the last street before Obalende, on neighbouring Ikoyi island. The two islands are separated by the MacGregor Canal, a sliver of viscous water a few metres wide, shaded by a flyover and so full of trash and human excrement that, to all intents and purposes, the two are one island. That gave Ataru a tenuous claim to being from Obalende. The Ajah Boys running the bus park, meanwhile, were from many kilometres away, and were resented as if they were colonial occupiers. If they could seize the terminus, the Obalende Boys would be cheered on as liberators.

Ataru assembled a few dozen reliable foot soldiers. They had already got the blessing for the takeover from the union chairman for all of Lagos State, who clearly saw the advantage of having indigenes in charge of Obalende. Enough police had been paid to look the other way. And there would never be a problem with the drivers. Of course, they resented having money taken off them by the union mobs, but why should they care which gang did the taking?

Hours before the assault, Ataru's boys met down the road near Onikan stadium to prepare potent spiritual fetishes. They put on leather armbands with pouches adorned with cowrie shells and containing white powder. The local babalawo (witchdoctor) had put the mixture together. He had chanted powerful Yoruba incantations on it, shaking his whole body and rolling his eyes. It was said a small amount of his stuff could protect you from up to forty bullets from a homemade rifle.

The witchdoctor had also made a sacrifice to Osara, goddess of the vast Lagos lagoon. Osara's role used to be to provide fishermen with abundant fish—back then there wasn't much around Lagos's swampy edge except fishing villages. Humanity had since arrived in such great numbers, vomiting such vast quantities of cement over the lagoon edge, that the goddess's fortune-bringing role had naturally diversified beyond fish.

Not that Toyin herself believed strongly in all this fetish stuff. 'Nothing shall ever happen to us except what Allah has ordained for us. He is our protector,' the Koran said, and Toyin believed it more than any black magic. She cupped her hands towards the sky and prayed to Him to deliver her safely. After praying and strapping on their various fetishes, the foot soldiers gathered in a dirt car park near the Obalende Bus Terminus around midnight. Toyin carried the weapons. There was the usual assortment for a street fight: cutlasses, handaxes, carpenter's saws, knives big and small, glass bottles. A couple of the boys had homemade, pump-action shotguns as a back-up, in case things got really ugly.

Toyin set down the bedsheet stuffed full of weapons and a zip-locked bag full of bottles at the entrance to the bus terminus. From outside the perimeter, they could hear touts laughing and drinking. Everyone took his preferred blade and each grabbed a bottle.

'Now,' Ataru shouted, and they hurled bottles into the garage with a smash, followed by shouting and commotion. After the first wave of missiles, Ataru and a handful of others ran in

22

through the open entrance. Their victims sat frozen in stunned silence. Ataru swiftly grabbed the chairman by the collar and pulled him out of the bus station into a side street. The rest of the gang charged in like a pack of wild dogs, blades raised.

There was more commotion as the touts scattered themselves across the park. Toyin chased one into a corner holding up a knife, and she delighted in his shock when he saw that she was a woman. Gasper, Jaga and the Ghanaian rounded up the others near an open exit—and they fled en masse into the night. There were a few still inside, but those who remained were well out-numbered. At least one was bleeding from having been struck by a bottle. One by one, they fled their attackers, and shot out of the exit.

The Obalende Boys cheered. They had done it: the 'indigenes' were in charge of Obalende Bus Terminus.

3

STATE OF BETRAYAL

Obalende, Adjacent to Lagos Island, 2003

When Toyin was young, her mother used to tell her a story about Tortoise. He had a wife, Yanibo, a female tortoise, who was unable to conceive. So Tortoise went to the Iroko (African teak) tree, which possesses a powerful spirit, for a cure. The Iroko tree gave him a concoction made from its roots and leaves and told Tortoise that if Yanibo cooked with the concoction and ate what she had cooked, she would get pregnant. She cooked a fish with it, and, as is the custom in Nigeria, she served her husband first. In his gluttony, he wolfed down the whole thing. The next morning, he woke up with a swollen belly—he had become pregnant instead of her. In panic, he returned to the Iroko tree.

'Nothing can be done to reverse what has happened, which was the result of your greed,' explained the tree. Enraged, the tortoise climbed the Iroko in an attempt to attack it. But the tree, which could move its branches like limbs, shook him free. He tumbled onto his back, cracking his shell into the grid pattern that still exists today.

The story always seemed to sum up to Toyin why the men in her life could never be relied upon. *Make your own way.*

* * *

A typical day for Toyin at the bus station, after her gang had seized it, looked like this: she would wake up at seven. By now her kids would already have made themselves—and her—breakfast. She would eat her cassava porridge and bean cakes or crayfish stew, and then pack her children off to Koranic school. The money from the racket at the bus park left her in the enviable position of being able to afford school fees for Aramide, Daminola and Tunde. She would arrange for someone to look after them when school ended so she didn't have to rush back— her mother, one of her aunts or even some of Bashir's other wives. Childcare is a nightmare for working single mothers in the West, relying heavily on scheduled, paid help. In Lagos, and in much of Africa, there are armies of female relatives to help out for nothing.

She would arrive at Obalende Bus Terminus around nine—by that time, most drivers have already been working for four or five hours. She would grab a Nescafé mixed with so much sugar you could use it to cement the cracks in the pillars holding up the Third Mainland Bridge. Then she'd sit on a stool at one of the shacks catering for the seething mass of humanity that squeezes through Obalende every day.

Obalende is a microcosm of Lagos's chaos: touts shout, impatient horns hoot, and women stir vats of bubbling, greasy food for hungry drivers. Dogs considered too old or rank for the stewing pot—the fate of tastier-looking hounds—hunt for leftovers among jettisoned scraps of meat and rice. Kiosks sell fan belts, engine oil, peanuts, football shirts, scarves, office attire. In one stall, a radio blasts out Nigerian gospel music; in another, Koranic verses. The bus conductors in their torn clothes and flip-flops shout destinations furiously at passengers to solicit them into the various 'danfos'—decrepit minibus taxis long since condemned in the European countries from which they are imported, but with extra seats added so that they cram in more passengers. In the 'garage' at the back—just a mud patch, really—men fix battered vehicles, welding car parts using just cheap sunglasses for eye protection.

As the day progressed, with Toyin still sitting on the stool, junior touts would come up to her with bundles of cash they'd extorted from the drivers. Toyin would count the money, estimate how many buses they'd hit, just to make sure there was no funny business going on, and stash it. This would carry on for pretty much the whole day, bar an hour or so for a lunch of, usually, egusi (melon seed) soup flavoured with dried fish and chunks of meat or perhaps eba, a starchy dough made from cassava flour.

Later, as the clouds pinkened and the fierce heat dropped, she'd swing around the back of a rusty shed, next to the MacGregor Canal. There the chairman sat, shaded by a busy flyover, with bundles of cash, handing out books of tickets to touts to give them as receipts. Would sit peel off notes to pay the touts, then lock the cashbox and take it home.

This was the best kind of business model, one favoured by oligarchs and criminals the world over, and indeed by Nigeria's successive governments. You might call it 'money for nothing except the promise of non-violence'. As long as the Obalende Boys and the other gangs in Lagos had the muscle to hold territory, they had a licence to print money.

Then, about three years after Toyin's gang seized control of Obalende, signs of trouble began to loom on the horizon. Lagos State governor Ahmed Bola Tinubu was elected for a second term on 19 April 2003, on a promise to clean up a city that had become *the* symbol of urban decay, a place visitors toured with a kind of fascinated horror. Cleaning up the transport mess was top priority. The private bus parks, with their unruly touts and beat-up old vehicles, were at the heart of the problem. Tinubu brought in consultants with clipboards and pens, and they pointed out what everyone already knew: Lagos was the only megacity in the world without an organised mass transit system.

These new buses they proposed would be nothing like the rusty old yellow minibuses most Lagosians knew. They would be shiny, red, Chinese-made, and, while not exactly new, handsomely reconditioned. They would be Lagos's version of Bus Rapid Transit (BRT)—a hopelessly optimistic label for anything that has to travel on Lagos roads. And so that they didn't become ensnared in a web of extortion like all the private buses, word was sent out to the gangs: leave the BRTs alone.

Explaining this to the touts, whose daily bread depended on the messy status quo, was going to be difficult. Tinubu managed to turn a fraction of them into traffic cops—dressing them up in yellow shirts and maroon trousers, and giving them licence to do pretty much what they did before (only this time they could also tax private cars, if they were violating traffic rules). But the other touts were going to be a problem. So the governor's officials approached the gang leaders whom they had paid to support them with muscle in elections earlier in the year. The Obalende Boys' leaders convened a meeting with the lower orders, including Toyin, to explain Tinubu's policy on the public buses. The foot soldiers complained bitterly.

'We are the few touts who helped Tinubu get where he is. He can't forget us,' someone said. He was right: most of the other gangs in the national transport union were loyal to the People's Democratic Party (PDP) of Tinubu's bitter opponent, Nigerian president Olusegun Obasanjo. But the Obalende Boys had supported Tinubu's Alliance for Democracy (AD) party right through his 2003 campaign, intimidating voters and guarding stuffed ballot boxes with unwavering loyalty. And now this was how he repaid them? So, in defiance of their bosses, a few dozen gang members organised a march to Tinubu's house. Toyin was among them. They crossed onto Awolowo Road, towards the leafier part of Ikoyi, passing the motorboat club, where Lagos's new rich park their mega-yachts on the Five Cowries Creek. Down they went, past expensive boutique clothes shops and banks, all the way to Falomo roundabout under the bridge linking Ikoyi to Victoria Island. Cars were hooting at the disruption.

They crossed onto Bourdillon Road, where the governor's official residence is, one of the most expensive streets in Lagos. Mansions shaded by mango trees towered behind black gates. Coconut palms swayed. The traffic was unbelievably light, save the odd black 4x4 whizzing by. There were proper pavements, instead of roadsides merging with dirt. Outside each forbidding gate was a patch of neat grass. She could never live here, Toyin thought. It's just too damn quiet.

Once outside Tinubu's leafy garden, the touts began chanting slogans: 'Tinubu doesn't care about the unions', and 'We won't be ignored'. The police guarding his residence cocked their rifles. Toyin was scared: Lagos police have a reputation for shooting first and asking questions later. Tense minutes passed. But after a stand-off, the union members slowly backed away. There was no point getting shot. They would need to find another way of sending a message. As they retreated back to Obalende, they agreed they would do what they did best: cause mayhem. Smash up the white 'city buses' that everyone knew were linked to Tinubu and that were seen as a prototype of the BRTs. Pelt their drivers with stones! Deflate their tyres! Toyin relished the prospect of a battle.

* * *

Segun Alabi was among the lucky few selected to drive one of the new 'city buses'. It was every bus driver's dream since they'd been introduced some months back, because the touts wouldn't be able to extort his earnings. Dealing with those criminals was the worst part of the job. Segun hated it.

After putting in his application, he had blown his savings on the sacrifice of a ram at a shrine to Sango, the Yoruba god of thunder. Back when Segun was living in a poor village in south-west Nigeria—which he had fled a decade and a half ago—a woman in his church who'd taught him to read told him there was One True God in Heaven and all the others were false gods. He wasn't convinced. Sango, with his tempestuous temper and thunderbolts, seemed just as real as Jesus. So after applying for the job, he hedged his Pascal's wager multiple ways: with offerings to Sango and to Sango's wife Oya—goddess of rainbows, winds, storms, death, destruction and rebirth—and with visits to his church to drop bills in collection buckets. It had been more than a decade since he'd escaped the slavery and violence of his village, and all he had to show for it were bruises from the thugs in the bus park. He needed something better. Whether by Jesus or Sango, Segun got the city bus job. It was a dream: his bus left from a separate, more orderly terminal from the main Obalende one. There wasn't a tout to be seen. Since arriving in Lagos as a penniless migrant from a destitute village, he'd never been so comfortable or hassle-free.

One morning, he was pulling out of the terminal and heading towards the Marina on Lagos Island. As he passed Obalende roundabout, a stone cracked his window. Then a few more. Then the bus started shaking. Outside, the touts from the garage were shouting and pushing. A bigger stone smashed through one window; a beer bottle through another. 'Down with BRT!' the touts shouted. Before Segun knew what was happening, they were forcing their way in through the entrance. One of them grabbed him, yanking him onto the ground, and began beating him. 'Get out!' they shouted at his passengers, who tutted but none of whom intervened as they got off. Some touts set to work trashing and setting fire to the bus; others were getting stuck into the really enjoyable business of beating Segun. Among those touts was Toyin.

Segun lay in foetal position to minimise the impact of the various blows. Toyin, meanwhile, was thoroughly enjoying herself, remorselessly kicking and beating him. That he wasn't even fighting back made her more angry. She kicked him again, and he rolled over. Then Toyin saw his face as he looked at her. Tears were running down his cheeks, showing pain, sorrow. And suddenly the lust for violence was drained out of her.

'Stop!' she shouted, and the thugs stepped back. 'That's enough.'

For weeks afterwards, she couldn't cease thinking about that experience, the sudden feeling of pity for the driver she was beating up. As often when she doubted things in her life, she consulted the Hadiths, the sayings of the Prophet Muhammad which she had learned in Koranic school. There was a passage on peaceful conduct: 'O Aisha, Allah is gentle and He loves gentleness, and He rewards for gentleness what is not granted for harshness, and He does not reward anything else like it,' one of the Hadiths said. Was it trying to tell her something?

A few weeks later she tracked Segun down at the city bus park. He was sitting underneath a flyover, smoking a joint of 'Indian hemp,' as marijuana is called on the streets of Lagos. His wounds were slowly healing, and she realised that she'd recognised him from when he used to be a driver in Obalende, under the old gang of touts a few years previously. Toyin had noticed something curious about him back then. He seemed to be able to gain the respect of the touts and the drivers without ever raising a hand to hit anyone. According to a perverse logic, somehow his gentleness won people over; the garage guys had accepted him as one of their own, until he moved on to drive the city bus. Even the women were suckers for his effeminate charms: such a contrast to the braggadocio that normally filled the park. He'd slept his way through most of the younger market women. Maybe violence wasn't the only way to survive Lagos.

'Peace, Segun.' She cautiously extended a hand to him. He glanced up through a bruised eye, and his scowl gave way to a smile. 'Peace,' he said, shaking her hand.

Later, she would look back upon this moment as the first turning point.

* * *

Broad Street, Lagos Island, 2007

For years after her experience with Segun, Toyin's discomfort at the violence swirling around her grew, but she kept it a secret. In fact, she did a superb job of hiding it: she participated in most of the beatings and humiliations dished out to drivers or rival gang members; she ruthlessly collected money and had little mercy for those who claimed to be unable to pay. Even the odd lynching of a robber—the screams and smell of burning flesh as they were incinerated under a jerrycan of petrol—didn't outwardly faze her. She made a point of cheering them on, even while her stomach turned inwardly. Her reward, when it came, was a chance to participate in Lagos's biggest political battle for half a generation.

The election cycle was in full swing again. Tinubu, the governor and ganglord presiding over Lagos State, had already served his two-term limit, so he did what all powerful Nigerian politicians do when they want to stay in the game: he became a godfather. He threw his considerable financial muscle behind his chief of staff, Babatunde Fashola. It was to be a close contest: both Tinubu's new Action Congress (AC) party, formed by the merger of his AD with some smaller political parties, and his arch-enemy, President Obasanjo's PDP, were mobilising every possible stick and carrot. For the carrots: rolls of naira bills in small denominations to be tossed to gleeful crowds from atop Toyota Land Cruisers, and 50 kg bags of rice to be handed out to feed the families of hungry voters. For the sticks: well, gangs like Toyin's were in charge of those. Cash—lots of it—had been set aside to pay them to intimidate opponents, guard ballot-box stuffing operations, and clash with rivals. Political violence in Nigeria looks chaotic, but it is in reality highly organised, with a chain of command stretching from politicians and paymasters at the top, to people like Toyin and her gang buddies at the bottom. The money will start in the political party's campaign office, and then the most senior of the group of thugs the party needs onside receives it and passes it down, each taking his own generous cut.

A few days before the election, Ataru gave them their marching orders. On this occasion, they were to guard the area around one of Lagos Island's oldest streets, Broad Street, a fusion of grand colonial-era buildings going mouldy in the humidity and skyscrapers housing big banks and insurance companies. The main target was Tinubu Square. It is a bustling roundabout at the junction of Broad Street and Nnamdi Azikiwe Street, on which the central mosque is situated, linking it to Ebute Ero wharf and Carter bridge to the mainland. It was named after Madam Efunroye Tinubu, whose bronze statue towers above it. She was celebrated as 'one of West Africa's greatest women liberators', in the words of one writer. She had escaped slavery to become a powerful businesswoman at the time when Lagos was being expropriated by the British in the 1800s. No one liked to talk about the fact that her wealth and power had come from selling slaves herself. As many of the gangsters, like Toyin, lived around Eko Idumota market, Ataru met them first at Breadfruit Street, near St Paul's Church, the first Anglican church in the city, built in 1880, which began life as a bamboo shed on the site where slavers tied their captives to breadfruit trees before selling them on to Europeans.

'I want you to be my eruku,' Ataru told them in Yoruba—a contraction of éru ikú, meaning 'fearless warrior', sometimes translated as 'messengers of death'. 'I want to see you everywhere for the campaign.'

So they set off down the street, passing UBA House, a cream-coloured sky scraper, one of the island's most prominent, and the glass cage that is Afriland Towers. They walked past the grand grey old African Church's Bethel Cathedral, a building of exquisite arches, pointy turrets, and stained glass windows turned almost black with the Lagos smog. They passed a turning towards the Marina, which faces the port over the busiest part of the lagoon for shipping, and walked on to Tinubu Square, where Madam Efunroye Tinubu's bronze cast loomed over the brick patio and water jets, a horse-hair whip in one hand and a fish-shaped club help up high in the other. The area was festooned with election posters. The PDP thugs had made an early advance to stake out some turf. Some of Toyin's gang clenched their blades and raised their homemade rifles. Tense moments passed.

The pro-PDP gang struck first, rushing towards the Tinubu loyalists. Within seconds the sound of war cries and crashing blades was blotting out the traffic noises. A couple of shots were fired from low-velocity hunting rifles. The street descended into an impenetrable brawl, and Toyin could barely tell which side was which. She thrashed someone wearing a PDP baseball cap with her nail-studded stick, and someone hit her with a wooden object. There were more gunshots, and screaming. And then suddenly she was on the ground with something wet and sticky underneath her and a tearing pain in her abdomen. She'd been shot ...

The next thing she would remember, vaguely, was Ataru letting out a cry and Gasper pulling her to the side of the street. She lay there amid the sounds of shouting and sharp metal hitting flesh and screaming. They had been badly outnumbered. The PDP fighters killed four of the AC fighters and lost only one of their own. Toyin and half a dozen other pro-Tinubu thugs had been wounded in the scuffle.

Someone had his mouth on Toyin's wound and was attempting to suck the bullet out of her abdomen—they did this in case it was poisoned. They then poured fiery schnapps on the open wound to sterilise it. Searing pain enveloped her, then unconsciousness.

* * *

She awoke in what was evidently a witchdoctor's shack. There was the familiar smell of rancid blood from sacrifices of animals offered to the various gods and ancestral spirits. Fetishes were dangling from the ceiling: a peacock feather, something bat-like. The bullet that had hit her was from the standard homemade pistol that touts used. Small steel ball bearings fired at low velocity, these bullets rarely killed on impact. They were fired from traditional hunting rifles used for downing pigeons or shooting grass cutters. But sometimes the bullets were poisoned. There remained another two lodged in different wounds around Toyin's ample belly fat. The floor was soaked in her blood.

It was believed the poison worked through black magic. The potion might simply be sand and water from the lagoon edge. The real power was in the magic incantation the witchdoctor pronounced on it. Devout Muslim that she was, Toyin normally ignored such claims, but who would want to take their chances? She recognised the babalawo delivering the cure. He was renowned among their small clan of Yoruba street warriors as a great sorcerer. She was dreadfully thirsty but wasn't allowed water: she could only drink once the spell was broken or else she might die. He reached out a hand, which she held.

The witchdoctor gave her a sip of schnapps, then poured some on the two wounds that still had bullets in them—both burned like the fires of Hell—and he readied a pair of tweezers. She bit her wrist as he rummaged around for the first one. She was

35

determined not to scream but couldn't help it. She fainted before he pulled out the second bullet.

'God be praised, I thought you were dead,' Ataru was saying when she awoke, pulling her up to his chest. The AC party had been successful in the election. For her role, Toyin received 200,000 naira ($1,600) in honour of her sacrifice to the cause, more than she'd ever seen. She could start to build a house with that, somewhere quieter and cheaper, on the shores of the lagoon. The thought briefly occurred to her that it was time to retire. Next time she might not be so lucky. But could she really give all this up?

* * *

A month later, she was back at Tafawa Balewa Square—where she had first impressed Ataru in helping his gang escape the police years earlier—watching the new governor, Babatunde Fashola, being sworn in. She was proud to have been part of what made his election possible. But if she had been listening, she might have noticed a veiled threat to the touts and all Lagosians who depended on the underworld economy. Fashola is a broad-shouldered man with high cheekbones that give him permanent dimples, and arched eyebrows, which, combined with his thin wire-frame glasses, conspire to give him a look alternating between the stern and the quizzical. As governor, he was bookish and technocratic, as well as having 'zero tolerance', as he told the cheering crowd, for disorder; he was preparing a drastic plan to tame the megacity.

He talked about 'a cleaner, safer, better-organised Lagos', he talked about getting tough on 'defiance of law and order,' and, most ominously of all, he spoke of 'enforcing the town planning and environmental laws'. Meeting these laws was, of course, impossible for most people in a city as corrupt as Lagos. You had to know the right officials or your plea for a building permit would go nowhere. The slothful bureaucracy of Lagos State could never keep up with the hundreds of people erecting shelters each day.

Tinubu's people had been shaving the edges off slums for years to make room for the odd road-widening or some pompous building, but he was also wary of draining the mangrove swamp that nourished his power. Fashola, by contrast, had no such qualms. His vision was almost apocalyptic: sweep away the dirt and the sheer maddening impossibility of Lagos. Bulldoze the shanties and replace them with orderly, air-conditioned shopping centres connected by light rail. Trying to adapt the current mess, trying to convert it into the Singapore of Africa he dreamed of, would be impossible. No, the slums had to go. And when the demolitions started, mere weeks later, Toyin would see them as a betrayal far worse than anything she could have imagined.

The first one she witnessed was near Eko Idumota. Eviction notices had been nailed to the doors, but the residents had nowhere else to go. The local market women protested by banging on pots as the Caterpillar approached building. When it was clear it wasn't going to divert its path, they scampered out of the way, carrying what few belongings they'd managed to salvage. The machine's arm crumpled the building like cardboard, and the residents cursed Fashola and screamed.

Within months, thousands of structures had been demolished. They knocked down the Sceptre Comprehensive College in Ogudu, just after where the Third Mainland Bridge joins the expressway. In September 2008, Fashola personally oversaw the tearing down of the rotting twenty-two-storey Bank of Industry skyscraper. A crowd stood in awe as it crumbled in a cloud of dust.

In Ajah, where Segun had recently moved to, the Overlord of Ajah, a powerful traditional chief, was seizing swathes of property and evicting the 'squatters'—mostly fishermen whose families had been there for centuries, but who lacked title deeds—from their plywood shacks. Whole fishing villages were being demolished, with help from touts from one of the bus stations on Lagos Island.

Then one morning Toyin awoke to the sound of her Nokia shrieking. On the other end of the line, her mother was frantic: 'They're going to destroy my house. Get here quickly.'

Toyin bolted out of bed. Orile, where her mother had spent years lovingly building a house after she became estranged from Toyin's womanising father, was sixteen kilometres away, on the mainland. It was already seven; the entrances to Carter and Eko bridges, the most direct routes, would be jammed by now. Toyin pushed through the market and hailed a cab. It crawled out of Idumota market, past the Central Water Tower to the main cloverleaf leading to the Third Mainland Bridge. They turned off the bridge, past swampy Oworonshoki with its huts on stilts in the sewage-green-tinged lagoon edge.

Orile Bus Stop made Obalende look organised. The road was always a sea of mustard yellow from all the minibuses jammed together. Even by Lagos standards, the air is poisonous with petrol fumes from stalled vehicles. This was hopeless. Toyin was never going to reach her mother in time.

When she finally arrived, Latifat was sitting on the side of a dirt road weeping and shaking while the machines finished off levelling her house. The bulldozers hadn't given her time to collect her belongings. Touts were smashing things with hammers and looting the debris. Toyin sat with her mother for a long while. That house was everything to her. It gave Latifat an independence that was rare among working-class Lagos women. She could have friends around for tea and homemade akara bean cakes with cassava porridge. She could store booze without anyone drinking it. Without a house, she was just another of Bashir's concubines living in his overcrowded apartment.

'Mom, it's OK,' Toyin tried to tell her, while her body was almost convulsed with grief. 'We'll build you a new house.'

Weeks later, Latifat was in hospital with a severe attack of hypertension, from which she'd suffered for a decade. Minutes after Toyin arrived, her heart stopped. For one of the very few times in her life, Toyin broke down in tears. It literally broke her mother's heart, losing that house. In a boiling rage, she resolved that never again would she fight for a Lagos politician, and that if she ever saw Fashola in the street, she would slice him open right there.

She thought again about retiring from the life of thuggery, which had become such a big part of who she was.

* * *

Two years later she was on her first hajj pilgrimage to Mecca— which all Muslims are obliged to undertake at least once in their lives. There she was, wrapped in a white shroud, at the tawaf ritual, in the al-Haram mosque, where Muslims honour the Black Stone set in silver. Suddenly she felt flooded with spirit, as if every sin were being washed away: the times she had lied to her parents, the times she had bullied weaker people, the violence of the bus park. She knelt in divine supplication, broke down and wept with joy, wept as she never had before—not even when her fiancé abandoned her or her mother died had she wept like this. At that moment she knew: she was done with violence. She would leave the Obalende Bus Terminus, taking the money she had earned, and set up a business around Ikorodu, on the northern side of the lagoon. Ikorodu itself was a heaving, traffic-smothered city, just like everywhere else on the Lagos mainland, but she would pick somewhere a bit quieter, away from the city, closer to Ijede, a village on a clay shelf whose main attraction was a terminal for ferries crossing the lagoon to the Lekki Peninsula. She was ready to retire: the only thing that really made her happy these days was seeing her children.

She spent a month on the plot where her house was to be built so she could retire. She had ordered the building materials:

a truckload of sand from the sand dredgers, the men who dive to the depths of the lagoon for sand to feed Lagos's endless construction boom. A lot of the other Obalende Boys seemed to be moving on as well. Ataru had helped the Overlord of Ajah in his fight for territory there, earning himself a plot of land. He was building himself a home, not far from where Segun now lived. She sat in a plastic chair on the sand. Fishermen in dugout canoes were casting nets over the lagoon. Small waves lapped the shore. Could she really live here, away from the chaos, the fighting, the sheer drama of Lagos Island? She put a sheet down on the sand, and fell asleep.

4

THE FIGHTING NEVER STOPS

Eko Idumota, Lagos Island, 2015

The city races and churns. Round and round the bridges and flyovers crawl thousands of tonnes of moving metal, cogs in a wheel grinding through an endless cycle: home to work, work to home, and back again. Millions of journeys, millions of passengers with their heads full of stress and trauma, with their small pleasures and amusements, their grief and bereavement. The maddening slowness of these journeys will rattle their nervous systems and balloon their blood pressure. But they won't complain: complaining gets you nowhere in Lagos. And though the stress will lead some to an early grave, it will put money in their pockets and food in their bellies.

Stepping out of her flat into the fuss and shouting of Eko Idumota, Toyin hails a keke napep (rickshaw) and we both get in. We zip through the anarchy of market stalls, narrowly avoiding knocking several over. In a clearing lit by the sun, a man in a dark grey suit and shiny shoes holds a frayed Bible in one hand, while his other hand wags a forefinger in Divine Judgement.

Minutes later, we are immobilised in a jam. These nifty little rickshaws are normally quite good at manoeuvring in and out of the little spaces between cars, but not when traffic is this bad. An area boy jumps out in front, and there is a look of fear in the rickshaw driver's eyes. The boy bashes the roof—he can't be more than 16, although it's hard to tell—and with his other hand he rubs his forefinger on his thumb.

'No money,' the driver pleads.

'Pay me my own share.' The boy gives him a fierce look, but the driver insists his ragged, torn trousers are empty. It's easy to believe him from the way he looks. 'You go balance me,' the area boy insists, using a colourful Nigerian pidgin English phrase for 'pay me what you owe'.

'I know this boy,' Toyin tells me, leaning out of the keke.

'Ah, madam.' The boy almost loses his balance while bowing in deference. She urges the driver to offer a little something and they settle on 50 naira.

We crawl past the 'Best Care Hospital', a shabby building that I hope I never end up in. A man in a kaftan and skullcap cries something in Arabic into a megaphone. 'It's not Muslim prayers, the guy's just begging,' the keke driver says. A woman wrapped from head to toe in a dark robe and headscarf drops a bill into the man's bucket, as does her friend, who, incongruously, is wearing a miniskirt and a strappy top.

After almost an hour of gridlock, we arrive at Obalende Bus Terminus. Toyin heads for Mama Tee's Cool Spot, a place for sipping golden beers that old Mama Tee somehow keeps cold with a tiny fridge hooked up to a sputtering generator. It is remarkably cool for a shack in one of the most crowded parts of a city with an average of humidity of 85 per cent, positioned as it is under a flyover that provides ample shade.

Mama Tee has hardship creased into her face. Her few possessions include a gold-coloured pair of flip-flops and a denim dress, although even on a bad day she makes an effort: lipstick and red toenails. Her bar, like so many small businesses in Lagos, is an invention of necessity. After her husband died, leaving her with nothing, she wandered around the bus park in despair—in Lagos, a woman in her mid-fifties in desperate need of a job is among the least sought-after to fill one. As she suffered refusal after refusal, she noticed an unclaimed piece of territory under the bridge, and a breeze tickled her face.

Toyin took pity on Mama Tee and, in her capacity as the senior Obalende Market Women's Association head (of course), leased her the space which neither of them owned at a heavy discount—and lent her 50,000 naira to get set up. It swiftly became a place of beer and banter and the occasional brawl.

Toyin, Segun and Gasper are sitting on the bar's plastic chairs as the lunch-time rush hour fades away. Mechanics weld battered minibuses back together. Everyone is dabbing sweat off their faces. Bus drivers fuss and argue. Touts collect money and issue threats.

'Segun, you wimp, fetch me a beer,' Toyin says. He obliges. They haven't seen each other in more than five years since he became a private chauffeur. He nods at a hawker who comes with a bucket of large, cold Star beers. After one, Toyin's pale brown face is becoming characteristically red.

After building her retirement home near Ikorodu, she quickly realised she could never live there. She tried to get used to the relative quiet, the lilting rhythms of insects after dark. But she missed the warmth and closeness of frenetic Lagos Island. 'I like noise and wahala [trouble] too much-o,' she tells me. She could barely sleep without the sounds of the city she'd known since birth. Within six weeks, she was back in Obalende. She kept her promises to herself not to do violence anymore, at least not unless someone attacked her personally—and especially never again to fight for a politician. But she couldn't stay away from the bus park. It was all she knew.

At Mama Tee's, various touts approach to shake Toyin's hand, giving her hearty slaps on the shoulder, as they do to the men. Gasper leaves to go dish out orders to some touts, leaving Toyin and me alone. For years now, men have been only friends or business partners for Toyin, but never lovers, she tells me—'I've no interest in that anymore'. As one of our many conversations about this topic progresses, she deflects a question about whether she might prefer female lovers, which would land her foul of Nigeria's homophobic laws and society. 'I don't ever think of that,' she says.

Gasper returns, overhearing some of our conversation. He is with Segun.

'She's the only lady we ever had working for us,' he says. 'She's the toughest lady in Lagos,' and she goes a little redder.

The clouds are dirty and grey. A man wheels a rusty barrow full of fat earthy yams to sell to the travellers, and a child of about seven or eight in a bright green dress holds a bucket of water on her head to sell to people needing to wash their hands.

'All of them have to pay to use this space,' Segun says, still sounding a little resentful. 'They have to register and after that the union takes some of their money.'

'Yes, that's just how it is,' says Gasper, as he turns to me, smiling.

Gasper and Toyin reminisce about the old days, how they used to get into so many fights, before the bus station got a bit more orderly. Under Governor Fashola's efforts to restore law and order, a lot of places that used to be overrun with thuggery have scrubbed up a bit, even Obalende. Just outside, there is now a visible traffic police presence. Toyin tells me two of the cops in view used to be thugs for Ataru's gang.

'I miss those days,' Toyin says. 'I used to get excited coming here. But now things are quiet. It's like the fighting just stopped.'

An engine growls and unbearably loud Nigerian pop music fills the air.

THE FIGHTING NEVER STOPS

'This is Lagos,' Gasper says, levering himself off his chair with his ample, tattooed biceps.

'The fighting doesn't really stop.'

PART II

THE SCRAPYARD BARD

Lagos's greatest slum, Ajegunle, exemplifies the worst of worlds: overcrowding coupled with extreme peripherality. In 1972, Ajegunle contained 90,000 people on 8 square kilometres of swampy land; today 1.5 million people reside on an only slightly larger surface area, and they spend a hellish average of three hours each day commuting to their workplaces.

Mike Davis, *Planet of Slums*

When supernatural forces are at work, it is not impossible for a hen's egg to crack a stone.

Edo proverb

5

ERIC

Olususun Dumpsite, Lagos Mainland, 2000

Every city is many cities. In Lagos, there are cities made of fine
brick with imported marble, and cities made of crooked drift-
wood with rusty iron roofing. There are cities assembled out of
shipping containers, cities floating on swamps. And then there is
Olususun: a city made of all things that Lagos's 20 million
inhabitants no longer want.

To most Lagosians, the Olususun dumpsite is a stinking monster, a bloated eyesore, a constant reminder of how unsustainable
the city's breakneck growth is. Things fester, decay, putrefy in
Olususun. As one of the world's largest rubbish tips, it is spread
over one hundred acres and rises as high as an eight-storey building in some places. In others, it extends as far as thirty-five
metres underground as rubbish heaped on more rubbish has
gradually compacted itself down into the dirt-like fossil layers.
Tens of millions of tonnes of refuse have moulded their own
kaleidoscopic geography of rolling hills, jagged gorges and lat-
ticed pathways formed of plastic bags, flip-flops, clothes, cardboard boxes and tyres. At the tip of this reeking iceberg, white

herons, rats, flies and lizards gorge themselves on fermenting food waste. When dust devils whirl through the site in the dry harmattan winds blowing south from the Sahara, the polythene bags caught in their gusts look like buzzards circling.

Olusosun is a collective effort, which every Lagosian has had a hand in creating. It doesn't matter if they are the kind who can afford to throw out gold jewellery when it's no longer fashionable or the kind who pick weevils out of rice. Whether they reside in a palace adorned with Corinthian columns or a shack adorned with nothing; whether they socialise with princes and oil tycoons or with their cleaners and gardeners; whether they wash themselves in a spa or in a gutter—regardless of who they are, every time they toss out an old pair of shoes, a tissue, a car tyre or a battery, there's a good chance it will end up on Olusosun. And if any part of it is still of value, someone will probably recycle it. Olusosun is the sight that richer nations try so hard to hide from their citizens, who produce far more rubbish per person than any African nation but have it expunged: buried, burned, flushed or exported to poor countries far from their precious view. In Lagos, a city expanding to fill every nook and cranny of the land on which it lies, the effluence of modern life simply can't be hidden.

When the site had first formed in the 1990s, a group of pioneers figured out it was a potential gold mine for anyone strong, resilient and willing to hold his nose. Almost overnight, a boom town sprang up as hundreds of trash pickers and scores of scrap buyers flocked to it. Today, fizzing with methane like an undersea volcano, this shadow economy lies barely five kilometres from Lagos State's main government buildings. The dumpsite is a market, a community, a village.

It was on Olusosun that Eric Obuh, lean, hungry and glazed-eyed, pitched up shortly after his eighteenth birthday. It was the turn of the millennium. Thanks to decades of neglect by a succession of Nigerian military dictators, Lagos was a serious contender for the title of the world's worst city to live in. Its reputation preceded it as a place beset by touts, robbers, kamikaze bus drivers and mountains of refuse.

But the new Lagos State civilian governor, Tinubu, wanted to be the first governor who actually got things done, instead of simply collecting money from various extortion rackets (though he did that, too). Of the mammoth tasks ahead, collecting trash was the most urgent, a lynchpin of the governor's vision of a modern megacity. At the time it was a vision as laughable as the city's 'Centre of Excellence' slogan brandished on car number plates. Lagos was literally disappearing under its own waste. So Tinubu ordered a herculean clean-up, sending forth thousands of orange-boiler-suited trash pickers to fill up trucks with refuse, much of which would end up on Olusosun.

There is an unwritten deal between the Lagos State government and the trash pickers: the latter work all day, every day, as often and for as long as they wish. They get no pay, no sick leave and no benefits, but they get to sell whatever they find to recyclers. In return Lagos State gets free recycling, reducing landfill and saving it the burdensome task of sorting the recyclables itself.

The scavengers at Olusosun will travel from their various slums for up to six hours en route and some stay several days in makeshift shacks before heading home, scouring recently dumped piles of trash for plastic bottles, glass, electronics, clothes. Scrap buyers arrive from all over the country with fistfuls of cash. Hundreds of others, mostly women, will sell them food, cold drinks, bath water, haircuts or medicine. Acrid smoke coils upwards from the site, a combination of fires burning refuse and women boiling pots over charcoal—the very smoke that Eric breathed in as he walked through the gate that first morning with empty pockets.

As with most ragpickers, this wasn't Eric's first choice of job. He dreamed of being a reggae singer. But he was broke. His friend Augustin, a fellow would-be musician, had introduced him to Olususun months earlier.

'Just come and see it,' he had said while they were eating bitter leaf soup and eba cassava dough, in Ajegunle, the most over-crowded slum in Africa's most overcrowded city. From the sec-ond the stench of rotting vegetation hit Eric's nose as he entered the dumpsite, he'd been horrified. Yet he was in awe of the sheer scale of the operation. Hundreds of workers sifted through fetid plastic like ants.

'You should set yourself up here. You can make good money,' Augustin had said.

A few days later, Eric awoke in his one-room 'face me, face you' apartment in Ajegunle and knew: he would take Augustin's advice. He said a prayer to Almighty God in Heaven to bring forth a new chapter in his life. *But never*, he continued the prayer, *please God, never let anyone find out*. If word got out that he was scavenging on a rubbish heap, he knew he would spend the rest of his life trying to live down the shame. Even in poor Ajegunle, scavengers were the lowest of the low: dirty, down-trodden, hopeless.

His head still full of sleep, he tiptoed past half a dozen snoring cohabiters squatting in his tiny room in the mouldy, unpainted building. He could imagine his father's disgusted look if he caught wind of it. Emmanuel had never given Eric much assis-tance beyond the highly incomplete schooling he'd funded. But fatherly disapproval is a powerful disincentive, and Eric knew the worst thing for a father picturing his son tearing open refuse bags would be the reflection on his own failures.

Eric shut the creaky door quietly, stepping out into the steamy air. He skipped breakfast: if he ate too early, he knew he'd be starving by mid-morning, and anyway he had no money. Neither, clearly, did he bother washing: as Augustin had told him, the dumpsite workers only needed to do that at the end of the day. His only concession to grooming was to polish his shoes until he could see the sun reflected luminously, an exercise which might seem pointless for a man about to wade through filth but which for Eric was a matter of pride.

He bought a tea of herbs and roots brewed by the local witch-doctor to ward off malaria—and bad luck. It was sold in abundance by female hawkers and taken as an alternative to expensive Western prophylactics, which in Nigeria—like many pharmacy drugs—are often fake anyway. The concoctions were usually prepared by Yoruba medicine men—leaves of a guava tree mashed up with mango tree bark, pawpaw leaves and lemongrass. Or else a fiery local gin poured onto bitter leaf and corn ears mashed up with the roots of the Neem tree. Eric swigged down the bitter liquid and set off to the central bus stop.

His walk passed open drains and the furious activity of slum dwellers who had started work even earlier than he did. He met Augustin and stepped into the first available danfo. Being one of the first in gave him a sense of spaciousness, which was rudely dispelled as the bus was stuffed with humanity. As usual, a blind beggar from the Muslim north guided by a willowy child was chanting something about the ascent of generous souls to heaven, but Eric had nothing to give him.

When it could fit no more passengers, the minibus crawled out of Ajegunle. It motored past endless fuel trucks queuing to get into the port and pick up imported fuel. After covering ten kilometres at a painfully slow pace, it passed the Mile 2 estate. A wasteland of burnt-out cars, traffic fumes and a rusting ferry terminal, Mile 2 was a haven for armed robbers preying on trapped rush-hour traffic and goods from the port. A second bus took him further north along the road to the frenetic Ojota bus terminal, next to the dumpsite. There, he and Augustin stepped into a yellow pandemonium of hooting minibuses that were somehow managing to move in myriad directions without colliding. The pair squeezed out of the informal bus station towards the dumpsite gate.

Olusosun was run by a group of buyers, one of Lagos's many 'associations' that fill the governance vacuum left by a dysfunctional state. 'The Scavengers Association of Nigeria' they called it, testimony to Nigerians' fondness for grandiose titles and also lack of political correctness. In reality, like all of Nigeria's 'associations', it was a little more like a racket. The trash kingpins that ran it charged almost everyone who worked there a fee based on (perceived) ability to pay. There was really no question of not paying. They knew who everyone was and they could be fierce with anyone who tried to resist or sneak out money without passing their cut to the association. Though they profited handsomely from it, they also provided a safety net of sorts: small loans, medical care, bribes to pay off bent cops.

On his arrival, the association registered Eric and, after some lobbying by Augustin, gave him boots with steel toecaps to protect against sharp objects, thick socks and the most vital piece of kit: a metal hook. The scavengers on Olusosun rake through the rubbish holding these hooks in one hand. Together they resemble a troop of Long John Silvers scratching around for buried treasure.

Eric set to work, scanning the jumbled rubbish heaps for iron, aluminium, rubber and copper wire. He focused on drinks cans first—not hugely profitable but easy to sort. He separated them into more valuable aluminium and cheaper iron—an easy task, since the latter would be coated in rust from Lagos's humidity. On several occasions he had to stop himself from vomiting, but as the day wore on he slowly got used to the stench. His muscles were aching.

By the end of his first day, he had managed to make 390-naira profit (then about $3.75), more than he'd ever earned in 24 hours, and he saw instantly what Augustin was making a fuss about. *Maybe I could do this.* But then the shame hit him on the minibus back, and he wondered whether he could bring himself to come back. Eric, who had hustled in recording studios since the age of 12 to try to launch himself as a singer, now found himself working in a landfill as he entered adulthood. Then again, it would mean a steady income, and he had two younger sisters to feed.

'You OK?' Augustin asked him while the bus was crawling through the gridlock, on a clogged freeway with muddy pavements down which people nonetheless walked in their smart business wear past crowds of hawkers. At this home rush hour, men in suits and ties jumped concrete barriers to dash across the expressway, stubbornly avoiding the purpose-built footbridges spanning the motorways from a safe height. Women shaded by parasols on the roadside did petty trade with the stalled traffic.

'I'm fine,' Eric said, but he wasn't. Even if it was good money, he just couldn't stand it: this was just not how he saw his future. He would find something else to do, even if it meant staying desperately poor before finally recording his big hit album. He made his weary way back to Ajegunle.

* * *

Eric had scrubbed up under a pail of water hired from one of the local women at the scrapyard before leaving. As well as these 'showers', as they were optimistically labelled, they offered haircuts and even manicures. When he got back home, he washed again. He wanted every whiff off his body before heading out. The Eric his friends knew was a musician, a playboy, a rapper, a hustler. 'Scavenger' did not fit with those epithets.

'Act big, even if you're small' was Eric's guiding maxim. Lagos slum dwellers have made dressing well and looking good an art form, even in the filthiest and most water-starved places. Eric was always immaculately turned out when he hung around Ajegunle's scruffy recording studios and bars. He liked to wear a polo shirt, sometimes with the collar up like the rich kids in the newspapers sipping pink Moët at the polo club. That club always looked so green, the kind of green Eric had only ever seen in a village or along a remote stretch of highway. He smoothed his hair and headed out.

The sun was dipping below Ajegunle's western shanties, the wispy clouds turning lipstick-pink. Some of the girls would be wearing that shade at the many nameless bars this evening. Eric was a hit with women, despite his poverty. They were drawn to his outsized confidence, philosopher charm and tendency to break into song. Eric is taller than average with high cheek-bones, a dimpled chin, thick eyebrows and red, glassy eyes from years of poor nutrition. His teeth seem crowded even for his wide mouth, but they give him a beaming smile, and a slightly lost look in his eyes lends him an air of vulnerability. When he lost his virginity at the age of 16 to a girl called Aduko, he was homeless. He had persuaded her to allow him back to her parents' house in secret. After that, he figured that finding women wouldn't be a problem.

But tonight Eric was out on the town for another reason: music. If you wanted to make it in the business, you needed to be seen where the DJs play it. The grimy nightspots of 'AJ City', as the coolest cats on the music scene called Ajegunle, had been experiencing a musical renaissance for a decade, a surge in creativity born of deprivation. In ragga and hip-hop songs, Eric's neighbourhood was called 'the Ghetto'. It was a fitting description for a place not far from the villas of millionaires yet so lacking in basic infrastructure like roads, power or sewerage.

As the twenty-first century wore on, Lagos was undergoing a makeover. Narrow roads were being widened into multi-lane highways; drains were being dug. Moss-covered colonial houses were being torn down, swapped for luxury flats in gaudy gold and silver, pink and orange. New high-rises sparkled. Yet somehow Ajegunle always seemed to miss out on the improvements. Its dirt roads were craterous; its trash-clogged gutters refracted the rainbow sheen of spilt petrol. The average daily commute on its hellish roads was two hours each way, even for people working at the adjacent port. Few homes were hooked up to the national grid, which anyway tended to divert power to richer areas like Victoria Island. Children had to trek miles out of town with jerrycans in search of water because the slum's few boreholes couldn't cope with the demand.

The ghetto's muddy streets were nonetheless proving an unlikely springboard for the success of local artists like Daddy Showkey, African China and Mighty Mouse. Each part of Lagos had its distinct sound, like Ikeja, the state capital running off the northern end of the Third Mainland Bridge, in the shadow of the deceased Afrobeat legend Fela Kuti. Ajegunle had taken a different route from that blazed by Fela's hypnotic, funk-infused music, with its blaring horns and dancing girls. Saxophones and trumpets are expensive in the Ghetto; Casio keyboards less so. Musicians there veered towards synthesised reggae-pop and especially its younger offshoot, dancehall. Singers emulated ragamuffin stars like Beenie Man and Sean Paul. They smoked copious weed and called God 'Jah'. The Rastafarian narrative, with its curious blend of pan-African nationalism and Old Testament prophecy, its talk of oppression by a greedy, self-serving 'Babylon', and its hope for redemption into an equitable 'Zion', always struck a chord in impoverished Ajegunle.

The nameless bar Eric was approaching comprised a few plastic chairs outside an unfinished concrete building with metal doors. Ragga was blasting out of speakers, loud enough to churn stomachs and damage eardrums. At this hour, Ajegunle's streets had a mellow hue, lit up by hundreds of woodfires cooking food. Like many bar-shacks in Ajegunle, this one doubled up as a convenience store, its shelves lined with milk powder, insect killer, tinned tomatoes, disinfectant. A surly bar lady was open-ing beers and, for one flashy customer, an expensive bottle of brandy poured into sugary Coke. Some of these guys would spend a month's salary on a big night, then eat cheap noodles in their windowless bedsits for weeks.

'Hey, Slender,' someone called out from a table. Eric had been nicknamed 'Slender' since boyhood on account of his skinny frame, and had adapted this to create a stage name: 'Vocal Slender'. Eric ordered his usual bottle of Alomo bitters—a herb-coloured local gin brewed from fruits and a dozen African medic-inal herbs meant to treat everything from impotence to belly-aches. Then he ordered his regular bowl of cow-tongue soup. The concrete space outside was slithering with Ajegunle's popular 'galala' dance: men crouching down, knocking their knees together and spraying out their arms; women rotating hips and chests with sexually charged fluidity. Eric's friends Edwin and Jerobi were there, as were musicians Maggy, Augustin and Prosper. A Rastafarian lit and passed around a joint.

Eric's tactic in bar conversation, as in life, was to dominate it with his overconfident, opinionated, booming personality.

'You know you just need one reggae hit to become a million-aire, if you get it right,' he offered. 'That's what I'm going to do: make a million. You'll see.'

'Slender, this is Nigeria. The only millionaires are oilmen,' said Maggy, dreadlocks flopping over his face. 'Anyway, when did I last see you in a recording studio?'

The barmaid brought out a plastic bottle of freshly brewed 'scoochies': gin mixed with iced marijuana tea and blackcurrant cordial. It was a favourite amongst AJ City's wannabe musicians. After the alcohol wore off, a slow-burn marijuana haze descended on everyone.

'You'll see,' Eric said, cutting off Maggy, as he does most people when he has something more important to say. 'I'm going to make my millionaire song.'

Eyeballs rolled skywards. Eric's friends always admired his optimism, even the ones who found his incessant self-promotion irritating.

The sky darkened. In the West, consumers fret about light pollution, but Lagos skies are so blackened by power shortages it is easy to forget they hang over millions of people. As the scoochies took effect, everyone fell silent, the collective consciousness warping into a hall of mirrors. Eric decided to turn in. He was exhausted from his day on the dump—at least no one at the bar had asked him about what he'd been doing all day. He stumbled home, crunching Ajegunle's plastic detritus underfoot, and wondering what hustle he'd have to take up next to pay his share of the house rent. Was he ever going to have enough money to record his hit song?

* * *

Eric's parents had first moved to Ajegunle from the Niger Delta at the end of the 1970s, a few years before he was born. Penury forced them to abandon their village in the delta's mangrove swamps, where the 4,200-kilometre river is shredded into thousands of creeks as it flushes into the Atlantic. The region had been producing all of Nigeria's oil for two decades when the 1970s global oil price boom turned Nigeria into the world's sixth-biggest crude producer. But aside from the pollution soiling their creeks—and the gas flares lighting up the sky every night in apocalyptic orange—the inhabitants of the delta could be forgiven for not noticing that they were at the heart of Africa's oil business. The money gushing into state coffers seldom came their way, and their riverine fishing communities remained as poor as before the first barrel was pumped.

Lagos, by contrast, was a 'land of opportunity', as Eric's father, Emmanuel, would constantly repeat. So, gathering up a sackful of clothes and a Bible, he and Eric's mother, Dora, headed by bus along rotten dirt tracks to the creek-veined slum of Ajegunle. In some ways it resembled the delta: creeks, palm trees and bogland prone to flooding. But it was then, as now, urban chaos in the extreme: rows of single-storey iron-roof kiosks selling everything from Western clothes to food to car parts; an endless succession of traders carrying buckets of flip-flops or sacks of rice on their heads; women grilling chicken on portable barbecues; and every inch of road space not taken up by a hawker jammed with minibuses and rickshaws.

Because of its proximity to one of Africa's biggest ports, Ajegunle is an electromagnetic field sucking in the poor and discontented from every part of Nigeria: Igbos from the forested east, Hausas from the north on the cusp of the Sahara, a patchwork of minority tribes from the orange groves of the Middle Belt. West African migrants from other countries also make thousands of toe-blistering journeys across sand, bush and forest to reach the slum: fishermen from Benin, cattle herders from Niger, desert-hardened Chadians. In this way, Ajegunle keeps squeezing more arrivals into a jumble of narrow streets spanning less than ten square kilometres. As he was growing up, Eric's teenage journeys to the recording studios would pass Beninese women hawking pungent fish smoked over charcoal in the traditional West African way, and butchered meat sold by pastoralists from Africa's scorched Sahel region in tiny wooden kiosks, with coils of shiny intestine dangling off meat hooks like shocks of red wavy hair.

It certainly makes for diverse ways to bother God. Even today the Pentecostal churches draw in West Africans from southern Ghana, the Ivory Coast, Togo, Benin. The central mosque, with its bulbous dome and beetroot-red minaret, meanwhile brings the Chadians, Nigeriens and other nationalities from the Muslim strip of Black Africa just below the Sahara, the legacy of centuries of Arab conquest. They kneel and pray on mats outside, hands cupped skywards, alongside Lagos's skullcapped Yoruba Muslims.

Ajegunle is, and always has been, a quilt stitching together an outsized chunk of West Africa's huge diversity: two major religions, hundreds of languages, and scores of ethnic groups all working, hustling, praying, sleeping, washing, marrying and eating in the same jumble of hastily erected buildings. Yet the elements in this colossal melting pot never quite melted, no matter how tightly they were pressed together. And, because of this fact, they can be highly combustible.

* * *

About a week after Eric's day of trying out work on the dumpsite, he was getting ready to perform at Reggae Night at a club on Lagos Island. A dozen acts competed for a prize every weekend. He had always been pipped by someone else, but he had a good feeling about tonight.

He would sing his latest composition, 'Post No Bills', with another Ajegunle musician from the Niger Delta called Palliman. They took a bus past the clogged Apapa port area, one of Africa's biggest and by far its most chaotic, a virtual city of containers piled up as high as multi-storey buildings along the edge of the lagoon, before it opens out into the Atlantic.

From the motorway running past it, through the gaps in the crumbling walls being consumed by weeds, the edge of the port complex is a post-apocalyptic Mad Max mash-up. Abandoned container lorries rust in scrapyards; highways loom over moulding apartment blocks occupied by squatters who hang out their clothes; silver hemispheres of fuel storage tanks cluster by bronze-hued canals. An intersection of flyovers past the port has spawned a makeshift community underneath, where dozens of traders, tramps and down-and-outs take refuge from the city's alternating humid heat and pounding rain—Lagos has only two kinds of weather.

The usual line of traffic inched passed the port roads—there were fourteen different bribe-seeking agencies holding up shipments while they 'inspected' containers, causing blood-boiling gridlock six days a week. The bus then crossed the Carter Bridge to the island, and the setting sun sparkled off the lagoon. *God, please deliver us a resounding success,* Eric said in silent prayer. He opened his eyes to see Palliman also bowed in prayer.

Before going on stage, they pulled their baseball caps over their heads and high-fived. As they grabbed the microphones and started jumping around, the crowd cheered and silhouettes of women in short skirts and tight tops danced. They didn't win the contest. Eric swiftly spent the little money he'd earned from his performance on drinks, then decided to leave—it was getting late to cross the bridges safely, and Eric didn't fancy negotiating with an armed robber with nothing in his pocket to give him.

Eric and Palliman took the night bus back together. It pulled up at Ajegunle Boundary, near a canal running off the lagoon. As usual, the lagoon edge was clogged with the plastic bags that people dumped because no trucks came to collect their rubbish, some of it twinkling in the reflected headlights. It was the tail end of the rainy season, when this part of town was always flooded so badly that it began merging into the lagoon. Eric started to drift off—until the bus came to a sharp halt.

Eric peered out of the window. Something was wrong. This was normally the most frenetically crowded place in the whole slum, yet everyone had vanished. Metal shutters on thousands of shops were pulled down; others had been ransacked. There was shouting and the sound of people running. Then Eric caught a glimpse of the bus driver's face: it was pure terror.

'OPC!' someone shouted, and everyone on the bus scrambled to get off as if it were balancing on a cliff edge. Outside, fires raged in the streets, lighting up angry faces and filling the air with car tyre fumes. Eric and Palliman saw twenty youths with machetes run into a side street. 'Shit,' Palliman said. They quickened their pace to get home.

ERIC

A couple of weeks earlier, the Oodua People's Congress (OPC), part vigilante movement, part ethnic Yoruba separatist group, who were fighting to split Lagos and the southwest off from Nigeria, had fallen out with migrant Hausa traders from the largely Muslim north. A wave of tit-for-tat killing followed. It was the kind of violence that had periodically convulsed Nigeria since independence from the British in 1960, when around 300 ethnic groups quickly realised they didn't really want to live together.

The OPC had been set up five years earlier by a medical doctor and hotel owner called Frederick Fasehun in response to decades of abuses by 'northern' military leaders in the 1990s. But as their numbers swelled with neighbourhood gangs of unemployed youths, known as 'area boys', the OPC grew factionalised and thuggish.

In the past two days, the OPC thugs had set up roadblocks and killed dozens of those deemed from the 'wrong' ethnic group—especially Hausas from the north. And the Hausas in turn had been killing Yoruba and other southern tribes. Eric feared them even more: his Edo ethnic group were sometimes allied with the Yoruba.

'What tribe are you?' a Hausa man holding a machete asked Eric and Palliman at a roadblock near the boundary. There were eight Hausas, some armed with bows and arrows, and all adorned with chains attached to magic amulets meant to harness the power of the occult to protect against weapons.

He could honestly say he wasn't Yoruba, thank God, but what if they had it in for his Edo people too? The various Niger Delta tribes, including the Edo, had fought bitterly with the OPC last year. But they were both southerners, at the end of the day. Better not tell them.

'Please, I'm from Cameroon,' Eric said. 'Near Calabar, on the Nigeria border.'

The skinny Hausa youth narrowed his eyes. Eric tried to beam his winning smile. He tilted his head sideways to indicate that they should let him and Palliman pass. Which they did.

'What tribe are you?' asked the OPC militiaman at the next roadblock, a few hundred metres down the road, next to one of the main junctions, which were never so deserted, even at night. Normally there would be crowds of night traders and women grilling meat over charcoal, and some revellers getting drunk on cheap spirit.

'Igbo,' Eric said this time. Yoruba and Igbo were allies against the Hausas, right?

'We could kill you right here,' the youth said. There was a pause: Eric knew he should have just said Ijaw. He felt a blade slap him— but it was the flat side, pressing coldly against his skin.

'I'm just kidding, man,' the OPC youth said, and he and Augustin scurried away.

Eric barricaded his room when he got home. More than a hundred people died in the next four days of rioting across Lagos. Mutilated corpses were dumped in the streets. In Ajegunle, Lagos's most dangerous slum at the best of times, the OPC looted and burned down shops while hundreds of people took refuge in a military barracks. Finally, the military stepped in to restore order. The sound of machete clashes was replaced with gunfire—and the militias melted back into their shacks.

'Let's go back to Olusosun,' Augustin suggested the following day, after they ventured outside to see weeping relatives picking corpses from the rubble. 'There's none of this wahala [trouble] there. You only tried it for a day. Why not go again?'

Eric really didn't want to go back. But it seemed a damn sight safer than AJ City right now. And he certainly needed the money.

* * *

He managed to suppress a retch when the smell hit him on the way back in. Then he set to work, putting on his special boots and his ragged overalls. First, he needed somewhere to sleep. So over the course of the day, he assembled a bed out of plywood and mosquito netting improvised from a discarded wedding dress that he found on the dump. He picked up his hook and starting raking.

He spent the next week searching plastic bags in stagnant puddles. After about three days, the smell had ceased to bother him at all. Even when the rains arrived, and flash floods engulfed the city, turning parts of Olusosun into a noxious lake of caramel-coloured sludge, his nose barely registered the stink. Rainy days were going to be the worst, he realised, as he joined the scavengers helping to push the rubbish trucks that got stuck, their frictionless wheels splattering their torsos with mud.

Most of the scavengers got up at six thirty to offload their scrap. They held off until ten or eleven before taking breakfast, then hungrily devoured rice, beans and goat or beef from the eating shack, or yams fried in palm oil red as fresh blood. After dark, they ate instant noodles with scrambled eggs and fiery peppers or morsels of fried fish, if the day had been lucrative enough. Those satisfied with their day's takings would go home. The others, which was most of them, would collapse on top of their wooden boxes on the dumpsite, their exhausted bones awaiting another punishing day of hustle. Some almost never left the dump. Here there was money; outside, just myriad ways of losing it—on demanding relatives, in nocturnal drinking houses, in myriad scams, on extortion at police or area boys' roadblocks.

On the bus back to Ajegunle for the weekend, Eric realised that even after a week or so he was saving money, not much but more than he had ever managed back home. For several weeks he made the same journey to the dump, and each time saved a little more, but still his doubts grew: would it ever be enough? In a decent studio a song would cost at least 40,000 naira (then $400), more than a hundred times what he'd made in a day, before spending was considered. An album could take years. With each lumbering journey to the dump, his heart sank, and was only slightly lifted at the end of the week, when he returned to Ajegunle with cash in his pocket.

A few weeks of this and he was almost ready to quit. As a child he'd known hunger, especially after his dad was swindled and lost all his money in what Nigerians call a 419 scam—a too-good-to-be-true business opportunity that involves an upfront payment from the gullible investor. Yes, he knew hunger, enough to be afraid of it. But he also had his pride, and his pride really didn't want him to be on Olususon. And then something happened that made him realise he was destined to stay on the dump. *God wanted him there.*

* * *

It was the usual start to the week. He was on his way to Olususon with Augustin at a painfully early hour. They sat together, eyes bloodshot, as the gridlock lumbered to the Ojota bus station. On arrival, they took a shortcut past a series of derelict buildings. The street, not the usual one, was full of overgrown bush and, apart from a mechanic fixing old cars, was eerily deserted. Eric noticed some area boys smoking weed in one of the buildings, sweet smoke puffing out of an empty windowpane, but he thought nothing of it.

Then the gunfire started. It would turn out later that this was a police raid, and that the cops suspected Eric and Augustin were members of the weed-smoking criminal gang they had been monitoring in the building. Panic took control of Eric's limbs and he ran towards the dumpsite without thinking, ignoring shouts of 'Stop there'. Barely ten metres from the gate, half a dozen policemen cornered him—and shoved him to the ground.

ERIC

As he lay in wet dirt with a policeman pointing an AK-47 at him in front of his guffawing colleagues, he cursed himself for ever starting work in Olususun.

The big-bellied cop took aim through the sights of his Kalashnikov, and Eric could see the man's eyes narrowing to focus on his target. Eric was lying in the dirt a few feet away. At first he didn't bother pleading. Police shoot hundreds of people every year in Lagos and no one much complains apart from the odd diplomat or local human rights lawyer. He started to get up.

'Lie back down,' the policeman barked, and he obliged.

A rain cloud was dissolving the dirt track on which Eric lay into a muddy stream. The cop unclicked the safety catch. He then joked that Eric would struggle to run away again with a bullet in his knee. Eric almost wanted to thank him for that: a leg shot meant he might survive.

He revised his opinion on pleading.

'No, I beg, don't. Please don't.'

The cop aimed his rifle at Eric's knee—left or right, he couldn't tell which one was the target. Eric shut his eyes and winced. There was a click, then a bang.

* * *

When Eric was born in December 1982, an oil price crash had plunged Nigeria's crude-fuelled kleptocracy into crisis. In a pattern that has been repeated ever since, its venal military and a few equally venal civilian leaders had drunk champagne instead of making hay while the sun shone, leaving the economy unprepared for the oil shock. In the climate of decay, Eric's father failed to find a job for long enough to keep up with the bills. Fed up with living in squalor, Eric's mother abandoned her husband and their five children when Eric was barely out of infancy.

Emmanuel initially managed to cobble together money for school fees, but barely enough for food. Eric found it hard to concentrate on his schoolwork with a rumbling belly. He would try to hold his attention on the tatty blackboard as the teacher droned on, but the gnawing would drag it away. When Eric's dad took a second wife, Shana, whom he met at his church, things only got worse. He swiftly moved into Shana's flat, came to see them less and less, and over a very short space of time supplies of food to the family home where his children remained dwindled to next to nothing. Eric was seven.

Shana would beat any of Emmanuel's kids who dared show up at the door. One time when Eric hadn't eaten anything since morning, he and his elder brother Gideon turned up in search of their father to complain.

'You are a foolish boy. What business do you have with me?' Shana shouted, eyes wide with inexplicable rage, before smacking Eric around the head so that he toppled to the ground. He left and resolved never to depend on his father for anything.

* * *

Eric opened his eyes. There was no pain, no blood. He looked at his knee; it was intact. Somehow the cop had missed. He would later wonder if it was all a bluff, and he'd been pointing his rifle at the sky.

When the man's supervising officer came in screaming, the policeman protested that he had caught Eric smoking 'Indian hemp', Nigerian slang for marijuana. It wasn't true, but Eric knew no one would believe that. He knew of people whom the police had carted away and they'd never been seen again. The landfill workers suspected several of their colleagues had ended up in Kirikiri, Nigeria's most overcrowded prison, next to the Apapa port, which human rights groups attack for its degrading treatment of prisoners, poor medical care and predictably high death rate.

The police bound Eric's hands with a cloth, tying it until it hurt his wrists. The van rattled over potholes to Ojota police station, and Eric and his eight fellow detainees bumped their heads on the chassis. They were stripped naked and lined up. The police officer in charge of the station told them they would be examined to see if they were criminals. Eric asked him what they were looking for.

'Scars', the man replied. Most of the 'vagabonds' the police detained had been beaten by them before. The beatings—using batons, steel cables and rifle butts—left distinguishable marks. The police were identifying the criminals, using somewhat circular logic, as people they had hit or tortured in the past. None of the detainees had scars, so they let them go—in exchange for a hefty 2,000-naira ($20) bribe that Eric and Augustin managed to get the Scavengers Association to cough up. Clifford Azemoh, a shorter-than-average man with a furrowed brow and wiry build, who was also from Ajegunle and had bonded with Eric on his first day, seemed to know the cops. He quickly peeled off the money and handed it over. Off came Eric's and Augustin's cuffs.

That evening in Ajegunle, Eric thanked God. Like most Nigerians, Eric was always grateful for his blessings, especially averted near-disasters. Eric saw the Almighty as he appears in the Old Testament: capricious, vengeful, capable of dishing out indiscriminate plagues, but sometimes merciful.

'When the Divine Being looks at us, we are like ants,' he would say. 'One day he could just squash us, like ants. But there is a divine plan, even if you don't understand it.'

Now, he felt he understood it. He had dodged a bullet and escaped jail, thanks to Divine Grace. It struck him, suddenly: God had a purpose for him. For better or worse, being on the dumpsite was what he had to do.

6

A WITCHDOCTOR'S MAGIC

Olusosun Dumpsite, Lagos Mainland, 2008

Light pierced through Eric's eyelids, and his head throbbed. He knew he shouldn't have stayed out drinking so late, downing that vicious white spirit with Nansa and the gang. It always made him feel like crap the next day. They'd been chatting to two women in that bar next to Ojota Pedestrian Bridge: that much he remembered. Nansa, one of Eric's best friends on the dump, was a womaniser of astonishing skill for a ragpicker. He had literally charmed the pants off one of them, taking her back to some seedy motel, as he always did. Of course, she was probably in that in-between space between a sexual conquest and a hooker, batting her eyelids and expecting some money the next morning. Nansa would have ended up parting with a chunk of his week's earnings. Eric had stayed out drinking late into the night with some of the other guys from the dump—Joseph and Jack, a couple of others. He had scant recollection of coming home.

The unforgiving Lagos heat and humidity were building up under his mosquito net. Time to get up. Eric lifted his head—

and was rewarded with another fierce skull-throb. He levered himself off his hard wooden bed, slipped his overalls on and prepared for another merciless day of raking through rubbish in the sun. Outside his net, the grey refuse mountains leaned in on Olusosun like the set in some bad black-and-white horror movie.

It had been about eight years since Eric's near-lethal encounter with the police, when he resolved to stay on the dumpsite as long as God wanted him to. After years of sweating and raking through smelly rubbish, he had, he thought, surprisingly little to show for it. Two years back he'd completed his first track in a studio. A popular local DJ called Master Lee repeatedly played it on Style FM to critical acclaim locally. But he had never managed to leverage it to make money—the pirates were the only ones who ever made cash out of recorded music in Lagos—or widen his circuit in the Lagos bars. He had also, about three years after his encounter with the police, wooed and met his sweetheart, Nana. She was the daughter of Yoruba Muslim market traders from the same rough streets of Ajegunle. Her parents had tightened their belts and sweated in the midday sun to push her through school and a polytechnic. That was more than Eric's dad ever managed—Eric had had to drop out as a young teen. Before he realised he was falling in love with her, he had confessed everything about his secret life on the dump, and, to his surprise, she wasn't repelled by it. She was the only one, apart from Augustin, who knew where his money came from.

A dump truck curved round the corner carrying a fridge glistening in the violent sunlight. The dumpsite's tough guys—whom everyone called the 'lions'—flexed their biceps ready for the scramble. You could get four kilos of copper out of the best fridges, more than a week's earnings. The lions were licking their lips, and Eric could see a fight brewing. The new Lagos governor, Babatunde Fashola, who was an even more zealous cleanocrat than his predecessor, Tinubu, had ordered a huge clean-up of this still dirty, unruly city, supplying extra trucks to carry the waste away. As the additional trucks brought in vastly more rubbish while recyclers sought ever more plastics, paper and metals, the flow of wealth to Olusosun surged.

'The shit those rich people throw away, we keep picking it up and then selling it back to them,' was how Eric's friend Joseph liked to put it. 'And when they buy it, they don't even know it's the same shit they threw away.'

But as scavenging became more lucrative, fortune seekers flocked in. Even with the association keeping order, competition was getting vicious, and disputes were settled by whoever had the stronger fist.

As the truck approached, fifteen scavengers ran towards it, hooks out. Four of them touched the fridge, and the inevitable fight broke out. Clothes were torn, faces bruised and blood spattered on sand. One of them was beating another on the ground with bloodied fists. His head still throbbing with booze, Eric had wisely sat it out. But he knew he would have to fight soon if he wanted to keep his place in the pecking order. He dreaded being one of the hyenas, the downtrodden, 'the weak ones, the ones too scared to hustle and who believe God will provide', as he called them.

Eventually a senior Scavengers Association member called Jide, who seemed to have a knack for keeping the lions from each other's throats, settled the dispute over the fridge. After a stern word with all three, two of them melted back into the valleys of waste. Jide was a big-time scrap buyer with a stocky build, square jaw, a neat, grey beard and a strangely pensive expression. Unlike others, he hadn't gravitated to Olusosun out of destitution. His mother, known respectfully as al-Hajja, had been a scrap dealer since the 1950s, before independence. She became so wealthy that she had real gold jewellery and had sent herself and five children on the hajj to Mecca. It was rumoured, admittedly mostly by Jide himself, that she was a cousin of the second-highest Yoruba king, the Alaafin of Oyo.

'My mom spent her whole life in scrap, yet she's an aristocrat,' he liked to say. 'There is blue blood in this business.'

From the association headquarters—a shack a few metres square, constructed from crooked planks of plywood, corrugated plastic, nails, wire meshing to keep out flies, and three shades of carpet, harvested from the cast-offs of rich Nigerians—Jide had introduced some quite medieval punishments for brawling, like forcing errant scavengers to lie down in the baking heat until they got sunstroke. It was usually enough to prevent fights getting too out of hand.

Eric had learned a lot from Jide. He once explained to him and Augustin how to track the most promising rubbish: by its smell. The richer the household, the more putrid the waste. A family in poor Ajegunle hardly wasted food, so its trash would smell like lavender compared with that coming from rich quarters. He headed for the foulest bags and, amid maggoty decay, would find cameras or phones in perfect working order, or intact porcelain toilet seats.

'Check the side of the truck to see where it is coming from,' Jide once told him while a scrum of them were blaring their horns in a backlog. 'If it is coming from Victoria Island or Ikoyi, there's money there.'

A week ago, a 'big man' from one of these two wealthy districts had hired his own mini-truck and sent it to the dumpsite with furniture and clothes cleaned out of his mansion: electronics, designer handbags, pairs of shoes. Eric swiped his share of this rich man's loot and counted the cash as it trickled in.

Back in Ajegunle, he poured his earnings from other people's cast-offs into recording. It paid for synthesisers to play brooding chords and simulated bass. It paid for sequencers to churn out breakbeats with rasping snare drums. It paid for his deep voice to rumble through microphones onto magnetic tape. Yet, no matter how much of his soul he sank into his songs, he never seemed to be able to break out of the Ajegunle ghetto.

* * *

Muezzin calls were echoing through Lagos for the evening prayer. The dumpsite's Muslim faithful knelt on raffia prayer mats with woven fractal patterns outside a scrap-iron mosque. As well as at least five such makeshift mosques—the Christians with their less rigorous schedules worshipped outside the dump—there were several eateries and, at any one time, at least two mobile cinemas. Everything was mobile in Olusosun. The dumpsite's geography was as shifting as a sand dune, its make-shift structures at the mercy of the Lagos waste management agency's Caterpillar machines. A few months earlier, the whole community had been on the west side of the dump. Then the Caterpillar had rolled in and demolished everything to make space for more trash. The scavengers didn't protest: they had no legal right to be there anyway. They simply salvaged what they could from the ruins and pitched up on the east side. Even with this constant destruction and creation, Olusosun's lived-in parts oddly resembled a more permanent neighbourhood, their narrow, mercantile alleyways bustling with commerce like a scrap-hewn Marrakech.

It was getting dark. Eric made his way to the Promise Land Cafe. In the darkness he liked to imagine that the mountains of refuse, barely visible in the dark, were like the mountains of Jerusalem he had read about in his Bible. The silhouettes of a few scavengers were visible in their flashing torchlights. Night was a good time for the weaker ones, as the lions were usually either sleeping or tipping their earnings into their beer glasses.

Auntie Anne's Promise Land Cafe, or this iteration of it since the last Caterpillar visit, was a shack with a few wooden tables and a seating area made of used tyres and broken wooden furniture. Tonight's special was isi ewu, an Igbo dish made of a whole goat's head with the brain removed and mashed up with chilli peppers, cooked with onions and stock cubes, then put back in the skull. Augustin and the association bigwigs Jide and Clifford were there, helping themselves to outsized plates.

A week ago Eric had won a fist fight with another ragpicker over an aluminium pot, and he had quite enjoyed it, spitting metallic-tasting blood from his split lip onto the ground as he swaggered off. But the association was trying to stamp out this kind of behaviour, and he could feel a lecture coming.

'You are not going to last here,' Clifford turned to Eric after a long silence, 'unless you calm down. Competing is OK, but all this brawling? Getting into fights? They will throw you out.'

Eric successfully resisted the urge to argue back—not something he often managed to do. He simply nodded. 'OK, sir.' Clifford was keen to help Eric. He also saw a bit of his earlier self in that volatile young man.

Later that evening, some of the cafe clientele moved on to the 'cinema'—a projector screen in a shack hooked up to a generator. It showed premiership football and pirated film CDs of the 'Nollywood' films that make up the world's most prolific film industry and are a hit in villages all over the African continent.

Tonight was *Missing Angel*, a kind of Dr Faustus story in which the angels of darkness hear a prayer from a poor orphan and decide to turn her life around, in return for her soul. She wins the lottery and becomes rich. When a dark angel, played by a chiselled Nollywood actor in a black shirt, is sent to take her soul in return, he ends up falling in love with her. Eric decided to give the film a miss.

Nollywood's obsession with 'juju', as the West African occult is called, often filtered through onto the dump. One afternoon Eric heard a terrifying scream. A teenage scavenger had unearthed fetish objects. There was a calabash, wooden carvings of deities, charms made of leather, bottles of concoctions. When anyone found such things, it was assumed that the evil would head straight into the hapless finder's body, bringing ill health, bad luck and maybe even death. Whenever someone on Olususun went mad, the scavengers would whisper that he had opened a bag with fetishes in it.

Eric had been raised a Christian but, like many Lagosians, he sometimes dabbled in the occult. During his early years on Olususun, he begged traditional Yoruba priests in Ajegunle to be initiated into their cults worshipping gods of water, fertility and storms. All had refused. He tried the white-clad cult of the Celestial Church of Christ—a kind of curious Christian and West African spirit religion hybrid—but after several years of worship he kept coming back home to the same leaky roof in Ajegunle, poor as ever. There seemed to be no supernatural power he could turn to.

* * *

The harmattan of early 2008 was one of the fiercest in living memory. The dry Saharan wind was blowing extra hard, beating back a moist coastal breeze that blows from the opposite direction off the Atlantic. Dust from faraway dunes thickened the Lagosian haze of car and generator fumes. You could almost smell the Sahara. The cooler harmattan season is the only relief Lagosians get from the megacity's oppressive humidity. But the benefit is quickly cancelled out when everyone gets nasty colds, the cold viruses hitching a ride on the dust grains floating down their desiccated windpipes. Coughing his way through his daily grind, Eric hated Olususun more than ever.

The new governor, Babatunde Fashola, had been in power almost a year and was taking the drive for a clean, orderly Lagos to new heights, sweeping the streets of area boys, touts and criminal gangs. A plan was emerging to kick all the scavengers off Olusosun and use its biogas to power turbines.

Jide was receiving threatening phone calls from some shady official, saying they would 'review' Olusosun's status. Eventually the man turned up on the dumpsite, leather briefcase tucked under his shoulder.

'Your association is not legitimate,' the man said when they were alone. 'According to our record, you don't exist.'

It was true but a laughable argument in a city where every possible means of making a living had organised itself into a cartel, none of which had any validity on paper.

They would need to register with him, for a fee, of course. 'You realise we can shut you down like that,' he snapped his pudgy fingers. 'You don't even have proper uniforms.'

Jide rolled his eyes. They were in the shack for quite a while before they evidently came to an arrangement. The man walked out with zero sense of shame and left in his car.

It was around this time of rampant extortion and harmattan winds that Eric finally struck gold. He was leafing through some trash from a Victoria Island truck when something yellow twinkled. He raked it out to find eight heavy-set gold chains and four gold earrings. He could scarcely believe his eyes.

One of the 'malams'—Hausas from northern Nigeria who traded gold and foreign currency at the dumpsite—beckoned him over. He was tall and wore a light-blue kaftan, the traditional Muslim robe, and his eyes lit up when he saw what Eric had. He paid him 200,000 naira (then about $1,700) for it. Eric almost burst into song. It was more than he had ever dreamed of owning. He took the bus back to Ajegunle daydreaming of how he was going to splash out big in its bars, then have enough left over to finally record an album.

Some days later, he had squandered everything on partying, clothes, a small TV and a CD player, and, conspicuously, nothing on recording his album. He hadn't saved a penny. And that was when it hit him: his future was on the dumpsite. He was stuck there, and his delusional dreams of being a musician were just that: fantasies. His music was at best an expensive hobby. For weeks, he sank into a deep depression.

* * *

Ajegunle, next to the Lagos port, 2009

The witchdoctor's shrine stank of the stale blood of thousands of slaughtered animals. Their throats had been slit over the years, drained to satisfy the vampirish thirst of gods and ancestors: a chicken here for the mermaid-like spirit of Mami Wata residing in the lagoon, a goat there for the river goddess Osun, a ram to placate the restless ghost of some grey-haired man who had been dishonoured by being incorrectly buried after death. The thirst of these spirits could at best be temporarily appeased, never truly slaked. They always wanted more blood.

As more and more and more blood had progressively crusted over the wooden carvings representing them, it had coated them in layers of what looked like black candle wax that stank of rotting meat. *This is my last chance for success*, Eric thought to himself, several months' earnings clasped in his hand. If this babalawo couldn't turn his luck around, no one would ever talk about Vocal Slender again. He would die a scavenger.

It had been about a year ago that he'd found gold and spent the lot on debauchery, and since then Eric had saved diligently in the hope of having one last shot at being a singer. He decided the best use of his funds would be to summon the powers of the occult—he'd been praying in church for years and Jesus, though he had saved Eric's soul, had yet to do much to improve his material well-being. If the myriad ghosts that haunted the wetlands of Lagos couldn't help him, then he'd have run out of options.

Outside the black gates of the medicine man's compound, a tree swayed. A horn hooted at the gate and a skinny security guard opened it, allowing the battered old pick-up truck laden with tied-up goats to pass through. The goats screamed as the pair offloaded them, as if they knew somehow, the way incarcerated animals so often seem to, that these frantic breaths were going to be their last.

Dr Mudi's clientele included rich, poor, Muslim, Christian, animist. Once, a church pastor whose Sunday sermons raged against the evils of witchcraft had asked him in private for help in defeating an enemy in a real estate dispute. The shrine was lit by seven candles. A breeze through his window set in motion various fetishes dangling from the ceiling by dirty threads: a pigeon feather, a pot of thin rope, a blackened corn cob, an Iroko tree branch, and some gilded leaves. Fixed to the wall were several tortoise shells and coconut halves.

'You need to pay 1,000 naira to the deities for the oracle to begin,' said the babalawo, referring to the process of calling up the spirits using fetish objects. His voice was like dry gravel. Eric pulled a note from his pocket and tossed it into the space where he was sitting cross-legged. A bronze amulet was suspended around the shaman's neck from a turquoise bead chain. The whites of his eyes showed as he began chanting in an arcane Yoruba tongue. After a pause, Eric was passed an 'oracle'. It consisted of a bone, evidently from some bird or other, attached to cowrie shells by several brass chains.

'Cast forth the oracle,' the witchdoctor said, and Eric's hands trembled as he tossed it onto the sacred raffia mat. The man picked it up and began chanting again, repeatedly throwing it against the wooden floor so that its chains fell in different formations.

'Ah,' he said finally in his scratchy voice. 'You have a spiritual wife who inhabits the waters of the lagoon. Her jealousy is holding you back. Take your sacrifice to the water, and she will leave you.'

It was a common diagnosis of ill luck by 'native' doctors: Yoruba folklore dictates that this dangerous demon of the opposite sex can disrupt your earthly life. This water spirit was especially dangerous, according to the babalawo. Eric asked him what he should do.

'Follow the river wherever you can. Whenever you pass or cross it, tip a bag of sugar into it,' he said. 'I will visit the lagoon and make the bigger sacrifice on your behalf. After that, your fortunes will change. It is written here, in the oracle.' He tapped the bone with the chains of cowrie shells attached to it.

To make the sacrifice, he would need ten cowrie shells, ten eggs, sugar, milk, bitter kola nuts and biscuits. The whole thing, including the babalawo's transport to a clear spot at the lagoon edge, would cost 36,000 naira. Eric folded the money into the old man's hand. The wizard gave him some powder meant to bring good luck but which tasted suspiciously like chalk. Then, with goats still screaming in the next room, he got up to show in the next patient.

* * *

The witchdoctor was a quack. Nothing changed. Eric sank even deeper into melancholy over the next few weeks, despairing at having blown his fortune on this hocus-pocus. He scavenged as hard as ever, but robotically, in pure survival mode. His days on the dumpsite were as uniform as the Nestlé 'Pure Life' water bottles he collected to sell to recyclers: long hours spent raking through black plastic next to puddles of stagnant, smelly water. He'd all but given up recording music.

Then, on one such day, a BBC crew arrived to film a documentary. Eric burst out laughing when they told him. He had hidden his secret for nine years, and now these jokers wanted to splash his mug all over the telly? Fat chance. But then he figured, since it was for broadcast in Britain, it was probably unlikely anyone in Nigeria would see it.

The following year, the BBC aired a three-part documentary called *Welcome to Lagos*, the first part of which was filmed on Olususun. Nigerian elites naturally hated it. The footage was the kind of thing that would turn foreign businessmen off just when the state government was attempting to portray the notorious megacity as a glitzy business hub. But in Britain, and across the world, it was a hit, being translated into four languages.

Months after the white journalists left, international numbers started ringing Eric's phone. Local journalists were showing up at the dumpsite asking after him. He got a call from a breathless Augustin.

'Go Google your name,' his friend said. 'You're everywhere.'

A furious state government barred journalists from Olususun without written permission, and the site manager chased Eric away. But the calls didn't stop, and Eric was invited to the BBC in London to be interviewed. There, he performed several gigs, including at the O2 Arena in Greenwich.

On his return, Eric—aka 'Vocal Slender'—got several requests to perform at bars in Ajegunle and among the fading colonial terraced houses of Lagos Island. A music manager called Adejuku had taken an interest in his story and had begun calling him about gigs. Out of kindness, he had also been promoting Eric's brand on social media and printing out posters. Whether because of the witchdoctor's magic or the manager, before long Eric was singing live at events in Nigeria and, as his profile grew, he was invited to give talks at youth groups and environmental conferences. He had two more trips to London to play gigs.

Back home, he did collaborations with iconic Lagos musicians like Nigerian-German singer Adé Bantu. Hearing of his defiance of the odds against him, corporate charity departments started hiring him as a 'motivational speaker' to tell his story to youths from the slums. A recycling company looking for sellable scrap hired him as a consultant—after all, he knew exactly where to find it. In Ajegunle, he was starting to appear on posters, wearing a white blazer and terminator shades. He cut and pasted from the BBC documentary to create a music video for his own song, 'Owo ti Yapa', a defiantly upbeat melody with pounding bass, silky keyboards and female backing vocals over which Eric sings in a deep ragamuffin drawl. Even with his surge into the limelight, it was hardly enough to make him rich, but enough that he knew he would never have to work on the dumpsite again. And it all happened so swiftly that even now he can scarcely believe it.

'So you finally made it,' Augustin remarked in Ajegunle, after Eric's friend had returned from another pungent day on the dump.

7

THE GOLD FROM DIRTY ROCKS

Freedom Park, Lagos Island, 2014

A sound wall of bass guitar ripples off the stage, shaking tables, vibrating through liquids in people's glasses and triggering a wave of hip-shaking. The live show, called *Afropolitan Vibes*, is hosted in a cosy, mildewed amphitheatre in Freedom Park, in a leafy part of Lagos Island where skyscrapers loom over beachy palms, splendidly tropical sausage trees and decaying Portuguese-style colonial architecture. Freedom Park was once a British colonial prison where convicts waited to hang. Now it is a place of art galleries, bars, fried chicken and live music. Gathered in front of the stage are the hip of the Lagos elite, the alternative, 'Afro-chic' crowd with their big Afros and funked-up traditional dress. Lagosians wearing dashikis and talking in English boarding-school accents mingle with loose-clothed expatriates. Together they sip palm wine, down cool bottles of Heineken, and criticise corrupt politicians. Cymbals clash, bass drums thump. And then out steps Vocal Slender. He is wearing jeans, a baggy white shirt and dark wraparound shades. A brass section consisting of a trumpet, trombone and sax bellows to the right of him; women dance to the left.

After a suitably dramatic intro, he launches into song. 'Burn de fire, burn de fire,' he sings, his urgent vocals punctuated with dramatic keyboards and lilting female backing singers. The crowd roars and claps. He feels at one with the crowd, and yet, for most, their origins could scarcely be more different than those of the ragamuffin singer they are cheering on stage.

Vocal Slender by this time has an album and several reasonably successful concerts behind him. His shoulders have expanded to make him barely recognisable from the skinny youth on the dumpsite, and so has that barometer of wealth in Nigeria: his belly. He certainly isn't well off by Western standards, but, compared with where he came from, his star has risen by light years. His paradox is this: in the end, it was a chance event at the very dumpsite he dreamed of escaping that would make his dream a reality.

* * *

'Do you believe in a human soul?' Eric asked me. He was selling bootlegged copies of the BBC documentary in Bogobiri, a poorly air-conditioned haven for struggling musicians and bohemians near the Falomo Bridge connecting Ikoyi to Victoria Island. Even after years of relative 'success', Eric still needed to hustle for a living. I was Nigeria bureau chief for Reuters news agency, and this was my local. I bought one of the copies: he charged me 2,000 naira, which seemed an obscene sum, but I wasn't going to haggle. He knew that.

'Um, in a manner of speaking, yes,' I replied.

'You, Tim, are not just flesh.' He pinched me. 'You are a soul, like an idea, not this body which will die one day.'

'Where did you learn that?' I asked.

'It's in Plato.' He pronounced it 'Plah-toh'. 'An immortal soul is separate. Plato understood it even though there was no monotheistic religion in Greece in those days.'

And I realised there must be something extraordinary about a man who didn't finish secondary school and spent a decade on a rubbish heap yet came out remarking on the finer points of ancient metaphysical dualism.

Eric had dropped out of school at 13, but he found that Olususun was teeming with reject books, so he soaked up everything he could get his hands on except fiction, which bored him. He especially sought books on philosophy. In an introduction to ancient Greek thinkers he read about Socrates and the oracle of Delphi exhorting visitors to 'know thyself'. From Plato's theory of forms, Eric learned that the soul was separate from the mortal body, like pure light.

'Plato taught me that my life on the dumpsite was a stepping stone to something better,' he told me.

He read about other ancient civilisations before Greece: the Babylonians, Assyrians, Egyptians. The Egyptians surprised him the most. The only story he had ever heard was of how Europeans brought civilisation to Africa, yet here was an African country that had developed it before Europe!

Over the years I knew him, Eric looked back on his days as a scavenger with a tinge of nostalgia, albeit moderated by dread at the prospect of ever going back. He still lived in Ajegunle, but he moved to a quieter, more middle-class area, on the outskirts. He still had to hustle, but he would never have to go back to the dump. He'd started up a charity, the Ghetto Love Foundation, to use his tale of overcoming to inspire Ajegunle's poorest youth.

'Do you know what gold has to go through to be gold?' he told me during one visit, while ten schoolkids in identical brown uniforms came rushing out of the next-door building to urinate in an open drain. 'It looks like dirty rocks until they put poison in to extract the metal.'

Satisfied with this metaphor, he reclined in his new sofa to read something from his library, then flicked on his large, mounted flatscreen television. His framed Google 'Africa Connected' award, which he won in 2014, sat proudly on the wall.

Mindful of past mistakes, Eric resisted the urge to blow his $25,000 windfall from that award, instead putting it in a savings account. But as with many Lagosians, the demands of patronage left him perpetually broke. He had five relatives whose college degrees he was partly footing.

'Don't you think it's funny? I didn't even finish secondary school and now I'm helping other people graduate from university,' he said. In 2015, he married Nana, the love of his life.

But he was in no doubt as to the ultimate cause of his changing fortunes.

'You think God does anything by accident?' he said. 'God Almighty was watching me singing on the dumpsite. He knew I would get out.'

* * *

When Vocal Slender returns to the dumpsite for the first time since he left five years earlier, it is with a business proposal for machine-aided recycling. He wears stone-washed jeans and a red-and-blue auto racing shirt. The air carries a whiff of mouldy plastic and something altogether more toxic, more metallic. Olusosun is quiet, insulated like a polythene fortress from the traffic horns and heated arguments reverberating through Lagos. Calls of 'Slender' ring out, as men in rags exchange swaggering handshakes with the homecoming celebrity.

A white minivan with 'Scavengers Association of Nigeria' printed on it rumbles past. Behind it an army-green jeep pulls up, crushing a broken wicker basket under its monster wheels. Its door opens, and a man wearing a traditional Yoruba outfit in psychedelic yellow-purple stripes rises to give Eric's hand a vigorous shake.

Emmanuel Ovba is vice chairman of the Scavengers Association. His wrist is adorned with a gold watch, his neck with a gold chain, and his feet—the only part of him that still makes contact with trash—are in plain black sandals.

'Slender, long time, oh. How you dey? What brings you back here after all this time?' he asks.

'I'm fine, vice chairman. I have a business proposal for you,' Eric says, smiling his broad smile.

'Then let's go to the office.'

They march past a rusted wheel and sacks of scrap, crunching bottle tops as they go. A photo portrait of the chairman—he is away on 'business'—with a Dubai gold frame hangs behind a wooden desk. The vice chairman sits in a faux Louis XIV chair—salvaged from the dumpsite—beloved of Nigerian big men, while Eric, Jide and Clifford take cracked plastic chairs. Clifford wears a scruffy work shirt; Jide, a black vintage biker T-shirt, baggy jeans, a gold-and-silver watch.

'Drinks?' the vice chairman asks, nodding at a minion to fetch a basket of nearly cold Heinekens and Guinnesses. Small talk over, Eric readies his business pitch.

'The association of scavengers is big, but you could be much bigger,' he says, surveying the ruined tyres and rusting pipes outside the door. 'Right now, you collect the scrap, then you sell to recycler for processing. What if you were to buy a processing machine and process it here?'

The question runs to the core of their livelihoods. The Lagos Waste Management Agency (LAWMA) plans to concrete over Olususun, inserting valves for the monstrous quantities of methane emanating from it. The gas will be used for desperately needed grid power. Landfill activities will be pushed out further from the city.

'The machine doesn't cost that much,' Slender continues. 'You would make it back very quickly. And you could employ people, maybe hundreds of—'

'Slender, you forget we are mere tenants,' Jide cuts him off. 'If we bring your machine, we need approval of the landlord. And then he will steal your idea and drop you.'

In the cut-throat world of Lagos, that is how it works.

'There must be a way,' Slender continues. 'The Chinese, the Europeans, they shred plastic, export waste and make business from it. We could do it here.'

Eric, Jide and the vice chairman then engage in the kind of talk seen in corporate boardrooms the world over, which seems surreal against the backdrop: they discuss figures, supply chains, shrinking margins from recycling companies.

'One day, LAWMA will move this dumpsite somewhere else,' Slender finishes his beer. 'We need to protect our future. If we have a recycling business set up, it is assured. Without it, what are you going to do?'

The vice chairman holds up a forefinger and shakes his head. Not today. There is a silence. A blue-and-orange lizard scuttles over the wire meshing towards a fly. Eventually Slender bows at the vice chairman, says goodbye and steps out into the open.

The sky is swaddled in wool. Lagos's fluffy clouds are a perfect heat trap: thick enough to incubate the humidity, too light to keep out incoming sun rays. A scavenger sheds goblets of perspiration as he eviscerates the rusting corpse of a car. As Eric leaves, a youth balancing a sack of metal on his head nods in deference.

'That used to be me,' he says, sounding nostalgic.

We board a danfo to head home, a journey that takes us a couple of hours, including an interchange at Mile 2. In the second danfo, there is a hole in the floor that enables you to see the road whizzing by.

* * *

Back in Ajegunle, Nana stirs a blackened pot. She is making fish pepper soup, a delicious local broth of catfish, onions, herbs and scorching bonnet peppers of the type repressive states use for quelling protest. Nana has broad shoulders, round eyes and a heart-shaped face. The only time she ever saw Slender on the dumpsite was on screen.

'To see him suffering, I couldn't stand it,' she says. 'You would never have known how tough his life was. He kept it so well hidden.'

They serve me first, doling out the shark-like whiskered head of the catfish, which always goes to the honoured guest or head of the household. Eric opens a beer for himself and me.

'Is Lagos what you expected?' Nana asks me after dinner, clearing plastic dishes into a washbasin.

'It was better than I expected, even more fun,' I tell her. 'But then people from outside can have a fixed idea about Lagos if they've not been.'

'Before you get to Lagos, you can have a fixed idea.' She pours water into the bowl from a stripy teapot. 'Then you get here and you find everything is here: the good, the bad, the rich, the poor. You get to realise it is many cities.'

A goat bleats and someone's generator rumbles into life.

'So many cities in one city,' she says.

PART III

GOD'S ENERGY

Money is a guest. It can go out the same way it came in.

Igbo proverb

*Financial value is essentially a degree of hope, expectation, trust or credibility
... Being transcendent to material and social reality, yet also being the pivot
around which material and social reality is continually reconstructed, financial
value is essentially religious.*

Philip Goodchild, Theology of Money

8

UJU

Ikotun Egbe, Lagos Mainland, 2013

Every Sunday she could make it, Uju Ifejika took her seat in the VIP section of the Prophet's church. This was her favourite part of the week, blowing off the stress from a hectic job as an oil executive, and there was no better church in which to do it. Prophet T.B. Joshua was a special kind of man. A man who knew things: things he couldn't possibly know; things nobody would believe, were it not for the evidence right before their startled eyes. He knew, before you said a word, exactly what had brought you to him. The Prophet predicted world events with uncanny accuracy: wars, calamities, plane crashes, sports results. He had many other supernatural powers, too. He could defy physical laws with the same disdain that Lagosians defied traffic laws. His Synagogue Church of All Nations, with its kitschy rock-wall design and glorious high windows, was a place that made miracles ordinary and saw demons massacred by the dozen. The sheer volume of prophecies and miracles emanating from him could fill books and, in fact, several had already been filled by the Prophet's own publishing house. He had healed people of

HIV/Aids, cancer, infected dog bites, burns, ulcers, high blood pressure, insanity, constipation, erectile dysfunction, physical deformities. He'd resurrected stillborn babies and made the paralysed leap out of wheelchairs. His cures fixed every misery that could be inflicted on a human being. Because all had the same cause: Satan.

Of course, some people, both in Nigeria and outside, claimed his miracles were fraudulent. There were those who argued that he was nothing more than a stage magician with a gullible audience. But then, as his faithful liked to point out, hadn't Jesus suffered the same from doubters during his ministry? The proof came from Joshua's remarkably international audience: people from all over the world came to see him, including plenty of whites. They included several African presidents and more than a few rugby players from South Africa's national team, the Springboks. His birthday was celebrated in dozens of countries, televised over his TV network from the main celebration event at his Lagos headquarters. It was said he was in his mother's womb for fifteen months, instead of the usual nine, and that his birth had been prophesied a hundred years in advance (though, admittedly, the sole source of both claims was his own ministry).

His signs and wonders certainly kept the tithes flowing into his bank account. *Forbes* magazine in 2011 estimated him to be worth up to $15 million, thanks mostly to voluntary contributions and subscriptions to his Emmanuel TV channel. Not bad for a man who began his life in a poor village in southwest Nigeria, who failed to complete his first year of secondary school, and whose first job—at least if his official biography is to be believed—was cleaning up chicken shit on a poultry farm. The Synagogue Church of All Nations, which he founded in 1987, would eventually attract about fifty thousand people every week—the combined number of visitors to Buckingham Palace and the Tower of London. Uju herself was a 'top contributor', who had donated many thousands of dollars over the years. As a result, she had often had communion with Prophet T.B. Joshua in private. Each time, she had felt his power, and had often been shocked by his clairvoyance. But on one Sunday in particular, the Prophet said something that would change the course of her life forever.

When she first told me about it—about the prophecy that changed her life—several years later, we were in her car on our way back from a T.B. Joshua service in 2013, one of several to which I accompanied her. Try to picture it. The headquarters of Joshua's Synagogue Church of All Nations is set up like a concert hall. A hangar-like roof hangs over seating for thousands of people, supported by pillars decorated to look like palm trees. There is light blue-and-white flowing material in the backdrop to signify life-giving water, while on one stage there is a giant open Bible. A gospel choir with a band plays with fast, thumping, syncopated and strangely hypnotic rhythms that seem to cause worshippers to collapse in ecstasy and chant in incomprehensible tongues. Then, once the choir has worked the crowd up into a state of excitement, the Prophet enters, his silk shirt sparkling in divine radiance. His voice lacks the booming, thunderous tone that normally makes a good Pentecostal preacher. It is almost a high-pitched squeal by comparison. Yet there is something mesmerising about it all the same. A state-of-the-art camera for his Emmanuel TV rolls up to him.

'In the mighty name of Jesus, receive that breakthrough that makes one to forget the pain,' he shouts, leading a prayer. 'When you receive that breakthrough, you will forget the past. Receive it now!' Joshua shouts. 'I say to your business, a breakthrough! Breakthrough in your career, in your finances, in your marital life, in your destiny! Breakthrough! In the mighty name of Jesus!' His voice is hoarse yet still high-pitched, like gravel scraping a blackboard, and it works the crowd into a state of total delirium, of jumping up and down, singing, chanting, shouting and cheering. Then he attends to the usual queue of people waiting to have their demons cast out.

A man with a shaved head and chocolate shirt is shaking and laughing manically. Joshua says, 'In the mighty name of Jesus Christ!' He closes his eyes and extends his forearm like one about to do magic. 'Don't touch me! You don't know me!' the demon inside the man shouts in a southern African accent. A dumpy, grey-haired white woman next to him is sobbing. The man starts convulsing and dancing and letting out blood-chilling screams. Joshua shouts the Jesus slogan at him again, knocking him to the ground with a theatrical punch.

'It's a snake, a python,' Joshua says, after he starts writhing on the floor. 'Who are you?'

'I'm his boss,' the demon inside the man replies in a scratchy voice. 'I'm the boss of the boss.'

'OK,' Joshua says. 'How many powers do you have?' and the demon replies, 'Countless.' He tries to stand up, but Joshua sends him back onto the ground just by looking at him.

'This guy is very dangerous. He's a king of wizards,' Joshua says, and then later, 'He has turned into a tiger. There are many things that live inside him.' As if taking a cue from this, the man starts making claws with his hands and growling. One of Joshua's assistants holds a microphone to the man's face, which is contorted somewhere between pain and maniacal laughter. And then, the climax: Joshua holds a hand up in divine majesty and the man's body flops to the ground as if his bones have just dissolved. It's over.

'Father, we thank you. The demon inside of him is gone. But he has to confess everything,' says Joshua, and the hall erupts into clapping. The man gets up slowly, looking dazed. 'Thank you, Jesus, I'm free,' he says to the camera, and he stumbles away.

UJU

The congregation collapse back in their chairs in an almost post-coital calm.

* * *

Ikotun Egbe, 2007

It was after a similar service, back in May 2007, that Uju made her way slowly up the steps behind the stage to the inner sanctum of Prophet T.B. Joshua's office for a private meeting. Every now and then she would go to see the Prophet for advice, when she was facing a particularly difficult obstacle in her life. But on this occasion Joshua had—unusually—instructed her to come. 'I have a prophecy for you,' he'd told her, on one of their regular private counselling phone calls, while she was in the office at Chevron-Texaco in its sprawling complex in Lekki, the large peninsula attached to the eastern end of Victoria Island. The Texan oil company was the second-biggest operation in Nigeria after Royal Dutch Shell, and getting a job there was many an educated Nigerian's dream. She had been with them for two decades, rising up the ranks to become head of marketing, and she was certain her unshakable faith in Jesus was responsible for her successes. 'Come without delay,' Joshua had said on the phone, and she'd agreed to meet him the following Sunday.

Uju climbed the stairs to the waiting room of his inner sanctum. T.B. Joshua's VIP room looks strangely like a kitsched-up corporate boardroom: it has a long, excessively polished table in the middle lined with leather chairs. On each wall, a TV projects his Emmanuel TV satellite station: a feast of Joshua's best sermons and most dramatic demon deliveries, the possessed shaking and dribbling like poison victims. There are Chinese plastic flowers on the ornate faux-ebony table. The lighting is low but still somehow white and harsh. Uju sat down in the VIP room and waited for the Prophet to appear, exuding her usual confidence. In her middle age, Uju had developed a buxom, full-bodied figure. She had high, bulging cheekbones and full, prominent lips always glossed with thick lipstick, often the colour of gold. Uju liked to turn heads. She often wore bright suits made of silk in a satin weave giving a metallic sheen, with gaudy colours: shocking pink or bright green. It advertised her bright, entrepreneurial spirit and her skills at networking—which in Nigeria entails remembering thousands of birthdays, taking out newspaper adverts to celebrate them, attending society weddings and funerals, and listening to tedious speeches of record-breaking length.

And yet she'd lately been feeling her talents were being under-appreciated in such a big firm. For years she'd dreamed of being CEO of her own petroleum operator, instead of working for Chevron, slaving away to make some Americans rich, but she'd never plucked up the courage to strike out on her own. Partly, that was because of her cautious husband, Emmanuel, an accountant (like her father, before he died). He reminded her that Nigeria's business world is a shark-infested sea, littered with the floating bones of many a small fish that has been chewed up and spat out by the oligarchs who control everything. The risks were enormous: you might not find oil, or you might find it and some big man decides he wants it, and nudges you out. You could fall out with a local politician over an unpaid bribe, and he could find a way of blocking you.

'This is Nigeria, not the United States: there's not the same rule of law,' he had said when she suggested it once at the dinner table. Apart from the risk of fraud, there was the fact that the Niger Delta, from where all of Nigeria's oil flows, had erupted into chaos in recent years. The chaos was born of desperation: the oil had blackened mangrove swamps, killed the fish that people depended on to live, turned tap water toxic, given children birth defects. And all this upheaval had brought close to zero economic development to a region where a lot of people didn't have shoes. Militants in the delta had taken up arms. They were constantly attacking oil facilities and blowing up pipelines. With their belt-fed machine guns and bandanas like Rambo, they had shut down so much production that, in September 2004, they helped to push oil over $50 a barrel in the markets in London and New York for the first time in history. She could be kidnapped, robbed, or worse. But the biggest threat would be that she'd join a start-up domestic oil company with a claim to territory that had no oil in it. In such a case, they would drill it, find it empty and then the company would simply fold, and they'd lose everything. 'Please, don't risk it,' her husband had said.

'And how are you?' the Prophet asked as she entered his office to greet him. He had his usual warm and slightly mischievous smile. T.B. Joshua had a round, handsome face and cheeks that bulged over his cheekbones and gave him a permanently childlike expression. This, combined with his small nose, intense narrow eyes and grin full of perfectly straight white teeth, lent him a warmth that could be very disarming. Uju had first come to him years ago when her mother was in a wheelchair after suffering a stroke. It had taken almost a year, but eventually the Prophet healed her. She had risen up out of that chair and walked.

'I am fine, Pastor Joshua, and yourself?'

'We thank God. Please take a seat. The good Lord has spoken. I have a prophecy for you.'

T.B. Joshua's prophecy was this: 'That God will make you the centre of your world.'

This cryptic phrase uttered, he paused for a moment, then he waved her away and prepared for the next VIP.

Now, a less devout soul might have been dismayed at this point: no further detail, no hint of what it could possibly mean. Just a vague prophecy with all the precision of a newspaper horoscope. But Uju knew right then what she had to do: she would become the boss of her own oil company. She had always thought she could succeed, but all this time she had never listened to her calling. *God will make you the centre of your world.* What else could that mean?

Uju stepped outside the Synagogue Church of All Nations to find her car, and her driver switched on the motor. As usual, the traffic was a mad rush of the faithful heading back from hours of fervent prayer, flashy jeeps competing with clapped-out old bangers and rickshaws. Ikotun Egbe lies deep in the Lagos mainland, past the spectacularly scruffy and congested slum of Oshidi. It can be a tiring journey from here to the islands where elite Nigerians such as Uju live, even on a Sunday. Her car crawled away. Along the street, touts handed out brochures for motels that cater for T.B. Joshua's international audience. They ranged from someone's cramped concrete shack with a few mattresses thrown on the floor to hotels that had a vague pretence to luxury: shiny faux-marble floors, and brand-new flatscreen TVs in every room. There were laundry services, car washers and mini-grocery stores selling sweets, cigarettes or corned beef. Street money changers—all Muslims from West Africa's dry northerly, Saharan places—exchanged wads of filthy naira for West African CFA francs, South African rands, dollars and euros. Hawkers resold tiny spray bottles filled with Joshua's 'morning water, anointed by Christ to heal, bless and save'.

Uju always carried a bottle of holy water with her, obtained from inside the church itself—lest the ones being sold by the hawkers were just ordinary water in a plastic bottle with Joshua's face on it. In moments of fogginess or indecision, she would shut her eyes and gently spray some on her face. And when she opened them, she could see clearer—physically, to be sure, but also in her mind's eye. Uju had sometimes given some holy water to female friends who were struggling to conceive. They must spray some of it onto their vaginas while also getting their husbands to splash some on their own genitals before sex. The water's blessed properties would ensure the union was fruitful. All the women had conceived, after years of failing.

They made their way out of Ikotun Egbe and turned onto the expressway. The state government had spruced things up on this mainland artery: trees sprouted in former rust yards, neat rows of tennis-ball-coloured hedges had been planted. As soon as they passed through Oshodi, though, it was back to the classic Lagos dystopian movie look: mechanics sat under sinister bridges salvaging scrap or usable parts from abandoned rust buckets. Minibuses crawled through craters filled with stagnant, stinking water. A thriving market clogged up a railway track, and then had to dismantle and scatter whenever a slow-moving train approached (but that was at most once a day). Trash permeated everything like background radiation.

The road curved round to Oworonshoki, at the edge of the lagoon, and they took the ramp onto the Third Mainland Bridge. Most elite Lagosians, apart from those working in the state government headquarters in Ikeja, rarely crossed the Third Mainland Bridge, except to go to the airport on trips to the United States or Dubai, or to church. Many elites avoided the bridge altogether—terrified of the armed robbers who often plied it. Some refused to go without armed escorts. In this, as in many things, Uju felt protected by the power of prayer. She would proclaim silently that her car was 'covered in the blood of Jesus'.

The floating slum of Makoko came into view: thousands of wooden houses on stilts, all enveloped in clouds of smoke from thousands of wood fires. The people's lives had changed little since the time of their ancestors. They still awoke in a wooden hut at the edge of water, defecated in the open, and set out to fish in murky waters. Uju sometimes thought about the whims of God's will that had enabled some Nigerian families to rise out of poverty. She came from 'good stock', as she called it. Even if the white man had never come to Nigeria's humid shores, her family would have been in the ruling class. But ruling over what? Would they have had superhighways and airports and shopping malls or shopping trips to Dubai for the people like her? Would they have found those huge black lakes of oil?

The route descended into Lagos Island, where shakily built shopping centres and apartment stores leaned in from the lagoon edge, and her car joined the flyover turning off into Lagos's exclusive Ikoyi island. Below the ramp that curled into this fabulously wealthy section, homeless Lagosians washed themselves out of buckets on rough ground in their bare feet. She pulled up at the gates to the Dolphin Estate, where she lived. The Dolphin Estate had been built to replace the dilapidated Jakande Housing Estate just opposite, which had been the pride of the city when its namesake military governor in the early 1980s built it as low-cost housing. Jakande had undergone the rot of tropical heat: even its sewerage system had broken down so that waste was piped directly into open drains. Its replacement of shiny duplexes had been aimed more at the upper echelons, though it included some high-rises to accommodate those who'd lost their Jakande flats. Dolphin Estate was starting to look like everywhere else in Lagos: tired and fume-stained. But in a city in which most people resided in squalor, its houses were still seen as exclusive, and Uju and Emmanuel had always felt at home there.

That evening, Uju successfully avoided telling her husband anything of Pastor Joshua's revelation. She knew it would upset him to hear the risk she was planning to take. As she lay awake in bed too excited to sleep, she knew she wouldn't delay. Tomorrow, she would act on the prophecy.

* * *

Monday morning. The sun was only just rising, and the palm and mango trees were alive with screeching insects, but already Uju was awake, excited about what she was about to do. Unlike many people who have to drag themselves out of bed, Uju loved her work as an oil professional. She always felt she was doing God's work, making Nigeria rich by helping extract the abundant natural resources that the Lord had bestowed on the country (the pollution and corruption it spawned rarely crossed her mind). She sometimes leapt out of bed singing hymns.

She got up to get dressed. Uju made a point of power-dressing to show she was at least as capable as the men. At work she would wear a suit with padded shoulders to give her a no-non-sense edge, but the ample jewellery she liked to wear would show she hadn't neglected her feminine side. The suit would be tied together with a brooch made of yellow or white gold. Another brooch, often diamond-encrusted, would sit on her chest like a badge of honour. There were always big chunky rings on her fingers and jewel-laden earrings dangling from her ears.

By mid-morning at the office, before she'd even finished her sugary Nescafé with powdered milk, Uju was drafting her resignation letter giving her month's notice to Chevron-Texaco. Her pen hovered over the signature. Could she really give up everything and plunge into such a risky venture? She pondered Emmanuel's warning. They'd met in New Jersey, where Emmanuel had lived for thirteen years. An accountant, he had got used to the cushy, salaried life of white-collar suburban America. He'd sought to replicate, as far as possible, this cosy security amid the Lagos rat race. People who enjoyed that kind of life were vanishingly few in Lagos, so the decision to up sticks and strike out on your own was a huge risk. But for Uju, there was no such thing as chance; everything was the product of God's will. It sometimes made her want to weep with joy when she could feel the Lord in action. She meditated on Joshua's words one more time: *God will make you the centre of your world.* Then she signed her resignation letter and sealed it in an envelope.

* * *

LAGOS

Victoria Island, 2008

Money and oil make the world go round, and, in the case of Nigeria, the two are inseparable. Much of the vast wealth that sloshes through Lagos, keeping the megacity awash with dollars and its citizens scrambling after them, begins underground—on a stretch of coastline lying hundreds of kilometres east of the lagoon city. The elites in their Lagos mansions, with whitewashed neoclassical pillars, swimming pools and collections of sports cars—useless ornaments in a city with roads like Lagos—are sucking wealth through a straw that leads to the Niger Delta. Oil pays for their shopping trips to Dubai, New York and Paris, and for the staggering volumes of champagne that Nigeria imports, the highest in Africa. It pays for the scions of powerful oligarchs to keep two dozen horses they can use on the immaculate green lawns of the Polo Club in Ikoyi. It funds a momentous property boom that has conjured new land out of water, on which have been built exclusive estates. Petrodollars built the staggeringly expensive estates on Banana Island—a man-made peninsula poking off the northern end of Ikoyi into the lagoon—and the Eko Atlantic city, both of them on land that used to be water. Oil pays for the monster speedboats parked outside the Lagos Motorboat Club, and the dozens of Porsche Cayennes splashing through potholes that politicians have been too busy filling their boots to fix. There are many ways to grab a slice of this oil wealth, but, as Nigeria's elite know better than anyone else, none are as sure-fire as having your own stake in an oil-producing company.

In less than a year after acting on T.B. Joshua's prophecy, Uju had taken control of local oil company Brittania-U, then a small outfit with little to its name but a marginal oilfield in shallow waters offshore. She bought out some existing minority shareholders, giving her 35 per cent of the company, with her own savings. She then proceeded to turn it into a profitable business.

Emmanuel had taken the whole thing surprisingly well, although there were flashes of scepticism in his conversations with her about it. Not that he was the only sceptic. Whenever a woman did something like what Uju was about to attempt, the sneer of sexism was never far. No woman had ever been the chief executive of an upstream oil company in Nigeria—at least not running the business, as opposed to just owning it and collecting the money while a Western oil company did all the work. She had heard the whispers: she didn't have the calibre to pull off something like this. And she was just a lawyer, with no technical experience. So she started by building an eighty-thousand-barrel storage unit and acquiring a shuttle tanker. She bought a lucrative interest in a fuel import operation to profit from imported refined petrol—basically a licence to print money, since one of Nigeria's many madnesses is that, despite producing two million barrels of oil a day, its own refineries have always been so run-down they can barely refine any of it. Revenue started streaming in.

That was all very well, but real success meant pumping your own crude oil. Brittania-U had acquired the Ajapa marginal field in the 1990s. It was part of a policy to put more of the oil business in the hands of Nigerians, instead of the sweaty-shirted whites who had dominated it since oil was found in the 1950s. But the block had yet to be drilled. For all anyone knew, it could be dry as the harmattan blowing down from the Sahara, with not half an egg cup of oil in it. You can own the rights to territory that looks promising, but until someone shoves a drill into the earth's crust to see if the black stuff comes gushing out, you own nothing. A foreign oil company seeking to buy a 40 per cent stake had offered to operate the block and fully finance the cost of exploring it, taking on all the risk themselves if it turned out to be empty. It would have been less chancy, but Uju said no. When the oil came gushing out of Ajapa, she wanted to show Nigerians what a woman was capable of. This was *her* project.

The main problem, apart from the growing insecurity in the Niger Delta, was that to hire a drill and prospect for oil, she needed serious money—it would turn out to be $120 million, all told. She knew she would need to put up some serious collateral to get anything from the banks. So, without telling her husband, she put up as much of her own worth as she could render liquid. She quietly mortgaged the family house in Maitama, the richest quarter of the capital, Abuja, the playground for Nigeria's rich. And she did the same for their home on the Dolphin Estate. That enabled her to raise 23 million naira (about $200,000) in a loan from two banks, enough to persuade folks she was serious. More money came trickling in and Brittania-U organised an oil rig. Within a year of leaving Chevron after her cryptic conversation with Pastor Joshua, Uju was running her own company searching for oil in shallow waters offshore of the Niger Delta.

* * *

One night while all this was going on, Emmanuel was doing something he'd sworn to himself he'd never do. It was three in the morning. He hadn't slept for a split second. He'd turned onto one side, then another. It was futile. He had to find out where Uju had got the money to fund her oil company. He tiptoed over to the cupboard where she kept her paperwork. She'd seemed dismissive when he raised the question, but as far as he knew she didn't have some mystery benefactor lavishing cash on her in return for a cut of the proceeds. Where had her money come from? He opened the cupboard and began rifling through her files, looking for clues.

Ever since he'd met Uju, she'd been a strong-willed woman. That was one of the things that had attracted Emmanuel to her in the first place. They'd met when he was at Rutgers University in New Jersey. She was visiting her cousin, who happened to be his classmate. They were a living embodiment of the theory that opposites attract: she was boisterous, loud, confident; he was a mild-mannered, softly spoken man. After getting married, he had continued living in the States for more than a decade, working as a government accountant, and they'd kept things going long-distance. They'd had three kids, all of whom were currently living and schooling in America. When he finally returned, she'd helped him set up an accountancy firm in Lagos. It was all very upper-middle-class professional: he, a bean counter for small companies in downtown Lagos; she, a marketing executive for a Western oil company. They lived well. But he could sense she was bored with her job.

Bills, bank statements, mortgage statements, *ah, there it is*, he thought, as he opened the file with the details of her personal transactions relating to the funding of Brittania-U. He scanned down the page: money going out here, money going out there, blah, blah, and then ... his heart nearly exploded. She'd mortgaged everything they owned to get the money! He had to reread it, then pinch himself in case he was in some horrific nightmare. If this venture didn't work out, they would lose everything. All her savings, the two homes they owned, all would be gone. Where would they live? How would they pay school fees? She had put their entire life on a roulette wheel.

'What?' Uju said, somewhat grumpily, as he woke her up.

'We need to talk,' he said. 'I notice you used this house as collateral.'

'And the one in Maitama,' she said, sleep still in her eyes.

'You don't think you should have discussed this with me first? What if you go to drill and you don't find oil? What if you go in and you're not able to operate the field, for any of the many reasons this could go wrong?'

'Look, I've made up my mind,' she said, rubbing her eyes. 'I have to do this.'

Emmanuel gave up. As usual, his anger and shock were mixed with something a little bit like admiration. He had to hand it to the lady, she was bold. But what if she was wrong? So he prayed: prayed to Almighty Jesus that his wife hadn't just ruined the entire family.

* * *

A few weeks after Emmanuel had discovered her shocking secret, Uju was sitting in her office on Victoria Island at a desk piled with papers and walls full of photographs of herself. She had come a long way since taking charge of the company. They had done a seismic study: heavy vehicles weighing tens of thousands of kilos had applied a giant plate to the ground and used powerful hydraulics to make it vibrate, radiating the waves deep into the earth's crust. They had bounced back to create a map of the underground caverns that might be lakes of oil. And the map looked promising.

Then they made the final move: assembling an oil rig and pushing a drill deep into the rock under the sea. The test well was near completion and the results would be in soon, today or tomorrow. If Uju was nervous about what they would be, she showed little sign of it. Staff saw her busily shuffling papers just as always. She had an urgent meeting with a Nigerian bank to ask for more money later that morning. If—when, rather—they found oil, the company would need a big cash injection to finance production. She decided to leave early for that meeting.

Her managing director, Kalu Nwosu, entered the office. He was an ethnic Igbo like her, charming and with a gentle sense of humour, who had also cut his teeth in an international oil company—in his case, Shell. But his usual airy, indiscriminate smile wasn't on his face. He looked worried.

'I'm going to get going to see those banks. We need to get the finance in soon, we're almost out of money,' Uju said, somewhat in a hurry.

'I can't let you go,' he blurted out.

'What do you mean you can't let me go? Who do you think you are?' she responded, reacting with typical forcefulness to this clear insubordination.

'Madam, there is something I want to tell you.' His face was a mixture of panic and hopeless sadness. 'I'm afraid we drilled a dry hole.'

Uju had been in the oil business in Lagos for more than twenty years, but almost all of that had been spent with Texaco, which had long-established oilfields. She still knew little about exploration, so the phrase 'dry hole' didn't register.

She said, 'Mr Nwosu, what are you talking about?'

Nwosu started talking about oil rigs and drilling depth and how 8,500 feet was a long way down and still they hadn't found anything. Then he talked about how unlikely it was, after all this effort, that they would ever find anything, and at some point during his talk, shock overcame her, so that his voice faded away into the background.

'It's over,' he continued.

'You can't be serious.'

'I'm telling you, it's a dry hole. There's no oil,' Kalu Nwosu continued, doing his best to ignore her look of utter bewilderment. 'I want to tell you because I'm telling them now to remove the rig, pull it up and send it off. We're done.'

'No!' she almost screamed. Her world was collapsing around her. 'Don't give that instruction before I tell you. Don't move the rig.'

'But, Madam, the cost ...'

'You hear me? Keep it there.'

Nwosu felt awful for Uju. Her pride, her future, her relationship with her husband: it was all doomed. All those people who had doubted her as a woman running an oil company, all those ill-wishers: they would be erupting into self-satisfied laughter. She was finished. Realising there was nothing more to say, he left the room for a meeting.

At the meeting, Uju was miles away. Voices sounded in the distance, like a dream. Her mind was racing. And she realised, in a cloud of gathering panic, that this was just not in keeping with the prophecy. The prophecy was her finding oil and being Nigeria's first female CEO of a successful oil business. She left the room and called T.B. Joshua on his mobile.

'Don't worry, you will find oil,' he said, on the fuzzy line. 'You will pray and come back to me.'

She hung up. He could be infuriatingly vague sometimes. She pictured what she'd have to tell her husband. 'Oh, by the way we'll have to move out of our house on Friday and sleep under the bridge. Sorry about that.' He had warned her this could happen, and now she would have to come clean and face up to losing this colossal gamble. Tears ran down her cheek, and she locked her CEO's office door so that no one could see them. *Lord, what am I going to do?*

9

SIGNS AND WONDERS

Igboland, about 450 km east of Lagos, late 1800s

Like everyone else's story, Uju's stretches back to a time long before she was born. But I'm going to start it near the end of the nineteenth century, when 'Jesus' first came to her ancestral homeland in the forests of what is now southeast Nigeria. The red-faced European missionaries wouldn't have looked like people about to conquer an entire nation. With their buttoned-up black waistcoats and appalling body odour, they were struggling in the heat and dying of malaria in their droves (this humid stretch of West African coast wasn't nicknamed the 'White Man's Grave' for nothing). There was, however, one thing about them that was appealing. It was this: by joining their religion you could escape the worst excesses of a military occupation by the richest and most powerful empire on earth.

Imagine: British soldiers are running amok in villages inhabited by the West African tribes collectively known as 'Igbos'. They are stealing their farm animals, raping women and trashing crops. Pasty-faced colonials with absurd moustaches are starting to impose onerous taxes. Igbo men are being driven into forced labour as porters for the new white masters, and those who refuse are publicly flogged. The complex Igbo pantheon of small deities and ancestral spirits, which has guided their lives for millennia, is under attack. Righteous Christian soldiers deal with these 'idols' much as they did with the Norse gods in the Middle Ages: by banning them. In what can only be called a holy war, in 1902 British troops attack the sacred Arochukwu shrine, a hundred and fifty kilometres southeast of the village. The shrine houses the oracle for the supreme Igbo deity, Chukwu, 'the Great Spirit'. Chukwu proves no match for a bunch of bawdy English pirates armed with pistols. The shrine is utterly destroyed.

But there is a quick way to escape this violence and humiliation: the Church. For in their quest for converts, the missionaries use their influence to shield their flock against the capricious nastiness of the colonial powers. Embracing the Good Book— and rejecting the traditional spirits as 'evil', as so many Igbos like Uju still do—becomes the only way to thrive or even survive the British onslaught. Within a few decades, millions of Igbos (like millions of Africans elsewhere) have abandoned their culture and embraced the religion of a bunch of long-dead, Greek-speaking Semites.

This was a story brilliantly told by the great Igbo writer Chinua Achebe, who was also from the same village as Uju's father and whose classic novel *Things Fall Apart* chronicled how his fellow Igbos had been gradually infiltrated by Christian missionaries until their own tribal customs collapsed. Today, the Igbos are one of Nigeria's big three ethnic groups. But when the Christians came here they found that, unlike the other two main groups, the Yoruba and Hausa, the Igbos had not yet been much exposed to that arch-rival brand of monotheism sweeping down from the Sahara, Islam. Igboland was virgin territory.

If there was another thing that made the missionaries irresistible, it was education. Thanks to this, a handful of Igbo converts were granted access to good jobs, European standards of living, and a mastery of that strange alchemy that seemed to make the British imperialists so irresistibly powerful: money. The connection between wealth, power and the Gospel was sealed in the Nigerian mind, a connection that still hasn't been broken to this day.

Now fast-forward to the middle of the twentieth century. Uju's father, Chief Clifford Ikpeze, the customary chief of the Igbo town of Ogidi, married Princess Elizabeth Chigo Aroh, daughter of His Royal Highness Eze, chief of the town of Abatete. Thanks to their parents' strategic embrace of the Gospel, they were both literate and highly educated. The rewards of his grandfather's decision to accept the Gospel were Clifford's first-class degree in accountancy and his coveted job in the colonial administration. Clifford was from a family of 'kingmakers'— Igbo nobles who performed magic rituals to determine who would be the next tribal chief. The British had suppressed the Igbo's magic rituals, but if anything they hardened their hierarchy. In the past, Igbo chiefs' powers were largely ceremonial in these village democracies; the British trumped them up into kings and lords of the new administration. And because he was smart and eager to do well, Clifford was swiftly made a sub-treasurer, one of the most senior civil service positions that could be occupied by a Black man.

In 1959, the year before of Nigeria's independence from Britain, Uju was born on the lush green islands of the Niger Delta that make up the town of Opodo, where Clifford's itinerant profession had taken him. She was the sixth of what would be ten siblings— six boys and four girls. The family had a huge house in the leafy 'government reserved area' (which had in earlier decades been 'whites only') and were almost as comfortable mixing with Europeans as with their own, a rare thing in a country run along race lines from its very inception. They had staff to clean their house and nanny their children, and a chef who could flit fluently between cooking foreign and local dishes: bitter leaf soup with pounded yam and pungent crayfish paste one day, bland beef stew the next. From an early age, Clifford taught Uju that failure—by which he meant not coming top of the class—was not an option. On Fridays, he would return from his job and test her homework in meticulous detail. Substandard work meant the cane across the backside. She would always remember those (few) pain-filled Fridays when he gave her lashes for second-rate homework (the classic English 'six of the best'). Her father was a wealthy man by Nigerian standards, but he always told his children they would inherit nothing from him, except education.

In the mid-1950s, in that same delta, something was found that would have momentous repercussions for the whole country. If there's any outside force that has shaped modern Nigeria at least as much as monotheistic religion, it's the oil business. Royal Dutch Shell and BP found the 'black gold' in the town of Oloibiri, four years before Uju was born. For a country comprising around 300 squabbling ethnic groups on the eve of independence, the flood of petrodollars couldn't possibly have come at a worse time. At independence in 1960, there was a brief honeymoon period before competition for that oil wealth between the tribes—but especially the regional power blocs aligned with the three main ethnic groups, Yoruba, Igbo and Hausa—began to foment trouble.

By the mid-1960s, after a shambolic election, Nigeria was unravelling. In 1966 a group of army officers tried to overthrow the government, murdering Prime Minister Tafawa Balewa. In the power vacuum, Major General Johnson Aguiyi-Ironsi, an Igbo, took power. In the same year, a group of soldiers from Balewa's northern region assassinated Aguiyi-Ironsi and installed General Yakubu Gowon, a northerner. The eastern Igbo region, which included the coveted oilfields, declared itself an independent republic, and one of the world's worst civil wars began. In classic Anglo-French rivalry, France began providing the rebels with weapons and mercenaries while Nigeria's ex-colonial master, Britain, funnelled huge quantities of arms to the federal government.

Over the next four years, a million people, mostly children, died of starvation because of a blockade of the self-declared Biafra republic. Yet while famine was wiping out whole families, Christianity was literally keeping Uju's alive. The state capital, Onitsha, fell to the rebels in 1967, and the federal government began shelling it heavily. A blockade prevented any food getting into rebel territory, while farming had more or less collapsed. Shocked Western audiences saw their first-ever pictures of skeletal children in live TV reports. When their hometown was captured by rebels, inviting a hailstorm of government mortar fire, Clifford moved his family to the rebel-held town of Nobi, where his older brother, the Reverend Ikpeze, was senior Anglican priest. Because of his connections to the Church, the Reverend Ikpeze had ample food rations to share. They never went hungry, not even for a day. There was even a school where the kids could carry on learning, and the family slept in the teachers' quarters until the Biafrans surrendered in 1970. Not for the last time, Uju would see the power of the Lord at work protecting her from the calamities that befell the world around her.

* * *

Falomo Bridge (between Victoria Island and Ikoyi), 2008

As her chauffeur drove her back home from the office, Uju thought about her extraordinary bad luck. She was ruined. She would have to explain losing everything they had to her husband, Emmanuel. She had told friends this venture could make or break their marriage. He had warned her, and she had gone behind his back anyway. How could he forgive her? They and their three children were about to be made homeless. And they could kiss goodbye to the fees for those fancy schools and universities in America. Uju rarely felt panicky, but now she was overwhelmed with sorrow and, more than anything, confusion. *God will make you the centre of your world*, Pastor Joshua had said, and yet the Almighty hadn't delivered when she'd most needed Him. Had she been misled by a demon?

Demons were everywhere, she knew that. Uju saw the world as alive with spirits all talking and making a cacophony of suggestions: you had to know how to tell good from bad. The evil spirits were the ghosts of the dead which had not departed for heaven but instead stayed to haunt the living. They had been improperly buried or had suffered some other transgression, and so they hung around to cause mischief. Often they were summoned by witches—you could be a victim of witchcraft and never know it. Your life would be going along fine and then things would inexplicably start going wrong. You could put it down to bad luck, at first: an accident here, a dead relative there. But you would soon realise, as the misfortunes piled up, that you had been cursed.

There were the good spirits, too, of course—the angels, which God sent down from heaven to help you. Uju had learned from experience to tell the difference. The malignant spirits were louder, pushier, nudging you hard to take a tempting course of action they knew would lead to ruin—in the next life, if not in this. *Go ahead and do this evil thing, nobody can see you*, they would be saying. And you would do it, whatever it was—theft, murder, adultery—and people would be saying, 'But how could she do such a thing?', but by then the spirit would have departed, leaving you only with remorse. The Holy Spirit, by contrast, spoke in a quiet voice, almost a whisper: you had to listen out for it carefully. Often, the only way to know the difference was by having a good pastor. Which was what Prophet T.B. Joshua was supposed to be ...

Her car curved round Bourdillon Road and made the turning into Dolphin Estate. That evening, Emmanuel noticed how obviously distracted she was. He wondered what was wrong, and waited for her to volunteer it. Of course, she didn't. 'What is it?' he asked, finally. She was just tired, she said. There was no way Uju could break her news to him before sleeping on it. She avoided his eyes and managed a choked 'goodnight' before shutting the door to their bedroom. She realised just how exhausted she'd been by the last few weeks. Weeks of furiously lobbying banks for money, the seismic study, assembling an oil rig: it had drained the last vital force out of her. Collapsing on the bed with a heavy heart, she erupted into floods of tears. Then, turning to her pillow so her husband couldn't hear in the next room, Uju cried herself to sleep.

* * *

It was General Ibrahim Babangida who had enabled Nigerians like Uju to run their own upstream oil companies. He had seized power in a coup against another military ruler in 1985. The general, a charming man and legendary party-thrower, known by his initials, IBB, had proved a master at using the Lagos financial networks. The result was that while tens of millions of Nigerians continued to live in poverty, a few hundred well-connected Nigerian individuals and families became rich. The message to Nigerians was clear: if you want to be wealthy and successful, you need to get a slice of that oil money.

Before IBB's reign, Nigerians had always played a secondary role in the oil business. They ran companies providing services, or petrol stations. The highly profitable business of extracting oil from beneath the earth was the preserve of 'white man' companies like Shell. For Babangida, that was an aberration. He decreed that local firms should be awarded oil exploration blocks. True to form, he used this policy to dole out oil blocks to companies owned by friends and well-connected individuals at his own discretion. Often the companies were set up just days before—or sometimes even after—the block was awarded. Perhaps the most famous was Folorunsho Alakija, who would later become Nigeria's richest female oil tycoon, and a model for women who wanted to break into this male-dominated world. Alakija was born into a relatively wealthy family and started her career as a banker, but this hardly provided an outlet for what she felt was her creative streak. She quit and moved to London to study fashion design. Upon returning, she founded Supreme Stitches, a premium fashion label exclusively for elites who could pay many thousands of dollars for a costume. Among her big-moneyed clients was a certain Maryam Babangida, IBB's wife. With access to her husband's fortune, Maryam was, in the words of one Nigerian writer, 'an icon of fashion and beauty'. Supreme Stitches was in the big league.

Spin on to 1993. Babangida is in his last days, and he knows it. Riots are erupting across Lagos after he cancelled the results of an election because he didn't like the winner, a southwestern Yoruba man. There are mutterings of a coup. So he distributes oil blocks to a number of people within his close circle (just as Russian politicians had been dolling out their state's assets to oligarchs after the fall of the Soviet Union). In May of that year, Folorunsho Alakija sets up a company and applies for an oil prospecting licence for one of those deep-water offshore concessions. She has no experience in oil and gas, nor even a university degree. Her qualifications for managing a 600,000-acre oil block are that she makes beautiful clothes for the president's wife. The block is granted. But unlike the other military bigwigs and well-connected businessmen, in similar possession of such generous gifts, she shrewdly decides not to simply sell her block on to the highest bidder. Instead, she invites Texaco to come in and prospect it, offering them 40 per cent if they find anything. They take on all the risk, while she gets 60 per cent of the proceeds. It's the kind of smarts they just don't teach you in college. In 2000, a newly merged Chevron-Texaco discovers a billion-barrel oilfield, and Alakija becomes the richest woman in Nigeria overnight. Years later, she will tell a Nigerian magazine that 'God Himself orchestrated and organised by divine intervention the beginning and continuation of our delving into the oil industry'. The paper will meanwhile gush that she is 'one of this West African country's most accomplished businesswomen', and praise 'the award-winning designer's entrepreneurial acumen', in acquiring an oil block. It will claim that her fortune is bigger than Oprah Winfrey's when the latter's is $3 billion. A more sober assessment by *Forbes* will put it at about a third of that.

Uju hadn't been so fortunate. Of course, she played the system like everyone else, and she certainly understood the importance of ingratiating yourself with politicians. But at the end of the day, it is an astonishingly lucky thing for any Nigerian to be able to grab a stake in the oil business, to join the few hundred people who oligopolise staggering wealth that, in theory, belongs to tens of millions. For Uju, the only way to get a seat at the table was by putting her hard-earned cash on the line. Too bad for her that, when the food tray was passed her way, it was empty. How could the Prophet have got it so wrong?

* * *

Dolphin Estate, Ikoyi, 2008

The night after Uju cried herself to sleep, after she lost everything, she had a dream. She was flying over a stretch of mangrove creeks with the midday sun shimmering off the water below, just as she had seen once on a flight over the Niger Delta, heading into the Gulf of Guinea where the oil concession was. As she glided over the swamp and it glistened, a calm, gentle and reassuring voice spoke to her. *Why are you worried?* the celestial voice said. *You went in the wrong direction. You should drill in the other direction. You will find oil.*

She awoke the next morning and she knew, as sure as the pillow against her head, that God had spoken to her in that dream. There was oil in that block; she just needed to drill again. Euphoria enveloped her. Emmanuel noticed her change of mood at the breakfast table but thought better of asking her anything. At least she was happy again. Uju dressed for work and got in her car. After her driver switched on the engine, she began singing hymns all the way to the office.

She called an urgent meeting with her managing director, Kalu Nwosu. Uju told him about the dream and how sure she was that they needed to drill into the other part of the oil block. The Lord himself had told her so. Nwosu went silent. He could see what was happening here: the desperate lady just didn't want to let go, couldn't face her failure. He tried to reason with her.

'Please, Madam. This is a technical enterprise, not a spiritual matter,' he said. 'There's no oil. It's a game of chance, a game of risk. That's the nature of the game.'

'No, we're going to drill again,' she said, and Nwosu rolled his eyes.

Uju started planning how she was going to find oil on the block that everyone else had written off. She would need to do another seismic. She managed to get hold of a geologist she knew from her days at Chevron to obtain new coordinates for drilling. They agreed on $150,000.

'That'll be done in two weeks,' he told her.

'No, I want it done in 48 hours.'

'What? Impossible,' he said, before agreeing to it for a further upfront fee.

When the new seismic study came back, it looked a little better than expected. But at the end of the day it was just a pocket in the earth: God only knew if there was any oil in that cavity. By now the banks were so invested—perhaps the executives in their lending departments were up against a similar loss of face— that they agreed to fund her crazy scheme to drill again. Nwosu bit his lip. If this second drilling came up dry, it would be a double humiliation: they would have to strip down whatever assets the company had that were still of value just to meet a fraction of the outstanding debt.

* * *

Five agonising days later. A huge drill has been plunged into the shallow seas off the coast of the Niger Delta, spiralling into the bottomless blackness. Uju is sitting patiently in her office, praying with tremendous intent. Then, in sweeps her managing director, Nwosu. Initially she can't tell from the look on his face what state of mind he's in: he is expressionless. Is he hiding something? But then he breaks into a smile, as wide as the Lagos lagoon.

'Madam, are you a normal human being or are you an alien?' he says, breaking into raucous laughter. 'I don't believe this. We found oil. Look.' He hands her the drilling results.

Uju smiles, then erupts into celebration. The Prophet had been right all along.

* * *

Synagogue Church of All Nations, Ikotun Egbe, 2014

Everywhere is rubble. Compressed layers of cement sit where a building once stood, with beams, columns and steel girders poking out of their mangled floors. The Synagogue Church of All Nations' new guest house, which was in the process of having floors added to it, looks like it's just been struck by a fifty-pound

123

bomb dropped from an aeroplane—and indeed, some days later, T.B. Joshua will try to point the finger at some mysterious aircraft he says hovered over the building before it crumpled like tin foil. Underneath the wreckage lie 116 twisted, mutilated bodies. The bodies belonged to devout worshippers who came to be saved by T.B. Joshua, many of them, ironically, with non-life-threatening health complaints. Most of them flew here from South Africa. All were crushed by six floors' worth of building materials. Red Cross workers are trying to salvage whatever bodies they can from underneath tonnes of concrete. Wind blows up some cement dust, and a smattering lands on a rescuer arriving at the scene. I close my notebook and return to the car to file a story.

It is now six years on since Uju's fortuitous oil discovery. Thanks to the gushing lakes of oil her company found in its concession, and the fact that oil prices have been averaging about $100 a barrel for years, she is now one of the richest women in Nigeria: a bona fide member of Nigeria's oil elite. Fittingly for a woman of her station, she has moved into the most expensive part of Lagos, to a flat in the exclusive Tango Towers in Ikoyi. A stark, modernist silver-and-copper building, it sits on Bourdillon Road, just opposite the sprawling colonial compound of Bola Tinubu, the undisputed Godfather of Lagos.

Uju believes she has three people to thank for her success: God Almighty, herself, and her primary link between the two, Pastor T.B. Joshua. For years she has faithfully attended his church and spent untold thousands of dollars on donations. But now, despite the fact she is convinced she could not have succeeded without Joshua, her faith is about to be tested. Because the Synagogue Church of All Nations has just buried scores of its own flock under an embarrassingly shoddy building operation.

A coroner will later conclude that the structure was inadequate in multiple ways: poor reinforcing materials, undersized beams, poorly anchored tension bars, and failure to build joints that could withstand movement. The Lagos State government will take T.B. Joshua to court for failing to get a building permit. Despite the damning evidence, the case will go nowhere. Days after the event, Joshua's media team will release a video depicting what appears to be a plane flying low over the building three times just before it collapses, implicating this 'strange aircraft' in the tragedy. To me, it looks like a normal plane in a part of Lagos that is under a flight path, pasted to repeat twice, but the belief grows among T.B. Joshua enthusiasts.

While all this controversy is swirling around, Uju is sitting in her office at Brittania-U. Outside her window, the financial district of Victoria Island is abuzz with smartly dressed professionals walking to chauffeur-driven cars and barking down telephones. Small traders wearing tatty clothes—the other side of Lagos's momentous divide—are desperately trying to sell windshield wipers and iPhone covers to stalled motorists. Uju shows the video that Joshua's PR team have released to one of her staff.

'You see, it's suspicious,' she says, glancing at the footage of the plane flying over the building before *whoosh!* it collapses in a cloud of concrete dust. But Uju doesn't sound convinced. She knows something is wrong with the whole affair, and the conclusion is incontrovertible: Prophet T.B. Joshua is fallible. She needs a new pastor. Thus ends Uju's decade-and-a-half attendance at the Synagogue Church of All Nations, as she quietly decides to seek spiritual fulfilment with one of its many Pentecostal rivals.

* * *

In early June 2021, T.B. Joshua dies, aged 57, of causes that are not made public. Tributes pour in from his congregation, who are despondent but also baffled, to say the least, at the loss of a man with such unparalleled supernatural powers.

His Facebook page, which has five million followers, says, 'God has taken His servant Prophet TB Joshua home.'

10

THE EXORCIST

Ojudo, on the outskirts of Lagos, 2016

'I'm going to break your family curse and cast that demon into the pit of Hell,' the pastor says to me. He's one of those preachers who is so charismatic he can make you feel as if you're going into a trance just by looking you in the eye. There's something hauntingly glazed about that look, as if his eyes aren't so much looking at you as through you. Like a big cat letting you know it could tear you apart at any moment but was choosing not to.

'So your wife is sick,' he says. Still that look.

'Yes, she is,' I say, stifling a yawn. I don't know why this meeting had to be so early in the morning. It was very kind of Uju and Emmanuel to line this up for me. Not everyone gets to see Pastor Chris Okafor in his inner office of bright light and darkened wood. It costs quite a lot of money—I didn't ask how much. Emmanuel, who drove me here, is in the room with me, smiling that warm smile of his.

After T.B. Joshua's guest house collapsed, Uju switched pastor. She will still always revere T.B. Joshua as a 'man of God', but all the same Pastor Chris is a more respectable, upper-middle-class chap. And he hasn't killed anyone in an act of construction neg-ligence. Pastor Chris—'the Oracle', to his flock—describes him-self as 'a dynamic multi-faceted preacher the Lord has decanted His Spirit upon, elevated ... high in the divine echelon of grace and power which has propelled him to mega-dimensions of barrier-breaking in Christendom', according to the first part of a long list of accolades on his website. He has 'a divine ability to decipher, decrypt and demystify the deeper meanings and mes-sages of the Bible hereby delivering to mankind God's epistle'. As with other popular pastors, his spiritual gifts have generated substantial material ones. He flies around in a chartered private jet, and wears a gold-trim tunic and gold-buckle shoes with a fancy Swiss watch.

Why did they send me here? My wife, Monica, a journalist like me, has been suffering from severe post-traumatic stress disorder (PTSD) from, well, take your pick of the various crises that we journalists have covered in West Africa over the past few years: bomb blasts, Islamist kidnappings, Ebola, a bloody civil war in Ivory Coast. I knew I'd find it quite hard to explain this to Uju, so all she knows is that Monica is 'sick', in a vaguely defined way that hints at mental illness. That's all Pastor Chris knows, too.

He continues talking in his deep, resonant, hypnotic voice. He is tall and light-skinned. He is still staring with that deep, pen-etrating stare.

'Where's your father?' he says.

'My father's in France,' I reply. 'He lives there.'

'Are you aware that he's having problems with his health?' he says.

Well, I'm almost 40 myself, which puts my father firmly in the senior-citizen category, so that was a reasonable guess. My father had a stroke a few years ago and he can't move around so well, but he's otherwise fine.

'It's my wife who's not well,' I tell him.

Undeterred by my attempt at keeping to the original topic, he says, 'But your father too is unwell. You need to pray. To summon the power of prayer for his health.'

'OK,' I say. He nods. His haunting stare has become something else now: his eyes are disengaged, trance-like.

'Your wife, your wife,' he says in low, hushed tones, like a stage whisper. 'Yes, I see it, now. There's a spirit oppressing her. This spirit is a resident spirit. It has taken over her body. And you realise, the same spirit that oppresses your father is oppressing her. Where is she now?'

'She's in southwest London,' I say.

After a long pause, Okafor says, 'Did they carry out any operation on her?'

'No, she's got trauma, mental trauma.'

'I see her in an operating theatre if you don't act soon,' he says.

Unless we're talking about electric shocks or a lobotomy, I seriously doubt it. Yet he's deeply absorbed in his vision.

'I see your wife in hospital, in a white robe. There is a drip attached to her. You can still avoid this. You need to pray so that it doesn't come to that, so that no operation takes place. We must pray and God will stop it. And while we are praying, you must get her and tell her to anoint herself with this oil.' He hands me a small bottle of olive oil branded with his name on it. 'No problem,' he adds. 'Your wife, God will heal her.'

'Thank you,' I say.

His latest book lies on his desk: it's called *Total Freedom from Spiritual Husband and Wife*. 'Spiritual spouses' are a perennial fear in Lagos. Eric's Yoruba medicine man, Dr Usman Mudi, once explained them to me. In West African folklore (and in many other cultures around the world), they are almost like a spirit companion from the netherworld, looking out for you. But they can also, like all animist spirits, cause trouble. They appear to you in dreams, and though they are dangerous, if you are a trained shaman they can bring you great supernatural powers which you can then harness to your advantage. For true Christian believers like Uju, they are always evil. How will I know if I've been visited by a spiritual spouse?

'Sometimes there are people, when they dream, they see themselves having sex in a dream. If you have sex in a dream, that is a spiritual husband and wife,' Okafor explains. 'That is very dangerous. It can cause a lot of problems. It can cause a lot of sickness, because it's a satanic operation.'

'So how do you exorcise them?'

'But we are here to talk about your wife,' he reminds me.

'Yes, of course.'

'It's about ancestral spirits. There's something that happened a long time ago that is working against the family. I see greatness, greatness, greatness in the family, but this spirit is an obstacle,' he continues, still in a borderline trance. 'The spirit will attack you because it wants to destroy that greatness. It's a family spirit, an ancestral spirit that came into the family many, many years ago as result of errors of the fathers. But God is breaking you out of it. Amen.'

'Amen, thank you,' I say, and with that I am whisked away into a VIP waiting room. When I enter, I appear to be the only person waiting for an exorcism from Pastor Chris. This gives me a vague feeling of being special. I sit down on the sea-blue sofa. The waiting room is lurid and space-aged. The floorboards are shiny brown with a raised black bit; the walls are 3D-panelled, a white maze pattern on one, the other a shiny golden sort of brick motif. There is a white plastic desk in a sideways, almost D shape with a metal bowl of plastic flowers on it, a golden sculpture of a horse and an empty copper vase. There are no windows. After what seems like a long time, I am beckoned down the stairs by one of his minions. Emmanuel descends with me. Now we are in a sort of hangar with a big roof, where some of Pastor Chris's senior disciples are casting out demons.

THE EXORCIST

'In Jesus' name I cast you out! Out!' one in a chrome suit says to a tall, mixed-race woman. The woman laughs a deep, sinister laugh.

'Out! I tell you. Come out of her!' Her eyes are vacant and her head is lolling about like a ball of mercury. She is possessed by a Mami Wata, a water spirit revered in traditional West African religions, which even has its own priestesses devoted to it. She is often represented as a woman with a sea snake coiled around her neck or sometimes as half fish, half woman, like a mermaid. As with other traditional spirits, to a Pentecostal preacher they are pure evil.

'Don't touch me,' she screams. 'I will fight you.'

He holds up a Bible as if he's about to strike her on the head with it. He brings it down in a sweeping, slicing motion. She starts to wobble. 'Speak up, demon. Stand up straight! Who are you?' the pastor shouts.

'I don't know if I'm comfortable with this whole thing,' I say to Emmanuel.

'Don't worry, it's not for you. You'll just get a prayer,' he says, totally at ease with the situation. 'They will help you.'

'Who are you?' the pastor asks.

'The Lord of Darkness.'

'A fire on you, in the name of mighty Jesus.'

'You are wasting your time. She's never going to be free. You should just go.' Her eyes are half closed and rolling backwards.

He grabs her by the wrist. Now he's ready for the *pièce de résistance*: holy water. He uncorks a bottle of water specially blessed by Pastor Chris Okafor, and sprays it on her.

'Oh, stop. No! Nooo!' she screams. 'Oh, it smells, it smells bad. It's disgusting. I hate it. What did you do to me?'

'I break the covenant. Now you wicked serpent, you wicked spirit from the water, Jesus has defeated you.'

And she collapses on the floor, writhing around like a serpent.

131

'I throw you into the water,' he shouts, and she screams, before her body goes limp and she opens her grateful, tearful eyes. The spirit is gone.

'I really don't want to do what she just did,' I say to Emmanuel. 'I don't have a demon in me. I mean, not like that one, anyway.'

Emmanuel says, 'No, he's just gonna pray for you. Calm yourself.'

But it's all academic now, because Pastor Chris himself has entered the room to cast demons out of the VIP guests, including me. I close my eyes as he approaches. I can hear his footsteps and his thunderous voice. OK, shit. This is it. I squeeze my eyes tighter. Am I going to collapse, like the others, slithering about like a salamander? Oh, hurry up and get this over with ...

'I'm sorry, I can't do this,' I say to Emmanuel, in a much more trembling voice than I wanted to. I gather up my pen and notebook and take the nearest exit outside. Emmanuel follows me, looking embarrassed.

Bright midday clouds floodlight the city. Electric pylons divide the sky. The ground is still wet from a rainstorm overnight. I glance sheepishly at Emmanuel. It's hard to tell if he looks relieved or disappointed. We get to his jeep, and the driver starts the motor. The privately hired police-escort pick-up truck, with two policemen in the front and two on the back, fires up its siren and flashing lights. Ostensibly it's a security measure to prevent VIP kidnapping, but Lagosians all know their real purpose is to beat the traffic. Even on a quiet Sunday, Lagos is humming. An unstoppable force keeps the city swinging like a mystical pendulum. The conversation turns to what I really wanted to talk to Emmanuel about: Uju.

'She's a woman of God, there's no doubt about that. And headstrong. Oh boy!' he says. 'She took a real risk. That bank loan, everything. It could have really messed us up.'

We prepare to take the ramp up onto the Third Mainland Bridge. 'You know, God has really helped us a lot,' he says, as we ascend the ramp. 'In sickness, Uju's pregnancy, in business. He could help you, too.'

The lagoon shimmers with the silver of reflected clouds as we zip over the bridge. Fishermen in ragged clothes are heading out from Makoko after the morning's church services.

'Amen, Emmanuel,' I say, unable to think of a way of changing the subject. 'Thank you for showing me what we saw today.'

* * *

Victoria Island, 2016

About a week after the church service in which I witnessed demons being chased out of people by Pastor Chris Okafor, I am in Uju's office on Victoria Island. It's the late end of rush hour. There is a chorus of bad-tempered hooting from the cars outside. The rain is heavy and stormy winds are lashing the palm trees on Uju's street. Victoria Island's streets are completely flooded, as they always are whenever there's rain, making the traffic immeasurably worse. You can hear cars splashing through puddles whenever there's a rare twitch of movement in the queue. Uju is wearing a bright-red jacket emblazoned with a diamond-encrusted pin. Her office a record of both her achievements and her extensive wardrobe. There are more than a dozen pictures of her. In one, she is in a black dress receiving some kind of award; in another, in a low-cut ballroom dress adorned with a large gold necklace, bracelets and handbag. The latter photo is completely black-and-white apart from her handbag and jewellery, which has been doctored to retain its gold colour. Another picture shows her wearing that same dress together with Emmanuel, who is in a black tuxedo with a black shirt and white bow-tie. In between the two photographs is a picture of T.B. Joshua, looking skywards and cupping his hands with his eyes closed. There are at least four awards sitting on that same darkwood chest of drawers. Her desk is piled high with papers from a court case to try to force Chevron to sell her an oil block she says they promised her (a case she will later lose). On top is a brochure for the glitzy Eko Atlantic city, the latest fortress that the elites are building for themselves on land reclaimed from water. The place hasn't even been built yet and she's already buying a flat—or the promise of a flat, since the residential tower block in which it will be located doesn't yet exist.

The queue of people wanting to see Uju today includes two Lebanese businessmen who are involved in building the said project. They are selling a flat in one of its opulent towers directly to her. The flats go for about $1 million apiece. One man is wearing an expensive-looking suit and an even pricier-looking bracelet.

'You look so cute, so handsome today,' she says to him, standing up to do a little flirtatious jig. He laughs coyly. Uju has them eating out of her hand. He shows her the copy of *The Economist* with the drawing of the Eko Towers and his face on the cover. It's Dubai meets the Jetsons: skyscrapers of glass and chrome, motorboats cruising along the artificial marina, palm trees growing on roofs. I ask him why someone would want to pay so much for an apartment in a building that doesn't exist.

'Oh, it will exist,' he says, agreeing to talk if I don't print his name. 'It's got all the essentials planned: shopping malls, restaurants, hotels, marina. People will not go out anywhere. It will be like Dubai mall. It's a city within a city.'

'So is that the idea—that you don't ever have to leave?' I ask.

He shakes his head, to mean 'no, you won't'.

'Won't people get bored staying in that place and never leaving?'

'You don't understand,' he says. 'Every entertainment will be there: your cafes, your swimming pools, your yacht or your motorboat, tennis courts, the beach, the cinema. Why would you ever want to leave?'

They put a pile of prospectus papers for the Eko Atlantic on her desk, then head for the door. 'Madam, it's a pleasure doing business with you,' the man who has been talking says with a wide smile.

After they leave, Uju turns to me, and the subject swiftly changes to my unwell wife. 'I hope you now understand that it's a spiritual attack. Not just on her, but on your family.'

I hadn't thought of it that way, I say.

'It doesn't matter what you think. You can be under attack from a fetish and you will not know it. They don't attack people who are not stars. Once they see that you're the star of the family, that your star is bright, they start making trouble.'

'Why?' I ask.

'Jealousy. They don't want you to succeed.' She fiddles with a ballpoint pen. I suggest that some spirits might have a positive influence, as when Nigerians summon them up using a witchdoctor, and the witchdoctor helps heal them or solve some problem.

'They don't,' Uju says firmly. 'They are not the right spirit. The right spirit has departed for Heaven. And the evil ones, the ones that stay behind, they only go for those who are doing well. You see a crippled man begging in the street ... Society has already written him off. No spirit will go after them. They have already fallen so far. But you, a chief bureau for Reuters, internationally recognised, you married into a big family, so that everybody will start hearing about this guy. No, the spirits are jealous. They want to bring you down.'

'What are these spirits? They're someone who was dead a long time ago?'

'A long time ago. You know, in the past, before the real Church, there were things that our grandparents believed in. They had their own religion. Then the Church arrives, but some of them try to mix it up. So they take the first, say, five books of Moses, they conjure the spirit in to make a covenant. But it's wrong.'

135

'You mean combining the Old Testament with traditional spirits?'

'That's it. So now, what you have is that the family has the spirit that they worshipped in the old times. They believe this spirit has been so nice to my grandfather. My grandfather, he dedicates his children to this small god that he believes in. And the spirits they believe in, the society, rightly or wrongly, once you make that acceptance, they start making demands on you, down the generations. And you as a young man, you don't even know there was anything like that. How can you start talking of appeasing something that you were never aware of?'

I tell her we haven't really had that kind of thing in Europe since medieval times.

'You do. It's everywhere. It used to be there, it's still there. That's why you see some people in Europe believe in ghosts and haunted houses. It's the same thing. There are white kids seeing ghosts, demonic possessions. Just because you don't believe in them, it doesn't mean they aren't there. This is what is happening to you, Tim, and to Monica. But you are lucky, because you now know.' She's been looking away, but now she turns her face and makes eye contact. 'You can only fight an enemy if you know about it.'

'How do these spirits find you?'

'Some, it's through friends. When you are growing up. They initiate you in it, but you will not know. They do a curse behind your back. They can give you chocolate or something, with poison in.'

We talk about her husband taking me to the church, and I say I was a bit new to it and I wasn't sure, that's why I chickened out and left before Pastor Chris could exorcise me. I hope he didn't mind, I add.

'It's your first experience now. That's what I'm telling you. Don't you feel something? A lot of people don't understand the power of a pastor like Pastor Chris. When you tell them, "Oh, let's see this pastor." And they say, "Oh no, no, no, I'm a Catholic." Well, I'm a Catholic, but they don't tell you these things in that Church. You will see people who have issues, who are clearly under spiritual attack, who are sick. They will just pray and say, "We pray for you." Nothing happens, you don't get healed. Praying isn't enough. There are people who are gifted at breaking the curse of these spirits. And that pastor is one of them,' she says.

She drops her lipstick into her handbag and prepares to head home. Outside, her police escort fires up the siren and flashing lights that will enable Uju to cut through the traffic.

* * *

Bourdillon Road, Ikoyi, 2016

One Sunday afternoon a few days later, we are at Uju's flat in Tango Towers. I'm with Segun Alabi, who has been driving me around all week. Uju asks him if he has eaten, and he says no. This isn't true—I fed him myself—but I can see why he wouldn't want to pass up the opportunity, with her superior egusi (melon seed) soup, jollof rice red from the tomato paste it's been cooked in, and crayfish stew. Uju is kind. No other elite Nigerian I have ever interviewed takes such care to make sure junior staff have everything they need.

Uju's living room is an opulent arrangement of black leather sofas and white-painted wooden tables with ornate gold trimmings and marble surfaces, all in faux-baroque style. Frilly, Italian-style curtains keep the bright midday sun from entering the room, which is instead lit by bulbs powered by diesel generators. Pictures of Uju are everywhere, some with her husband, in gold and bronze frames, but there are no other wall decorations, save a Piaget platinum wall clock. T.B. Joshua's Emmanuel TV beams from her flatscreen. A 25-year-old woman testifies that Joshua's 'anointing water' cured her asthma.

'You might just see it to be water but it is not. This is the blood of Jesus,' she says. Documentary evidence is presented showing her diagnosis before and after she started using the water. On the 'before' sheet, her diagnosis with asthma. On the 'after' sheet, the asthma has gone. Standing next to her is Antonia Ude. 'She suffered from barrenness for fourteen years before she took the anointing water,' a female pastor, one of Joshua's underlings, says ...

Uju walks into the room, and immediately Emmanuel, their three adopted young children—the children they had together are all very grown up now and living far away—and various nieces and nephews stand up, as you do when someone important enters. She waves to them to sit down as she herself takes a seat on the couch. They all find chairs around the dining table. Uju prepares to give a Bible reading, opening her black leather-bound copy while leafing through its gold-edged pages. Today's readings are from Jeremiah and Malachi.

'For every single individual, you are born with a vision. That vision is not about money. It is about your whole self ... This is your reason for existence on earth,' she begins, pouting slightly as she lifts her Bible up. All eyes, especially Emmanuel's, are transfixed on her. 'But vision is nothing if you don't sharpen it. There has to be that inner commitment. When you discover it, and you know God—because it is God who makes that vision manifest. Jeremiah 1.5 clearly stated that—let me read—"Before I formed thee in the womb, I knew thee. And before thou camest forth out of the womb, I sanctified thee. I ordained thee." So you now see that even your birth is preordained. Your existence, your formation in the womb, God already knows what you are supposed to come into the world to do.'

The woman who was barren for fourteen years breaks down crying as she tells the cameraman: 'Finally, I missed my period. What was not possible for so many years was possible that time. I was even thinking God forgot to put a womb in my system.' Tears are stream-ing down her face. 'People said, "The Anti-Christ is in you." But now I have a child. People of God, I'm telling you that this God of T.B. Joshua is the true God.'

'Can we see your belly, the pregnancy?' Joshua's female pastor says. 'Show it to the world so we can see that the Almighty has done it,' and the woman points to her belly under a T-shirt. For a religion based on faith, there's an awful lot of empirical evidence wielded in T.B. Joshua's Church.

'I lost a lot of money,' Uju says. 'And it is only through God's direction that I got it back. That's where the solution is: kneel down, talk to God.'

'Her daughter was suffering from epilepsy for many years,' Joshua's female pastor says of Mrs Keshinro, who is standing on the stage with her daughter, as the camera pans towards them. 'Now she is cured,' says a male pastor with an English accent. 'Let's put our hands together for Jesus Christ.'

'But if you learn how to revere God, you pay your tithe,' Uju says. 'It is clear here.' She finds a passage in her Bible. 'You have sickness, you have failure, you have lack of progress. Even if you have nothing, your payment of your tithe is something you must do. It is what comes back to you. So Malachi 3, let me read it for you.' Her audience is utterly rapt. '"Ever since the time of your forefathers you have gone away from my ordinances and have not kept them. Return unto me, and I will return unto you, says the Lord of Hosts ... Yet you have robbed me. But you say, where have we robbed you? In tithes and offerings. Bring me all tithes into the storehouse that there may be meat in my house. And prove me now, says the Lord of Hosts—"' Her phones trills and she answers it, telling the caller she'll get back to them later. '"—And I will rebuke the devourers." So now, how many of us pay our tithes? You say the money I take home is little.

Nevertheless, ten per cent of that is your holy Father's money, it's God's money. When you are able to do that correctly, then you now see God at work in your life. He's going to open up doors of opportunity for you.' She shifts her weight in her leather sofa.

A woman possessed with a spirit says: 'I am the evil spirit. I have destroyed her life. I have destroyed everything.' They spray her with holy water and she falls onto the ground. A man talking in a gruff voice says: 'I am the spiritual wife. I have destroyed his life.' He writhes around while two people hold him back. He also gets a dose of holy water and collapses.

Glancing at the TV, Uju says, 'See, there are more things out there than we even know about, spiritual things.' She continues the lecture: 'Where people want to bring you down, those are the devourers that God talks about here. Have you seen the Devil? Devil is man, because he uses man to operate. Just like God uses man to operate. God speaks to us every minute ... But if it's God that put it in you, you will never lack. You will not be sick, not the sickness that can deplete you. Whoever does not pray, who tries alone, will die a miserable death. So when God singles you, you must understand that it's for a reason: to glorify Him. Everything I've done in my life, I've tried to glorify Him.'

The lecture ends. I close my notebook and thank Uju for allowing me to join her family prayers. Outside, the sun mellows as it skirts lower, bathing the lagoon in sacred light.

PART IV

GHOSTS

What we often call the Northern Protectorate of Nigeria today can be better described as the poor husband whilst its southern counterpart can be fairly described as the rich wife or the woman of substance and means. A forced union of marriage between the two will undoubtedly result in peace, prosperity and marital bliss for both husband and wife for many years to come.

Lord Frederick Lugard, 1914, in a letter to the British government just a few weeks prior to northern and southern Nigeria's amalgamation

Orunmila! Witness of Fate, Second to Oludumare (God),
Thou art far more efficacious than medicine, Thou the Immense Orbit that averts the day of Death ... Thou Equilibrium that adjusts World Forces, Thou art the One whose exertion it is to reconstruct the creature of bad lot; Repairer of ill-luck, He who knows thee becomes immortal.

Prayer to Orunmila, the Yoruba god of divination, fate and prophecy, sung by witchdoctors in the morning, as transcribed by Philip John Neimark in *The Way of the Orisa*

11

GOLDEN CHAIN OF THE SKY

Up in the Sky, at the Beginning of Time

In the beginning, there was no Earth, and all the beings of the Universe lived in the Sky. These divine beings lived an ethereal existence of pure light, floating among clouds. Olorun (also called Oludumare), the Supreme Being and Creator of all things, lived around a great baobab tree in the blue, misty dome of the sky. Living with him were many lesser gods, or orishas. The orishas wore only the finest cloth and jewels. Their bodies were shrouded in gold-laced agbadas decorated with the most elaborate embroidery or, in the case of the goddesses, majestic geles (silken head wraps) fanning outwards. They were adorned with beaded necklaces, gold pendants, and cowrie-shell bracelets. Olorun allowed his pantheon to reign over the vastness of the Heavens, where they could explore unhindered, striding across the skies with grace and ease. But, in truth, all of them were perfectly happy not to stray too far from the great baobab tree, where there was every kind of food and drink they could possibly need. All, that is, but one: Obatala.

For Obatala was the curious orisha, never content just to stay at home in comfort, always wanting to explore. He stared down through the mists in the Sky, and noticed that below there was nothing but a vast, desolate ocean. After a while, the colossal emptiness of that ocean began to oppress Obatala, and he wanted to lay down something solid in that expanse of salty water. Seeing that Obatala would remain restless if not granted his wish, Olorun agreed. Obatala then asked Orunmila, who was also called the Seer because he knows the future, what he would need for his descent into the watery world below. Orunmila produced a sacred tray and dusted it with a fine powder ground up from dried baobab roots. Then he threw sixteen palm kernels onto the tray and examined the patterns they had created in the powder, which was how the Seer predicted the future. After repeating the experiment eight times, he told Obatala to construct a long golden chain, then pack a snail shell full of all the sand he could find in the Sky. He would also need palm nuts, maize, seeds from the baobab tree, and finally the Sacred Egg, which contained in it the spirits of all the orishas. In order to make the chain, Obatala went to the other orishas and asked them for all the gold they had, which they gladly gave him.

He took it to a goldsmith, who minted it down to forge the numerous links of the Golden Chain. Obatala gathered all the sand in the Sky and put it in an empty snail shell. He then packed the other things, as he had been instructed by the Seer. Dressed in clean white robes, he removed the Sacred Egg from the baobab tree and clutched it to his chest under his shirt that it should stay warm. When the goldsmith had finished the Golden Chain, Obatala lowered it into the chasm leading to the ocean below, and he began to climb down, link by link. Down, down he went towards the dark-blue swirling waters for seven days. On the last day, when he got to the end of the chain, he realised it was too short to reach the sea. He swung there for a while, unsure of what to do next, until Orunmila, the Seer, called down to him, 'Remember the shell!'

So Obatala removed the shell from his bag, pouring the sand out of it into the ocean below. As the sand hit the water, it formed a sandbank, which rose up hundreds of feet and spread out for miles, turning into vast stretches of land. So enraptured was Obatala with the beauty of his creation that his heart pounded and cracked the Sacred Egg against his chest. Out of the cracked egg flew Sankofa, the great golden bird bearing the spirits of all the orishas, the gods who would later control the forces of nature. Their spirits blew like wind, shaping the sandy land into various landscapes, including mountains, hills, plains, deserts and islands. Obatala let go of the chain and dropped it onto the sublime new land, which he called Ife, the place that divides the waters. He decided to explore this new place that he had created, so he walked through it, scattering seeds as he moved. Great trees rose up from the places where the seeds fell. Obatala bent down over some water and saw his reflection, which pleased him a great deal. In a burst of creative vanity, he decided to mould some shapes out of clay and water into beings that looked like him: humans.

After fashioning several of these creatures, he was thirsty. So he tapped one of the palm trees that had just sprung up, for its juice. But in the heat it had already fermented into palm wine, and in his raging thirst he drank several gourds without realising. He swiftly became drunk. He continued to mould more human beings, but in his drunkenness he was doing a sloppy job of it, and several of the beings were birthed with misshapen limbs or other deformities. Even the deformed ones Obatala thought were beautiful, but he was aware that his carelessness would cause great suffering down the generations, and he deeply regretted it. The other orishas heard him cursing himself for this foolishness, and they reassured him. After all, he had created these beings so that he could share his infinite wisdom with them, so what did it matter that they were flawed? And the orishas promised to each bring gifts that would help these imperfect beings navigate their treacherous lives, lives that would be filled with uncertainty and pain. As long as this world existed, the orishas would make themselves available to the humans, provided they carried out the necessary sacrifices and rituals.

Obatala smiled. Things were going to be fine in this new world. After some time, Olorun, the Supreme Being, dispatched a messenger, Chameleon, down the golden chain to see how Obatala was doing. Uncurling his long tongue, Chameleon reported back to the Almighty that Obatala had made clay figures which had form but were lifeless. So Olorun gathered all the winds from space, beyond the Sky, and sparked a ball of fire. The fireball shot down towards Ife, now a town in southwest Nigeria, where it dried up some of the swampy land there and baked the clay figures that Obatala had fashioned. Then Olorun inhaled deeply and blew his life breath onto Ife. The clay figures became animated. These people were the first people of Ife, the capital of the Yoruba nation, about two hundred kilometres northeast of the Lagos lagoon.

* * *

In a second version of the Yoruba creation story—just like the book of Genesis, Yoruba culture has more than one creation myth—Olorun assembled all his wealth in one place. He then sent his messenger to summon the 401 supernatural beings of Heaven, called the irunmoles in Yoruba (including, but not limited to, all the orishas). The purpose was to assemble all Heaven's treasures to bring to Earth. He told them to sacrifice a big pile of pounded yam, a pot of soup, kola nuts, sheep, chickens and pigeons, and 3,200 cowrie shells (the main currency in coastal West Africa before the white man came). But when the messenger went to the various beings, none of them provided the required sacrifices. Only Orunmila (the Seer) laid on the required feast, entertaining the messenger with a hearty meal and gourds of palm wine. Eventually, the irunmoles assembled in front of Olorun with what they hoped would meet the requirements for sacrifice: money, food, and other things valuable to them. Then they distributed these among themselves to take down to Earth, which at the time was nothing but a vast ocean. The messenger told Orunmila, 'Sit patiently. The most important thing is the snail's shell underneath Olorun's seat.' And so he did, until the other supernatural beings had gathered up all the things they were to carry to the unformed Earth.

After they left, Orunmila went up to Olorun's seat and took the snail's shell from under it, departing for Earth. Orunmila met the other spiritual beings on the way down between Heaven and Earth. They looked despondent. He asked them what was wrong and they replied that Earth was covered with water, leaving no place for them to land. He dipped his hand inside the shell and threw down a fishing net onto the ocean; then he brought out some sand, which he tossed down. Dipping his hand into his bag a third time, he brought out a five-fingered cockerel, and threw him on the net to spread the sand across it by running around in different directions. Olorun then descended and commanded the land to spread itself more quickly. Then the spiritual beings brought the forces of nature to Earth, imparting the energies that keep the natural world moving. Orunmila, having created the land, chose which of the spirits could come and join him.

Of the original 401, Orunmila chose 256 of them. They included Obatala, son of Olorun and god of creation; Olokun, the goddess of the deep ocean where sunlight cannot penetrate and the keeper of secrets; plus her counterpart, Yemonja. There was also Sango, the god of thunder, Yemonja's son, who sparks lightning from his double-headed axe; Oya, Sango's wife, the goddess of storms, rain, death and rebirth; Esu, the god of justice and law; Osun, the goddess of sweet waters and especially of the river Osun, running from its source in Yorubaland's interior rainforests into the Lagos lagoon; Ogun, the god of iron, weaponry and innovation; Oshosi, god of hunting; and Osanyin, god of medicine and healing. These beings became the orishas, or small gods that people worship. Once they had brought Olorun's treasures to Earth, they departed again for Heaven. But with their knowledge of Earth, they remained the link between the spiritual and physical worlds. Human beings would forever be able to consult the orishas for guidance and help in overcoming adversity. And the orishas would decide, through the sacred oracle of Ifa, which among the humans should rule as kings and lords. Those kings and lords would control all the lands of the Yoruba, from the northwestern-most city of Bassila to the southeastern extent of Itsekiri; from the northeastern city of Isanlu, to the southwestern lagoons of Lagos.

* * *

Like the creation myths of Europe and the Middle East that shaped the thinking of the West, Yoruba stories reflect the fears and dreams of complex farming societies forever just one crop failure away from famine. There is an obsession with the future and how to foresee it; a fear of natural forces—like rain, winds, fertility, and sickness—over which they have no control; and a related idea that these forces need to be appeased to work in your favour. They also speak to a sense of awe at the sheer vastness and wonder of Creation, the mystery of how it came to be, but also a sense that something must have gone wrong with it for there to be so much suffering and deformity. They reveal a conceit that human beings are somehow special, more divine than other animals, and that this whole cosmic show is really all about us. We are not just another animal among many struggling for supremacy like all the others, because our dramas are somehow divinely ordained. And therefore—and here's where most sacred stories find their real purpose—the inequalities in power and wealth between fellow humans must also have a divine basis.

Again, as with farming peoples everywhere facing potentially lethal hazards, Yoruba culture is strongly wedded to the idea of fate. In Yoruba, someone's destiny is called her ori, which literally means her head. The Yoruba say everyone has two heads: a physical, visible one and an invisible one, sometimes called a 'guardian spirit', that determines one's fate. But unlike in the Abrahamic religions that would later make such a huge mark on Nigeria, fate is not a straight line stretching from creation to an apocalyptic future. Fate is rather more like a circle: part of the cycle of birth, growing up, death and reincarnation through the rebirth of ancestors in later generations down the family. Because of this circle, individual fates are never distinct, but always bound up with the fates of the family and community. There is no separating someone's fate from that of his people.

* * *

Nigeria, as strangers eventually labelled the tropical expanse around the Niger River's last leg, comprises some 300 ethnic groups speaking 530 languages—between a third and a quarter of Africa's estimated 1,500 to 2,000 surviving tongues and about three times as many as those of all Europe. Yet while all of this vast melee of people have at one point or another made their mark on the Supernatural City, there is still one dominant group whose myths and meanings have had an outsized effect on how people think, behave and worship: the Yoruba. There were more than 20 million Yoruba at the turn of the twenty-first century, and according to some estimates there may now be more than double that number, most of them in southwest Nigeria. Even today, after a frenetic influx of millions upon millions of migrants, more than three-quarters of Lagosians identify as Yoruba. The Supernatural City is today, as it was always, a spiritual vassal of the Yoruba empire. That has never changed, even though its most powerful chieftancy, the throne of the King of Lagos, originally comes from the neighbouring Bini culture.

Despite people never learning to read or write, from as early as the eighth century AD Yoruba city states were every bit as sophisticated as early medieval European civilisations. They had ironworking, bronze sculpture, and a mythology with a pantheon of gods prone to antics as scandalous and intriguing as those of classical Greece or medieval Scandinavia. So influential was their religion that when Yoruba slaves brought it to the New World, it amazingly survived centuries of repression, and many of its sects persist to this day, especially in the Caribbean, where a version of it was blended with Catholicism.

According to one legend, the Yoruba originally came from ancient Egypt, migrating across the dry, stony Sahel, thereby explaining some striking similarities between ancient Egypt and Yoruba culture (not that the Yoruba ever mummified their dead kings). Another says the great king Oduduwa travelled from the 'east' (usually interpreted as Mecca, although some Yoruba historians dispute this, saying in fact he only visited Mecca and then returned to claim his throne) to settle in the forests of West Africa, and founded Ife, the Yoruba's holy city. At his death he became an orisha. Clearly, the reference to Mecca owes much to the influence of Islam on Yorubaland. Many Yoruba converted to the religion of Mumammad after jihad of the Fulani warrior Usman dan Fodio, although some Yoruba scholars trace the earliest influence of Islam to as far back as Mansa Musa's 13th Century Mali empire. Usman conquered a swathe of northwest Nigeria in the early 1800s and pushed down into the forest zone of the southwest. He was utterly defeated by Yoruba warlords around the city of Ibadan, but in another way his jihad couldn't have been more successful. For it cemented the influence of Islam over Yorubaland and its aristocracy for generations. To this day, many of the traditional rulers who wield such power in modern-day Nigeria are both Muslims and polytheists. They pray to Allah while making sacrifices to their patron Yoruba gods. Even the few who later converted to the white man's Christianity have retained their links to their traditional deities, the ones that for centuries gave them dominion of these humid, forested lands.

In the Yoruba chieftaincy system, it is the Oba, or king, who rules by divine right (because, like some medieval European kings, he is believed to be descended from the gods). Before the European colonists carved out West Africa between themselves, everything was pretty much decided by the Oba, in collaboration with a council of senior chiefs who offered sometimes limited, sometimes substantial checks on his power. The Oba decided whether his people should make war or peace. The Oba decided who had flouted customary law and who had kept it, who should be punished and who rewarded, and with what. The Oba could marry any woman he wanted from any community over which he ruled. The Oba settled disputes, passed judgements and pro-tected his subjects from each other's depredations. As sacred ruler, he was the official high priest of all the various sects wor-shipping the orishas. The Oba decided who among his people should be chiefs and lords, and he was also the primary link between the living and the dead. Because of this, the Oba and his chiefs and lords had total control of the land. In twenty-first-century Nigeria, the obas and chiefs have lost a lot of these func-tions to the modern state, but they still intercede between the natural world and the supernatural.

They also still control vast amounts of land. And land—in crowded Lagos more than anywhere else in Nigeria—is money. Money, meanwhile, is power. And power, in the Supernatural City, just like everywhere else, is something worth fighting for.

12

BIRTH OF A MONSTER

Lagos, late 1400s

Centuries later, Lagosians would look back on it as the day their lagoon-side settlement became 'Lagos'. The pale-skinned sailors appearing on the horizon for the first time came in ships which, like Lagos itself, bore a striking resemblance to the 'man-of-war' polyp, hence the creature's name. At that time, in the late 1400s, the Portuguese had the most advanced ocean-going vessels in the world, and they weren't afraid to use them to chart the 'dark' spaces on the maps that no other European nation had explored.

Whether anyone living on these palm-cloaked islands—little more than a swamp dotted with tiny fishing settlements— noticed the Portuguese adventurers mooring on their perilously shallow sandbanks was never recorded. And though the sailors made some observations about the lagoon and the scattered wet-lands around it, they quickly drew a dismissive conclusion: 'There is no trade ... nor anything from which one can make a profit,' the explorer Duarte Pacheco Pereira, one of the first Europeans to map coastal West Africa, wrote after a trip there in at the turn of the century. Still, the magnificent harbour protected by sandbanks from the sea didn't escape his notice. 'The channel has two fathoms at high tide ... but its entrance is very dangerous, with shallows of sand on which the sea breaks ... Only small vessels of thirty to thirty-five tonnes can enter it,' he wrote.

Dangerous and unprofitable. Not an obvious draw, then. The sailors would have had no idea, but Lagos's first inhabitants were a hotchpotch of refugees from warring Yoruba clans in the interior. If they'd bothered to find out more about the people already living in their 'discovery', they might have noticed an uncanny resemblance to Venice: a group of muddy islands around a lagoon that was relatively easy to defend, occupied by refugees fleeing war and civil strife on the mainland.

Yorubaland's oral traditions tell a story about the creation of Lagos and its countless snaking waterways. The goddesses Olokun and Osara were best friends. Both married Oduduwa, the god-king who founded the Yoruba nation in Ife. But it was Osara who blessed him with a male child and heir, which swiftly meant that she became his favourite. As so often in polygamous arrangements, the wives' friendship morphed into a bitter rivalry over their shared husband. Eventually Olokun tried to distance herself from her rival, but Osara pledged to follow her around forever—whether to try to patch things up or just to annoy the hell out of her was never clear. In the end, Olokun fled south from the holy city of Ife, passing through the Yoruba towns of Ilesha and then Abeokuta, finally arriving in Lagos. Osara followed her for the entire journey and wouldn't leave her alone, which annoyed her even more. Exhausted from their long travels, both of them collapsed and dissolved into water. Olokun became the vast Atlantic Ocean. She gave birth to Yemonja, guardian of all oceans, and also Aje, the god of great wealth and riches, which have so often seemed to flow from across the seas. Osara meanwhile transformed into the Lagos lagoon and its various tributaries and creeks.

Another Lagosian oral tradition says Lagos was uninhabited until the arrival of Ogunfunminire, a fierce hunter who used guns and magic amulets to kill his prey. Ogunfunminire left the holy city of Ife on an adventure, which eventually took him to a town that is now on the outskirts of the megacity. His two wives, Akesan and Ajayi, joined him. Ajayi failed to conceive a child, so he consulted the holy Ifa oracle, which told him to move to the edge of a river. He continued on his journey until he stopped on the sandbanks of Ebute Metta ('the three jetties') on the mainland side of the Lagos lagoon. He then proceeded further south to an island just off it called Iddo. No one who tells the story knows exactly when he arrived, but they usually date it to shortly before the arrival of the first Europeans. The move was successful, and Ogunfunminire had many children. His eleven male descendants then became the 'white cap chiefs' (idejo, in Yoruba) whose generations of families have produced the current obas or kings of the various parts of Lagos. On this somewhat dubious basis, those families still control swathes of its land to this day, much as the dukes and lords do in England (on an equally dubious basis).

However it was first settled, the early Lagos would hardly have shown any promise of one day becoming Africa's biggest city. Its sparse population was eking out a living on fishing, a little trade and some farming, at least on the land that wasn't too swampy—one of Ogunfunminire's sons, Chief Aromire, did establish a pepper farm on Lagos Island. And, unlike the Venetians, the settlers seemed to have no interest in expanding, whether through conquest, trade or anything else. Such a lack of ambition can leave you vulnerable. So the Benin Empire, a civilisation lying about three hundred kilometres east of Lagos at the point where the Niger Delta starts to fan out—and which definitely did have an interest in expanding—conquered Lagos in the seventeenth century. They absorbed it in an empire which at one stage covered a swathe of coastal West Africa right up to the border of the infamous slave-raiding Dahomey kingdom to the west. No one seems sure how they did it, or how violent it was, but it's fair to assume the indigenous Lagosians needed at least some forceful subduing to be persuaded to give tribute and taxes to their more powerful neighbour in exchange for nothing. The King of Benin, having subjugated Lagos, sent his most fearsome warlord, Ashipa (according to some accounts also his grandson), to rule it, as the first Oba of Lagos. Cleverly, he allowed the Yoruba white cap chiefs to keep their territory, so long as they accepted being vassals of the Benin Empire. The new rulers called the island Eko, meaning 'encampment', and Lagosians still call it that today when they're not speaking English. The Portuguese seafarers who had been so dismissive of the place swiftly changed their tune after that. For Benin was just the sort of sophisticated, top-down monarchy—with palaces, slaves and hoards of shiny metals—that hierarchical European nations could do business with. Benin's haunting bronze sculptures of their deities still make up some of the most impressive African loot in the British Museum (which is why, every now and then, it continues to come up with some lame excuse for not returning them). But back in the seventeenth century, before any European had much of an interest in African *objets d'art*, trade with Africa mostly meant one of two things: elephant tusks or (you've guessed it) slaves.

It was slow at first, and then unstoppable. Within two centuries of its conquest by Benin, the trickle of slaves flowing into the hands of Portuguese traders from the Lagos harbour had become a deluge. As British and French slavers joined in, the scramble for slaves became relentless by the mid-eighteenth century. Defeated rivals in Yoruba clan wars were captured, women and children were kidnapped, chiefs' servants were carted off. Some of the things they were traded for, like kitsch brass trinkets, seem bitterly laughable now. The hapless human commodities were put in chains and locked in sweltering cells. Half died from suffocation or thirst. Survivors were then packed into ships heading to the American cotton and sugar plantations—and about half of them again died on the journey. It was during this time—in the second half of the eighteenth century—that the name 'Lagos' starts appearing in the historical records.

Now fast-forward a century, to the mid-1800s. Britain was at this time settling into a new role as an unparalleled global super-power. Flush with a new anti-slavery fervour, it was determined to use its new powers to enforce a slave trading ban imposed in 1807, albeit from a position of shaky moral authority (the French had banned it fourteen years earlier and had impounded several British slaving ships, before Napoleon revived the trade). As Nigerians today are often keen to point out, in reality the anti-slavery fervour was mostly a sanctimonious cover for a colonising project, one that would simply replace the physical manacles with figurative ones. Britain's jingoistic prime minister Lord Palmerston—a man of such moral rectitude that ten years earlier he'd bombarded the Chinese for trying to stop British drug deal-ers from bringing opium into southern China—set the tone. In 1851 he sent a dispatch to the King of Lagos, Oba Kosoko, a stubborn and unrepentant slave trader. In it, he told an envoy to remind the King that 'Lagos is near to the sea, and on that sea are the ships and cannon of England; and also to bear in mind that he does not hold his authority without a competitor, and that the chiefs of the African tribes do not always retain their authority to the end of their lives'.

When Kosoko refused to sign an abolitionist (anti-slavery) treaty, Palmerston made good on the threat. The first British military expedition failed, underestimating how well defended Kosoko's encampment was, but on the second try they were dev-astatingly successful: Royal Navy gunboats obliterated half of Lagos in a single Boxing Day afternoon. The Brits kicked out

Kosoko and replaced him with his uncle, Oba Akitoye (who, according to some versions, had a stronger claim to the throne anyway). A decade later Britain annexed Lagos outright, putting a consul in charge and relegating the power of the King of Lagos to that of a vassal (as so often with their conquests in Africa, the British feared that if they didn't do it, the French would). Lagos Colony became Britain's gateway to a land stretching beyond the mighty Niger River, promising untold riches, not least vast quantities of the palm oil Britain needed to grease the creaking machines of its Industrial Revolution.

Ending the slave trade, and making Lagos a part of the world's richest empire, almost guaranteed it would start to become the cosmopolitan city it is today, as returnee slaves from Brazil and Sierra Leone brought new cultures to this overwhelmingly Yoruba place. The Brazilian returnees erected what remain some of the most beautiful buildings in Lagos (the ones that haven't been torn down to make way for modernist monstrosities). They, alongside the rising numbers of British missionaries, managed to convert quite a few Lagosians to Christianity, although their insistence that they abandon their Yoruba gods in favour of the newcomer Jesus was a tall order. Sufi Islam, which always seemed more attuned to local sensibilities and less spiteful towards traditional African spirituality, was still a lot more palatable for most. The end result: even though embracing Jesus was the obvious way of advancing oneself under the colonial powers, only about half of Lagosians converted, the rest sticking with Islam and their traditional gods.

* * *

It wasn't until 1914 that one of the fiercest architects of the British empire in Africa joined together in his imagination 640,000 square kilometres of West African territory, which included the so-called northern and southern Nigeria protectorates, to form Nigeria as we know it today. Sir Frederick Lugard, a man with a chest full of medals and a handlebar moustache the size of a small furry animal, had pioneered the British policy of 'indirect rule'. This was the ruthless system whereby the military and taxes were controlled by London and everything else would be run by local aristocracies—as long as they agreed to subject themselves to the authority of their colonial masters, of course. To make it work, rebellions by African kings who didn't accept British 'protection' were dealt with especially harshly in scorched-earth campaigns (as Lugard did to Abeokuta, in the Yoruba hinterlands just beyond Lagos, following a pattern he'd used in East Africa). Lugard publicly admitted that these diverse peoples had nothing in common. But the administrative convenience of stitching them together was too tempting. His girlfriend, the journalist Flora Shaw, had coined the name 'Nigeria' in a 1897 essay, and Lugard reluctantly made Lagos, the mosquito-ridden port he hated, its capital.

As with elites all over Africa, the British policy of 'indirect rule' had the effect of cementing the power of the oligarchs who ran Lagos. 'Take me to your leader,' the British liked to say, and, having arrived at his throne, would tell the leader he could keep his authority and land (or much of it) as long as he did everything they said. Thanks to this policy, the tenuous claims to vast tracts of land of a few aristocratic Nigerian families now came under the protection of the world's most powerful empire. No wonder so many of them played ball.

Of course, as even Lugard himself must have realised, the creation was doomed to rupture. It should have been no surprise that when Nigeria was hastily granted independence in 1960, it was quickly followed by quarrelling, assassinations of the leading political figures from rival ethnic groups, military coups and a civil war in the east that killed up to a million people by the end of the decade. Later, in the early 1980s, after a decade of recovery and oil-fuelled growth during which Fela Kuti recorded some of his most memorable songs, the head of a 'master plan' for Lagos named Oyesanya Oyelola drew up an ambitious blueprint for the city. It was to be financed from Nigeria's fat and swelling oil wealth. Oyelola foresaw thirty districts across the mainland to house booming factories and ease overcrowding on Lagos Island, which was bursting at the seams. It included plans for the Third Mainland Bridge, but also a fourth one connecting the swampy eastern Lekki Peninsula, which was about to undergo its own construction boom, to the mainland.

That plan died when soldiers led by Muhammadu Buhari seized control of Nigeria in 1983, followed by another coup by General Ibrahim Babangida two years later. The next fifteen years were marked by military misrule. Soldiers feasted on the public purse and vast amounts of money meant to spruce up Lagos and other parts of Nigeria went missing. Babangida did manage to finish the Third Mainland Bridge, but it filled up so quickly that within a year it seemed as if it had barely dented Lagos's unbearable traffic. He carried out some 'improvements' on the megacity, but his crowning achievement in that regard was the brutal eviction of 300,000 people from the vibrant slum of Maroko, on the Lekki Peninsula, to make way for fancy houses and shopping malls for the wealthy. Unsurprisingly, his soldiers 'cleared' the slum with spectacular violence, killing, raping and looting their way through this city on planks suspended over a swamp. History might have put it down to the usual excesses of a military government, but the attack on Maroko set a precedent that continued: dozens of other slums would be given the same violent treatment in the following decades, even by ostensibly democratic governments.

It happened like this. There was a wealthy land-owning family under Oba Idowu Oniru, the chief of Iruland, which included Maroko and some other parts of the swampy Lekki Peninsula east of it. Oniru laid claim to the entire area as the homeland of his ancestors. Never mind that nearly a third of a million people were living in Maroko. Babangida's military governor in Lagos, Brigadier-General Raji Rasaki, had had his eyes on Maroko for some time. It was right next door to Victoria Island, which was flourishing but running out of space as banks, insurance companies and oil companies were relocating from the utter chaos of neighbouring Lagos Island. One day in July 1990, dozens of houses were reduced to rubble while soldiers barking orders, blowing whistles and toting guns chased the residents out. They smashed skulls with rifle butts, beat men with whips, and raped young girls in front of their relatives. The inevitable negative publicity forced the government to make a half-hearted effort at relocating a handful of them. This they did by dumping them in a boggy estate about ten kilometres away that had been abandoned after the lagoon waters got the better of it. There was no power there, no road but the odd dirt track, and no piped water or schools. In that regard, their plight was hardly unique among Lagos's poorer margins.

As Lagos's population exploded, it became so dysfunctional that in 1991 the capital was moved to the newly constructed (and incredibly soulless) city of Abuja. Two years later, presidential elections took place that were meant to bring an end to military dictatorship, but General Babangida annulled them when he didn't like the winning candidate, Moshood Abiola, a Yoruba businessman from Lagos. The city erupted into bloody rioting, which then morphed into tit-for-tat killing between migrant Hausas from the north and Yoruba. Babangida wisely stepped down, but a transitional government lasted less than three months before his army chief, General Sani Abacha, seized the reins. Now Abacha was a caricature African dictator who wore aviator shades indoors, executed alleged criminals by firing squad, and is thought to have siphoned between $1 billion and $8 billion into private bank accounts in Switzerland and Liechtenstein (banks which are even to this day trying to keep the money). When Abacha died mysteriously in the company of two Indian prostitutes in 1998—some said of a Viagra overdose (if such a thing is possible); others, poison—democracy finally returned to Nigeria.

By then, Lagos was well and truly broken. It had a population hovering around 10 million, with a road, power, water and sewerage network suitable for less than a tenth of that. Bola Tinubu, the new civilian Lagos governor, really had no choice but to start fixing up the city and making more room for more people. That meant sand-filling and developing the useless tracts of swamps and sandbanks that lie further east of Maroko, which the various Yoruba aristocrats had been sitting on for generations since before colonial times. With Tinubu's bright new vision of a modern megacity that would require vast amounts of space to realise, all of a sudden the lands of these aristocrats were potentially worth billions of dollars.

PART V

THE OVERLORD

Isola, the scion of Agbo, he who dreams daily of wealth, he who thinks daily of the good things of life, he who looks unto the sky and says, 'I can hold you if I want to.' Isola, the mighty tiger, the elephant that shakes to disturb the forest ... Isola who says he is not ready to marry. When he is ready, girls will line the street from here to Hausaland.

Yoruba chant to Isola, the bringer of wealth, transcribed by
Toyin Falola in *A Mouth Sweeter than Salt: An African Memoir*

The Lekki–Epe corridor in Lagos is unarguably the fastest growing construction corridor in the Nigeria today. Almost all affluent Nigerians and those in the middle-income bracket want to build or own properties in this highbrow corridor. The once dreaded swampy neighbourhood [is] the toast of property investors.

Vanguard newspaper, 25 September 2012

13

FATAI

Lagos Island, 2002

On the day the sacred oracle declared Fatai to be Olumegbon of Lagos, the most senior chieftancy title in the whole city, he could scarcely contain his joy. Fatai had known for a decade that he was special, after discovering as a young man that he was a prince of the royal house of Olumegbon, one of the six most powerful chieftaincies in all of Lagos State. That had been quite a shock after his modest upbringing as an orphan on the Lagos mainland. Some said the title was so hallowed that only the Oba, the King of Lagos himself, had more authority. And, in fact, the newly named Fatai Olumegbon was also now one of the six 'kingmakers' who, after the death of the Lagos king, would select the next one from the ranks of his extended family by consulting the Ifa oracle. That wasn't going to be too far off: the current Lagos ruler, Oba Adeyinka Oyekan II, was already in his nineties.

In modern times, the authority of all these kings and lords and chiefs was largely ceremonial, at least in theory. In reality, they wielded huge power because their titles to vast tracts of prime

Lagos real estate enabled them to control local politics behind the scenes. Fatai's predecessor, his great-uncle Lamidi Yesufu, had died a decade earlier, and for a long while the royal house had not filled his throne. Once the time was right—which meant when the sacred oracle decreed it—five priests who specialised in divining royal succession were called in for a ceremony to choose the next Olumegbon. In Yoruba religion, the Ifa oracle is a gateway to the supernatural realm. It passes directly through Orunmila, the god of divination—the one who told the creator god Obatala what to bring with him when he descended the Golden Chain of the Sky to conjure Earth from a formless ocean. According to Yoruba folklore, Orunmila lived on Earth for many years after creation, until he became sick of humans and their petty-minded ways and returned to his seat in Heaven, under the baobab tree. Disaster followed, since humans could no longer predict events, and so he returned to dwell among them. Before departing again, he left behind a spiritual relic to enable humans to divine the future: the sacred palm nuts, which are used by priests even today for consulting the oracle.

The priests had had to undergo years of training to be able to interpret it. They'd learned hundreds of sacred tales and fables. Sitting in a special room in the palace, they took an envelope containing six names from the royal house of Olumegbon, and for each name asked the oracle what would happen if that person was declared Olumegbon. They took the sacred wooden divination tray, with some carved odus—the sacred sayings that reveal the nature of the divine to humans. They placed it at the feet of the head priest, who sat in front of it facing east, the direction from which Ifa always travels from the spiritual plane. The priest drummed on it rhythmically, then scattered white iyerosun across it—a dust harvested from a termite mound on the Irosun tree. He took the sixteen sacred palm kernels and shook them in his hand eight times, asking Orunmila to indicate which name he favoured before throwing them onto the tray so that each landed either concave up or concave down, making different lines in the white dust. 'If you choose this one, there will be fire and you'll have a lot of enemies,' came the answer for one name. 'He will bring famine and trouble,' it said of another. But when it came to Fatai, the oracle said there would be employment for the youth and a long and happy life for his subjects. The priests then declared Fatai the next Olumegbon of Lagos. This meant he was the spiritual leader of the idejos, the white cap chiefs who had ruled Lagos since it had been inhabited, until the British colonists annexed the city and turned them into mere wealthy figureheads.

His title also carried with it the designation of 'Overlord of Ajah', a stretch of the Lekki Peninsula running east off Victoria Island between the lagoon and the Atlantic Ocean. Fatai was now the interloper between Ajah's people and the very gods they depended on for good fortune. That meant there was also a more concrete, material reality to be considered alongside this spiritual role. For the Lekki Peninsula was about to become the hottest new development in Lagos, and Fatai's title to Ajah's 1,400 hectares was potentially worth billions of dollars. The developers, hungry to make money from the insatiable demand for housing in Africa's most overcrowded metropolis, had chosen the Lekki Peninsula for a simple reason: it was the only place in this whole mess of a megacity where they could start almost from scratch.

* * *

Lagos was running out of space, again. Developers looked at maps clouded with grey splodges representing the explosion in informal housing across the vast, burgeoning mainland. They looked at the islands, already bursting with commerce and condos. Property ownership in all these old parts of Lagos was a Gordian knot of trickery. People would buy a plot of land to develop on Lagos Island from someone who they thought was the owner, then four other people would turn up with rival title deeds, in this way holding up the project for years. There had been so much fraud and double-dealing over the decades, no one knew who really owned what. Ikoyi district had the most expensive real estate in Africa, and yet practically every other house warned buyers against fraud with 'this house is not for sale' graffitied onto it. One particularly audacious scam involved breaking into someone's house while they were away on holiday, faking or photocopying their title deeds to the standard of a master forger—fake documents were often so well done in Lagos as to be undetectable—and then posing as an estate agent selling their property. You'd come back home to find three or four different sets of people with keys to your house, all claiming to have bought it.

Even assuming the developers had managed to buy the land or property from the actual owner, they would then have to deal with the 'sons of the soil' (omo onile) gangs, who roam Lagos looking for landowners and property developers to extort, on the grounds that they are not 'indigenes', as Toyin's 'transport union' gang did in Obalende. You would have to pay them off, or they would keep coming back, beating up your builders or sometimes occupying your property. If you were connected to a powerful politician, you could usually get them to stop, because the politicians always maintained their connections to the gangs to fight election battles. If not, good luck to you! It was all a massive headache.

Newly developed Victoria Island, with Nigeria's biggest mall and cinema, trendy restaurants and banks, was anyway reaching its limit. There was only one way left to expand: the Lekki Peninsula, a stretch of sand and swamp free of such thorny encumbrances—or so it seemed—and ripe for developing. Lekki had been attached to V.I. ever since British colonialists filled in its easterly swamps with sand to mitigate the scourge of malaria in the early twentieth century. The peninsula is many times bigger than V.I. itself. Lekki was where Lagos's new governor, Bola

Tinubu, saw the greatest potential for realising his dream of a Singapore of Africa, a modern megacity and shipping hub that would end Lagos's reputation for filth and squalor. And Ajah, the Overlord's new domain bequeathed by divine right, was bang in the middle of it.

The front end of Lekki had already undergone a multimillion-dollar boom. The most elite part was Lekki Phase 1, built in the late 1990s. It was all neat mansions with copious classical columns protected by black gates, fed by fast-food restaurants, massage parlours and fancy waterside bars. Chevron had already relocated to a compound in Lekki with palm-lined avenues and yellow-bricked bungalows. Now even Phase 1 was getting full, spurring developments further along the peninsula, like Victoria Garden City (VGC), a completely self-contained gated community of 200 hectares with green lawns and a tree-shaded park. And immediately to the east of VGC, primed for the next such luxury developments, was Ajah.

The evening after the oracle chose him, Chief Fatai Olumegbon sat in his modest house in the sardine tin that is Lagos Island, with every inch of space taken up by hawkers and miscreants. A tall, stoutly built man with a handsome face in which sat deep-set almond eyes, pouty lips and flared nostrils that gave him an air of authority, Fatai had long dreamt of this day. He saw his future as ruler of a clean, orderly, model megacity in Ajah, with spacious housing estates, motorways, a light-rail link, a fourth mainland bridge across the lagoon, a new airport and a Chinese free-trade zone linked to a state-of-the-art deep-water port.

There was just one problem: Fatai's claim to be the ruler of Ajah was disputed by a rival chief and his clan who, unlike the Overlord, actually lived there. The rival chief's name was Amida Kareem, the Baale (paramount chief) of Ajah. Their dispute was generations old: almost as old, in fact, as Lagos itself.

* * *

Legend has it that Lagos's founder, Ogunfunminire—whose other name was 'One who uses concoction powers to become a boa constrictor'—parcelled out all of Lagos's land to his eleven sons. Ogunfunminire's eldest child, Olumegbon, was decreed the owner of a part of Lagos Island and the stretch of the Lekki Peninsula to the east of it known as Ajah. He was also made the head of all the other chiefs, the so-called idejo class, and the name 'Olumegbon' became the official title of that position.

Since then, Lagos had been conquered by two mighty empires—one from a neighbouring civilisation in West Africa, the other from a medium-sized island in the North Sea that happened to be (then) the world's most powerful nation. Despite its conquest by Benin and then Britain, Lagos's traditional land-owning class had done well at keeping hold of their territories. After their annexation by the Benin Empire, the installed Benin ruler, Ashipa, realised he would need cooperative chiefs to maintain his tenuous claim to Lagos, so he allowed them to retain their territories, so long as they sent taxes back to the ruler of Benin. Ashipa installed his palace on Lagos Island—on top of where Aromire's pepper farm used to be—shifting the city's centre of power away from the mainland to the islands, where in many ways it has remained ever since. Later, the British, too, could see they would never control this territory unless they had local elites to manipulate, forcing them, equally, to recognise the claims of all the leading Lagos chiefs.

The band of Yoruba fishermen and farmers who arrived to settle Ajah a good century after the Benin conquest could have been forgiven for not realising it had an absentee landlord. Apart from the abundant Nile crocodiles, mona monkeys, woodland kingfishers and treefrogs, Ajah was empty. According to their oral tradition, Ogunsemo and Ojupon were sons of a nobleman from the Yoruba's holy city of Ife, who had fled south during a war in the early eighteenth century—one of many civil wars that would engulf Yorubaland over the next 150 years. Trekking on foot with an unspecified number of followers, they reached present-day Lagos Island, and consulted the Ifa oracle about what to do next. It advised they continue their journey to a place where they would hear the ceaseless roaring of Olokun, the goddess of the deep sea, and the calm, lapping waters of Osara, the goddess of the Lagos lagoon. They followed the sliver of land between the lagoon and the sea—now known as the Lekki Peninsula—until they reached a lush mangrove forest. According to one version of the oral tradition, they named the place Azale, which in the language of the Benin Empire in control at the time meant 'treasure island', a name which was later corrupted to Ajah. When the oracle was consulted for a second time, it told them this was the place where they would live in peace and harmony (a prophecy that would later turn out to be a real howler).

Ogunsemo and Ojupon erected a hut—which their descendants would later claim to be the first dwelling laid down in Ajah—and slashed a footpath through the jungle to the sea. Two days later, the brothers, who like most Yoruba nobles were fierce hunters, killed a buffalo. Its tail became a wand to be used in magic rituals for generations, which remains with them to this day. Other settlers from different parts of Yorubaland joined them, and they established several prosperous fishing villages. They built a shrine to the gods and ancestors in the forest, which still stands, although the forest itself has been swallowed by concrete. The most important of these deities was also called Aja (spelt without the 'h'), the patron goddess of forests, of the animals within it, and of herbal healers, whose tradition of making plant potions had originally been brought to Earth by her. Under the patronage of these gods, the title of Baale of Ajah has rotated between the two families ever since.

It isn't clear at what point the settlers discovered that a powerful chief from Lagos Island claimed Ajah as his own territory—

theirs and Olumegbon's versions are wildly at odds. At some point at the end of the nineteenth century the Olumegbon family and the then Baale of Ajah, Chief Ojomu, took their dispute to court—and the court ruled in Olumegbon's favour. Ojomu ignored the ruling, and the British didn't intervene to enforce it. For the entire hundred years that they held sway over Lagos, the British imperial masters failed to resolve the row, because there wasn't much in it for them: Ajah was just a swampy outpost on the lagoon.

Then, in the 1940s, the Olumegbon family petitioned the then King of Lagos, Oba Falolu, to appeal to the colonial authorities to enforce their claim. On that occasion, a British commissioner to the colony apparently sided with the Ajah residents. But another court ruling in 1955 also recognised the Olumegbon family's claim. And so it went on, well into Nigeria's independence from Britain, generation after generation, until the rival families eventually signed a settlement in 1991. In that settlement, representatives of the Ogunsemo and Ojupon families both recognised the claims of the Overlord in exchange for a fee agreed between them.

That should have ended it, but other members of the two resident families claimed that the people representing them were not the real chiefs. The purported chiefs had also, predictably, pocketed the fees. So shortly after Fatai was declared Overlord of Ajah in 2002, the two families went to court yet again. This did nothing to solve the dispute but must have been wonderful for lawyers hired to repeatedly spin this merry-go-round. Again, the judgement was unequivocal: Chief Fatai Olumegbon was declared Overlord of Ajah, just as his ancestors had been. The two families of the Ajah chieftaincy would have to cede all claims on its land to him, and pay him for any portion of land they had already sold or leased.

Again, they ignored the judgement. Chief Fatai did manage to use the ruling to get land back from reputable companies who had bought it from the two Ajah families, including a major bank, which relinquished its building, only for it to be leased a few months later to the fast-food chain Chicken Republic. But apart from a few small victories, the Ojupon and Ogunsemo families were still holding a lot of territory, including every petrol station in Ajah, a place about to become the location of a major expressway. The Overlord realised there was only one arena left to fight this out: on the streets.

* * *

Fatai knew he'd hardly be welcome if he just walked into Ajah. Apart from passing through it once or twice, he'd hardly ever been there ('Overlord' was an unusual title, in that it enabled his aristocratic family to rule a territory to which they had little personal connection, much like the way Britain's dukes and earls lay claim to distant tracts they rarely visit except to aim their rifles at luckless herbivores). By contrast, the two rival chieftaincy families had always lived in the area and had a lot of local support. Fatai would need some muscle if he wanted to seize the place physically. In Lagos, you can wield as much authority on paper (or in Heaven) as you like; your real power lies on the streets: along pavements, in car parks, at roundabouts, inside minibus stations, on the fists and knives and crude shotguns of the city's restless youth.

So, shortly after he was proclaimed Overlord, he held a discreet meeting with a gang leader. The mafia boss went by the name Abija, and he ran one of the 'transport unions', the extortion rackets targeting bus stations across Lagos that our street fighter Toyin joined. Abija's territory was on Lagos Island. He was a tall, well-built man with a shaven head, a menacing glare and the languid gait of a man with great self-confidence and little fear. He was also known to fight for whoever was the highest bidder, and with a degree of ruthlessness that marked him out.

Fatai offered the gang leader a deal: plots of land in Ajah for him and his fighters if they joined him in his quest to secure the land against the illegitimate gangs of the Ogunsemo and Ojupon families. The Overlord's family had tried all legal means for generations, and they'd ignored the courts every time. What was a reasonable man supposed to do? Abija took up the challenge with pleasure.

Over the following months, the gang leader raised a small army of a dozen of his toughest boys, mostly from the Adeniji Adele Bus Stop, his main operation. One night, they gathered in a backstreet next to the bus stop, on Lagos Island, not far from the King of Lagos's palace. It was late enough for even this throbbing area to be quiet. The toughs were Abija's fiercest fighters, carefully chosen. They included a bus tout called Tunde, a short, stocky, muscular figure, although with ample fat around the middle, who who worked in the Adeniji Adele bus park. As Abija arrived in his immaculately washed 4x4, Tunde shuddered slightly at the thought of what they were about to do: the Olumegbon had a lot of enemies in Ajah, and they weren't likely to give up easily. Tunde knew all the tricks of the trade: how to aim and fire a homemade shotgun, how to wield a cutlass. He knew how to use a knife to badly disfigure his enemy, but without drawing so much blood that he died, so his mutilated form would send a message back to his kin. All the same, he feared his battle skills would be put to the test on alien territory. Abija hushed the crowd.

'I have a job for all of you,' he told the eager thugs. 'The Overlord has requested our help to reclaim what's rightfully his. He offers his land. You will each get one plot. It is very valuable. The Lekki–Ajah axis is where the Asiwaju of Lagos is building a whole new, great city,' he said, using the honorific title of the governor, Tinubu. At that the foot soldiers cheered; whether at the thought of a new great city or the personal booty they would get from this raiding expedition wasn't clear.

FATAI

For Tunde, the thought of owning territory in the brave new Lagos was a dream he had never entertained. He'd dropped out of school after his father, a poor market trader, died suddenly. He was 15, but he left school with only enough literacy to write notes and read instructions. And now he was the bread-winner, as his mother's itinerant perfume-selling business hardly brought in a meal a day. He looked around Lagos Island's insanely over-subscribed job market, and after some desperate weeks' pleading, he managed to get training as a plumber's apprentice. The plumber worked for the 'area boys' who ran the streets of Lagos, helping them fix leaks in the outside public taps. The area boys had de facto privatised these vital water points—charging people to use what was meant to be free—so it was only fitting that they patched up water pipes themselves when the council failed to do so. But Tunde had quickly found that legitimate trade scarcely covered the rent in his 'face me, face you' apartment near the King's palace. He could see the area boys, charging dubious parking fees and tariffs for each jerrycan of water, were doing much better. If you want to make a living in Lagos, he reasoned, you need to grab dollars, not slave for cents. He was 23 when he finally got the chance to join the 'transport union' at the Adeniji Adele Bus Stop, around the time of Fatai's confirmation as Overlord of Ajah. That was after he'd participated in a fight to chase away a gang who'd seized it for a few weeks. A short battle at the garage, mostly involving cutlasses, had enabled Tunde to demonstrate superior gallantry. He'd slashed a few people, not fatally, just enough to show his ruthlessness. It paid off: after they'd re-established control of the bus park, he landed himself a job. Tunde had won several fist fights at the bus park, even against bigger opponents, but he'd never taken a life. Soon, he would have a chance to prove himself on the battlefield and, if necessary, kill.

'Be patient, my warriors. It won't be tomorrow, maybe not this year,' Abija continued. 'But soon we take Ajah,' he ended his speech, provoking a loud cheer. The toughs melted back into the busy streets of Lagos Island.

* * *

Over the following months, Fatai Olumegbon bided his time. By 2003, a year after he was proclaimed Overlord, he had a mobile police unit lined up for his protection during the raid. He had also secured approval from the King of Lagos, Adeyinka Oyekan II, his father-in-law (without whose blessing no territorial claims could be truly defensible). Fatai might have gone ahead with it, but on 1 March the King, who'd been the ceremonial ruler of Lagos since shortly after independence from Britain in 1960, died suddenly. He was 91. His spirit would need to depart to the next world before anyone could get on with the grubby business of fighting over land. The King, unusually for such a prominent Yoruba nobleman, was a Christian—only the second time Lagos had had a Christian king out of the twenty-three who had thus far ruled the city—so there would be no Islamic three-day deadline on his burial. It could be months before his body was interred. A successor would need to be chosen, and that meant there would be an Eyo Festival.

* * *

The King's Palace, Lagos Island, 2003

The Eyo Festival is the night in Lagos on which the veil is lifted between the visible and the supernatural realms. Back in the day, only the death of a prominent Lagos figure—a top 'white cap chief' or the King of Lagos himself—could trigger one. These days they could be done at the request of the Lagos governor to bring in tourists: money was Lagos's true God now. But this was to be a festival as worthy as any in the more hallowed past. The six kingmakers, including Fatai, held a sacred rite to choose his replacement. They'd asked the Ifa oracle to ask Orunmila, the god who is witness of fate, who would be king next. The oracle had selected the dead Oba's nephew, Rilwan Akiolu. So the festival marked the final rites of passage of the old king to the spirit world, but it also invested supernatural authority in the new one. Funeral rites had to be done correctly or else the undead spirit could become restless and haunt the living. The festival would include a procession with wild, terrifying dancing. Ghostly figures in masks would act out a play—the *Adamu Orisha*—in which the different gods clash for supremacy.

The festival date was confirmed when the 'Adimu', the collective ancestral spirits, positioned himself in the streets of Lagos a week before. He was clad in white sheets with a black broad-brimmed hat and white veil, and thrust a long staff into the ground. He stood motionless for hours, a fearsome shape in folds of cloth, a white shadow. Then the other prominent secret societies had sent out a masked figure, dressed in the same white cloth but with different coloured hats: red, yellow, green, purple. The most important Bini dancers, known as masquerades, represented the deity Olokun, god of the deep sea and giver of luck. He was depicted as male in Bini culture and increasingly among coastal Yoruba—unlike the female form she took in the Yoruba hinterlands. To the Bini culture from which the King of Lagos hailed, Olokun was as important as the war goddess Athena was to the ancient Greeks. It was said the kings of Lagos were all his descendants.

On festival day, market traders on frenzied Eko Idumota closed their stalls. Thousands lined the streets, from Onikan, with its old stone walls caked in moss and sausage trees, past Tokunbo Street, with its jumble of wooden shack-shops. They thronged past the Marina on Lagos harbour, with its decaying Brazilian-inspired structures like Vaughan House, characterised by big round arches, up to Iga Idunganran, site of the Oba's palace. The Benin imperials had built the palace in the seventeenth century on top of the pepper farm of Aromire, one of the children of the founder of Lagos. Later, Portuguese slavers, allied to the King of Benin and his Lagos vassal, built a spectacular turreted castle. But like so much of Lagos, the palace suffered a modernising project in the 1960s that had left much of it looking like any sprawling big man's compound of nondescript box-houses.

The masked figures, dressed in white cloth, chanted poetry in terrible, scratchy voices and danced furiously, twirling their staffs. Sometimes they formed pairs and their staffs would clash like those of ninjas fighting a duel. They beat people for wearing the wrong kind of shoes, for smoking or for getting too close. Fascinated white tourists snapped illicit photos of the procession of masked figures in flowing robes. As with Halloween in the West, the masquerades represent a portal between the occult and the visible world, where the normal laws are suspended, and plans for mischief can be hatched.

Chief Fatai took his seat next to the new King of Lagos and other white cap chiefs, the aristocrats who were, like him, preparing multimillion-dollar real estate deals with their traditional land. All wore long, flowing robes and sat alongside diplomats and politicians flown in from the capital, Abuja. Among them was another group that would have looked very out of place: the gang leaders who ran the lucrative bus stations, including Toyin, her mafia boss, Ataru, and Abija himself. It was a mark of the power these street thugs wield: even the King needed this informal muscle to maintain his territory and fend off rivals. Without 'boys' to protect him, a Lagos big man was powerless. The gangs brought the correct gifts for the new king to sacrifice to his deities: schnapps, kola nuts and bitter kola. The night got more drunken and frenzied, and Fatai sidled up to Abija. In May, Fatai had met with the heads of the two Ajah families to try to resolve the dispute, and both had agreed to put it behind them. The Baale, Amida Kareem, had even signed an out-of-court settlement. But when he returned to loud protests from the two families at the paltry sums involved, he'd reneged on it, saying he had signed the settlement under duress. That had only confirmed to Fatai that he must take Ajah by force.

'I trust I can still count on your support,' Fatai said to Abija, as the dancing and drinking continued.

'It would be an honour to help you secure your rightful claim,' Abija replied. 'And I know another who could help,' he added, before later walking up to Ataru and whispering in his ear. In another time, Ataru and Abija would be natural enemies, as supporters of rival political parties, but nothing unites rivals in Lagos like the smell of money. Fatai smiled: these Lagos tough guys could easily take Ajah.

Later that night, a dispute between two groups of masquerades from rival chieftaincy houses spawned bloodshed. One group tried to pass another but were refused access, the other group said, because their deity was invisibly holding court in the street with some other ancestral spirits. A brawl left one of the Eyo performers lying hacked to death in the street, his white robe soaked in blood. Another masquerade threw a heavy gin bottle at the rival group in retaliation, smashing it on someone's head and killing him. No one was sure how the third man died, but a newspaper would report the next day that he was 'beaten to death with charms'.

* * *

Ajah, Lekki Peninsula, 2003

On the last day of the month of the festival, Fatai struck, with the blessing of the new king that Fatai had helped select. He had to be swift: the Ajah families were already parcelling out land illicitly to reputable businesses in the hope of complicating efforts to force them out.

Three days before the gathering, Tunde and twelve other gang members selected for the mission prepared Voodoo potions, which a few of them had learned how to make from some Egun people from the neighbouring Benin Republic. The Voodoo religion of the Egun and Fun peoples, who are found across Nigeria's neighbour, Benin, as well as in next-door Togo, presented some unique twists on the Yoruba magic used by most Lagos touts. They centred it around a god that the Voodoo religion shares with the Yoruba pantheon: Ogun, the god of iron, metalwork, technology and weapons of all sorts: spears, knives, hunting blades, and every type of firearm, as well as less lethal items like the ploughshare.

The witchdoctor prepared the medicine to make them impervious to bullets: it was green, acrid and heavily alcoholic. He had chanted Voodoo incantations on the leaves, with prayers to the god Ogun, before mashing them up into a pulp and mixing it with schnapps. They each made eight small incisions, four on each side of their faces, with a cutlass. Then, dipping the dagger in the potion, they put a few drops on the cuts. The concrete floor in the witchdoctor's house was spotted with blood droplets from all this enthusiastic self-immolation. They drank some of the liquid. The effect of the Voodoo magic put them in the state of okigbe, meaning in Yoruba 'when sharp objects cannot penetrate you': cutlass-proof. It also made the warriors ayeta, meaning 'bullet-proof'. Knives would not pierce them, and bullets would bounce off their bodies like rubber. Just in case the magic wasn't as powerful as the witchdoctor claimed, some of the boys, Tunde included, wore metal amulets chain-linked together over parts of the chest and belly to form a crude body armour.

Abija had supplied only three homemade shotguns for the fight and a limited number of bullets—this was meant to be a show of strength rather than a bloodbath. Like a standard mafia boss, he was long past getting involved in these scuffles himself. The local blacksmith had made the guns to order from scrap steel and wood, salvaged from rubbish dumps. The rest had just their cutlasses. Tunde was one of the three men armed with both.

Fatai had assembled a few trucks of police from privately hired police units to protect him. The convoy sped along the motorway running around the edge of Lagos Island from the King's palace, forcing other traffic off the road. Fatai himself was in a 4x4, and the touts he'd hired to take control of his territory lay near the front, in a minibus. They passed the rundown skyscrapers like UBA House and along the Marina, where the Yacht Club faced the container terminal on the opposite side of the harbour. Then they crossed the link bridge connecting Lagos Island with Victoria Island, at the westernmost end of the Five Cowries Creek—the sliver of water running the whole length of the islands—onto Ahmadu Bello Way. They ground along the brick roads, past the high-rises and posh hotels of V.I., where the business world had moved after Lagos Island became too dysfunctional and shabby for it. The road hugged the edge of the creek all the way to Maroko, which had been developed in the 1990s from a vibrant slum into an upper-middle-class area of shopping malls, housing complexes and international schools. The developments on V.I. and Maroko had made the royal house of Oba Oniru, who owned the land, one of the richest families in Lagos. The Oniru housing estates, and the massive Palms Mall complex, were worth millions of dollars. To get those developments under way swiftly, it had certainly helped that Crown Prince Adesegun Oniru was Commissioner for Waterfront and Infrastructure Development: a happy marriage of money and power. The same thing was about to happen for Oba Elegushi, who owned the western part of the Lekki Peninsula through which they travelled next. It was already being sand-filled and developed into expensive housing.

As the convoy rolled into the sandy streets of Ajah, Fatai's boys jumped out and began putting notices on the huts and brick houses of slum dwellers, which read: 'This land belongs to Chief Fatai Olumegbon, Olumegbon of Lagos. You have 24 hours to vacate.' They tagged two dozen houses this way. They would be first in line for the bulldozers when Ajah's development projects started. Fatai pulled out a megaphone and began calling out to people that their Overlord had arrived. On arriving at the roundabout south of Ajah market and just next to the Overlord's modest 'palace'—really just a large house in need of serious renovation—the gang members set out on foot to seize the territory, only to be surprised by a gang of youths attacking from the tall grass behind. Dusk was approaching and Tunde couldn't see them well, but he knew these were the Ajah Boys, led by Kazeem 'All-Rounder' Salami, a notorious thug and owner of several petrol stations in the area. Salami was close to the two ruling families who rejected Fatai's claim to the land. Tunde swiftly realised that they were outnumbered, with about thirty men on Kazeem's side against their thirteen. The police, meanwhile—a few dozen officers distributed between three or so trucks—hung back. Their job was not to get involved in the grubby business of fighting, neither was it to prevent it: just protect the Overlord in case things got out of hand. Fatai was confident he would prevail: the gods were on his side, as was the law, and Abija's gang included some skilled fighters.

One of the Ajah Boys fired a bullet from a pump-action shotgun in their direction, and they fired back. Within seconds, Ajah erupted into shooting. Tunde realised their best option was to scatter into Ajah market and then into the bush that edged the lagoon, a muddy stretch of tall elephant grass marked by the odd uncompleted building. He made a sweeping hand signal, and the warriors ducked down and dispersed. But the Ajah Boys knew all these stretches of elephant grass much better than Abija's gang.

Bullets banged and whizzed through the greenery, and Tunde threw his heavy body to the ground with a thud, plunging his face into a mound of mud. After some more rounds, the shooting seemed to die down for a minute.

Charily, he peeped over the top of the grass—and within minutes was smacked in the shoulder by a ball of lead, as the firing swiftly started up again. He fell to the ground. His shoulder was bleeding and in pain, but not broken or disabled—these homemade guns sometimes didn't inflict too bad a wound if fired from a distance. He edged up again and fired several rounds from his gun, until the clicks told him he'd run out of bullets. Between the grass he saw that the other two shooters had managed to kill a man each, shooting up their chests at close range, until they too were out of rounds. They all ducked deep into the grass, while more shooting came from the side of the Ajah Boys for what seemed a long time.

'Retreat,' someone shouted, and a group of Tunde's gang pulled back to the rusty entrance of the market. While he was running, two more bullets hit Tunde in the lower back, lightly piercing his armour. At some point during the commotion, the guns fell silent, as it seemed the Ajah Boys were also out of ammunition. When the Olumegbon's gang charged forward wielding cutlasses like crazed warriors at the Ajah Boys, the market descended into something akin to a medieval battle, with the wounded strewn across the ground. A dozen Ajah Boys descended on them from the side flank, firing shotguns. This was hopeless: they were all going to be killed at this rate. 'Pull back,' Tunde shouted, nursing his wounds. They were chased from several directions as they fled until they wound up, somewhat ironically, in Ajah police station. Fatai and his police protectors joined them, in a silent admission of defeat. Four of the gang, including Tunde, were injured, all with multiple shallow bullet wounds. None had been killed, unlike the two Ajah Boys they'd seen dropping in the grass—a fact which would later be confirmed.

Either way, they'd failed to seize all but the land near the roundabout south of Ajah market. For now, the Overlord had lost the battle for Ajah.

14

ANCESTRAL REAL ESTATE

Surulere, Lagos Mainland, 1960

The man who would seek to become one of the richest and most powerful landowners in Lagos was born in the year of Nigeria's independence from Britain to a family whose means were comfortable though not lavish. Nothing that would make you think he was a prince. As far as he knew while growing up, his sole connection to royalty was his mother, Alhaja Sikirat Eko, who was from the royal house of Elegushi. The Elegushis would later become fabulously rich, after profiting from the beach-side property developments they owned at the front end of the Lekki Peninsula. But back in 1960, when Fatai was born, the Elegushis' land was a combination of worthless swamp, on its eastern side, and, on the western side joining Victoria Island, Maroko: a muddy, noxiously congested shantytown which they shared with three other rival chieftaincy families. Sikirat was anyway a peripheral figure in this royal clan. Their family lived the life of Lagos's tiny middle class. His father, Akanni Eko, was a marine engineer earning a decent wage. His mother, partly through her aristocratic connections, was a moderately successful trader and businesswoman. She pampered and fussed over him like a little prince, giving in to his whims and taking him with her on her business trips to buy items for import in Accra, Ghana's capital. Fatai would later see that in many ways his sense of entitlement stemmed from his mother's doting. They lived in Surulere, then a very respectable middle-class part of the mainland for those who couldn't afford to live in the posh island suburbs of Ikoyi or Victoria Island, with neat, newly built government housing. Surulere lay just to the west of Yaba, and north of the Apapa port, making it well connected to the bridges over the lagoon. Fatai never wanted for anything during his early childhood.

Then, when he was 10, both of his parents died within months of each other. The orphaned Fatai wound up living with his mother's cousin Sade, a senior civil servant in the Lagos State government. Sade had far less patience for this somewhat spoilt boy's indolence. Her elder brother, Adedapo, frequently beat him for his stubbornness, and they sent him out to work for the yams and fried beef they shared at the family table. He woke at five every day to buy bread for breakfast; at other times, he sold charcoal and kerosene on the street. He tidied the house and cleaned up after their lunch. None of these chores could form an excuse for not doing his homework—for which he was soundly beaten if he did not complete it. Much later, during his long battle to seize Ajah, he would realise just how much they had helped him by toughening him up.

There was something else whose significance would only later become apparent: Fatai's father had been a pious Muslim who never drank, philandered or smoked, and who had no space in his spiritual worldview for traditional Yoruba religion. He was a kindly man who rarely judged others, but he disliked what he saw as heathen worship of small gods. There was one true God, Allah, and while Akanni was alive, he had told Fatai not to bother with the likes of the thunder god Sango, or his incestuous sister-wife, Oya, goddess of winds and rainstorms, of destruction, death and rebirth. Had his father still been alive when the sacred oracle declared Fatai a traditional ruler in 2003—a role steeped in ancestral worship—he'd never have allowed him to take it up (parental authority extends well into adulthood in Nigeria). Perhaps, Fatai would later reason, that was why his father had never told him that he was a prince from the Olumegbon family.

* * *

Fatai was already in his twenties when he made this discovery. It was the start of the 1980s, when Nigeria was settling into a deep economic crisis. Fatai was to perform as a white-robed masquerade at the compound of the Elegushis, his mother's family. It was similar to the Eyo Festival, but a much smaller affair than the one performed for the King of Lagos. Masked figures representing spirits of the dead from various noble families engaged in theatrical displays of dominance in their white robes and different coloured hats. They would parade along the expanse of sand, dirt roads and swaying coconut palms that the Elegushis owned before any of it was developed into a concrete jungle of hotels and shopping malls. Before the performance, Fatai spotted an uncle, Akiolu, from his father's side, whom he didn't know well. His uncle's eyes widened as walked up to him.

'What are you doing here?' he said, almost accusingly, glancing at the embroidered deep-purple hat with the orange crest with a purple lion representing the house of Elegushi, which Fatai was carrying with his white kaftan.

'I'm coming to perform at the festival,' the young Fatai replied, averting his eyes as it is polite to do when addressed by an elder.

'From which house?' Akiolu demanded.

'From the Elegushis. It's my mother's house.'

'So no one has told you, Fatai? Your father didn't tell you?' Akiolu's eyes seemed misted up with tears. After a long silence, he said, 'You are a prince from the royal house of Olumegbon. My boy, how could you still not know?' Fatai wasn't sure why the old man seemed so emotional, but it was something he could never ask. Something must have happened with his father that had prevented the rest of the family from revealing to him his true lineage. He knew how his father disapproved of the traditional rituals. Later that night, as the festivities wore on, and the masquerades representing the hallowed spirits of the ancestors got drunker and bawdier, his uncle took him to see the Olumegbon of Lagos, Fatai's great-uncle and one of the most prominent guests at the Elegushi masquerade. The chief tossed his extensive folds of white cloth aside as Fatai kneeled in front of him.

'Baba, do you know this boy?' his uncle asked of the Overlord, and the old man nodded. 'He came to perform as an Elegushi masquerade.'

There was a long pause before Chief Lamidi began to speak. 'So I guess your father never told you that you were from our family?'

'I didn't know,' the nervous prince answered, averting his eyes. Lamidi gestured to one of his servants to bring the sea-green hat with a black leaf pattern and white-edged rim so he could represent the house of Olumegbon as a masquerade at the next festival. Fatai felt a wave of pride wash over him: he was a noble.

The following night in Surulere, Fatai was eating suya by a roadside shack, a tongue-scorchingly spicy, high-fat, barbequed beef snack grilled and served by Hausa Muslims from the north. He could barely taste it, so absorbed was he in a daydream about being a king. He sat at a plastic table with his best friend, Noah Olufumni, and four others. The Hausa men were grilling heart-stopping quantities of red meat on a barbeque in the corner of the street. Fatai used a toothpick to skewer a piece of rubbery cow fat into his mouth and sipped his soda.

'I never knew you were from such a powerful family,' Noah beamed. 'Wow. You see this guy,' he shouted at the other customers eating their suya. 'He's a prince. Take note! He's going to be the Olumegbon of Lagos.' Fatai feigned embarrassment, but his heart beamed with pride.

There was no guarantee he would become the next head of the idejo class, of course: it would depend on what the oracle said when his great uncle finally passed away. Yet he somehow felt that he was destined to be a white cap chief. That night, Fatai dreamt the oracle had selected him and that, furthermore, the new Lagos king had crowned him as Oba of Ajah, fulfilling an aspiration long coveted by his many predecessors. He awoke happier than he'd been since before his parents' deaths. He vowed to learn the ways of the gods, and train to become a high priest of the Ifa oracle. His dead father would be crying from underneath his tombstone, but Fatai knew this was his calling.

Over the next few years, far from settling into aristocratic privilege, Fatai suffered worse deprivation than he'd ever known. He was laid off as a clerk for the Lagos biscuits company, with no redundancy cheque, after it got into financial trouble. He set up a trading concern, but business was slow in this rocky period in Nigeria's history, marked by military coups and recession, after a crash in oil prices. He had married in his late teens, and now he was struggling to feed his wife, Jumoke, and their three children. He sometimes ate one meal a day so they could have three. That sour taste of poverty would later add a layer of desperation to his drive to be a wealthy landowner, an almost pathological need to put permanent distance between himself and penury.

* * *

Ajah, Lekki Peninsula, 2007

The conflict for control of Ajah was long, sporadic and often futile. Sometimes Olumegbon's boys seemed to gain the upper hand; at other times, the Ajah Boys chased the wounded soldiers from Lagos Island down alleyways, until the latter had to take shelter in shabby hotels and police stations before fleeing back to the island. Over time Fatai seized enough territory to put a buffer around his Ajah residence, which he proceeded to upgrade to the sumptuous palace he'd always dreamed of. He built a perimeter around it of concrete interspersed with columns of bricks zigzagged in different shades of grey. Each stretch of wall between the columns had a single golden letter attached to it, collectively reading 'Olumegbon Palace'. The centrepiece of his throne room was an ivory throne in the ornate Louis XVI style, with lots of baroque curves. An ivory disc at the top had 'Olumegbon of Ajah' carved in it in blue letters. It was guarded on either side by gold-plated and not terribly realistic sculptures of lionesses. There was something sphynx-like about them, as if they harked back to the alleged ancient Egyptian origins of the Yoruba people.

Fatai took a second wife, Olori, a young daughter of the late King of Lagos Adeyinka Oyekan, having two kids with her. The marriage had been arranged to cement these two powerful aristocratic families. Fatai was sure that soon the current Lagos king, Rilwan Akiolu, would finally crown him as Oba of Ajah, granting him the title that King Akiolu's predecessors had for so long withheld from the Olumegbon family. The Ajah palace, right in front of the main market, stood as testimony to Fatai's territorial claim. It was secure, as was the front end of Ajah market and the Ajah Motor Park, the bus station along the express-way that he had set up as a base for Abija's touts, where they ran a flourishing extortion racket on the buses in this increasingly busy transport corridor.

But in the Ajah hinterlands towards the lagoon, Fatai was still Overlord only on paper. By 2007, four years after his first attempt to seize the area, his boys were struggling to hold on to anything between the south end of Addo Road, in front of the palace, and the shores of the lagoon. A year earlier, former governor Bola

Tinubu had signed a deal with a Chinese consortium for a 16,500-hectare tax-free trade zone that he envisioned being filled with bustling garment factories that would create tens of thousands of jobs. That triggered a fresh round of gun battles in Ajah, which lay right in between the planned 'free zone' and the bits of Lekki that had already been developed into the Lekki Phase 1 luxury estate bordering Victoria Island. For much of 2006, there were weekly battles between the gangs. But the Ajah Boys were still too easily able to retreat among the marshes, shacks and half-built concrete edifices along the lagoon side, and then return to counterattack.

By 2007, energetic Lagos State governor Babatunde Fashola took the helm and made Lekki the focus of his efforts to reimagine Lagos as an African Singapore. A Chinese free zone would seek to replicate China's industrial miracle in Africa's megacity, with vast warehouses for storing millions of products churned out by factories. Lagos State officials in grey suits gave presentations in overpriced hotel conference rooms. Their computer-generated images presented a futuristic vision so high-tech that the free zone looked like some kind of circuit board, with neat lines and silver cylinders among patches of neat lawns between motorways. It was hard to picture it amid the mayhem of the real Lagos. Chinese builders began scoping out the marshlands on the far end of the Lekki Peninsula to lay down foundations for the site, spurring a further round of speculative landbuying. Next to the free zone, they planned to build the Lekki deep-water port, the most advanced Lagos had ever seen—and there were also plans for a brand-new international airport costing half a billion dollars, to relieve congestion at the jam-packed Murtala Muhammed international airport on the mainland. To ease the inevitable surge in traffic through the peninsula, work began to renovate the fifty-kilometre Lekki–Epe Expressway, the artery running its whole length, into a multi-lane superhighway.

Property prices were rocketing all along the road and, with them, the value of Fatai's claimed estate.

There were some big developments planned in Ajah, especially south of the soon-to-be-renovated expressway, but investors were reluctant to pump in millions of dollars before the land dispute was resolved. Even the Lekki Scheme II housing estate, encompassing 3,000 residential plots and some 500 hectares in the part of Ajah south of the expressway over which Fatai had better control, was stuck in the mud. A planned 'model city' which he had wanted to build, modelled on developments that had already made a fortune for other Lagos nobles, was struggling to get bank finance.

To make matters worse, the Ilaje, a clan of Yoruba fishermen, had staked out a claim to a part of the lagoon edge where several had lived for generations in straw-hut villages, pitting them against both the Overlord and the Baale. Their claimed patch was exactly the site of the planned Fourth Mainland Bridge—a thirty-eight-kilometre mega-project three times as long as the Third Mainland Bridge, which would connect the Lekki Peninsula with the mainland, and which was already pushing up real estate values at the lagoon edge. There was just too much at stake to let the fighting go on.

So the Lagos State government set up a panel led by a retired judge to inquire into the causes of the Ajah conflict. Unlike the courts, which had always seemed to hold the Overlord's family's land claims sacrosanct, it concluded that maybe the Ajah families had a point, seeing that they, unlike the Olumegbon family, had actually been living there for three centuries. The panel recommended that, to smooth things over with the aggrieved parties, the Overlord immediately release fifty hectares of land as a gift to them, the first instalment of around a quarter of the property he owned right on the lagoon front that they'd recommended he part with, where his claim was most contested.

Fatai was furious, but he saw a chance to come to an agreement that would halt further bloodshed and make him look good in the process. He publicly promised to give them the fifty hectares around the lagoon edge just as soon as it was sand-filled, quietly ignoring the recommendation to give up a full quarter of his lagoon-side estate. The Baale of Ajah, Amida Kareem, whom Fatai saw as one of the more amenable from the two families, had died the previous year, and no successor was chosen. The hardliners running things in his absence were unequivocal: they could never accept the offer, because accepting it meant accepting Fatai's authority as Overlord, which they would never do. And so it went on ...

* * *

In 2009, a new Ajah Baale was crowned, three years after the death of Amida Kareem. The sacred oracle selected Alhaji Murisiku Oseni Ojupon to be the next chief. When the time was right—which meant when the oracle decreed it—the two ruling families, the Ojupon and Ogunsemo, called a meeting of the kingmakers of Ajah, the elders who had to preside over the ceremony to decide who should be the next Baale. The elders called in a fetish priest who lived in a barnacled beach-shack on the peninsula's seafront. A 4x4 took him to the Ajah shrine in order to consult the sacred Ifa oracle. He was never told of the purpose of his summoning; they just gave him a list of seventeen names and told him to pick one. The priest performed an elaborate ritual using cowrie shells. The chosen Baale, Chief Murisiku, was a man in his late middle age with a wide and fleshy bulbous nose that pushed his eyes far apart, a warm smile, cavernous dimples and a lump the size of a golf ball in his lined forehead. He often wore silken robes with intricate embroidery and large colourful beaded necklaces. Murisiku turned out to be significantly more intransigent than the last Baale, refusing to sign anything or even accept any settlement made by his predecessors. He frequently mocked the Overlord's claim to Ajah. When Fatai pointed out in public that his grandfather's body lay in a shrine behind Ajah market— macabre proof of his ancestral claim—Murisiku retorted that the tomb was in fact empty, and that the only time Fatai's family had ever even been to Ajah was in 1820, when a previous Overlord had had to flee Lagos Island as a fugitive accused of robbery. That infuriated Fatai even more, and his relations with Murisiku hit a lower level than with his predecessor, if such a thing could be possible. Both responded by hiring more soldiers.

* * *

In early 2013, a decade of on-off bloodshed seemed to be coming to a head. The Overlord made one final push to secure his divine right. By May, sporadic battles, mostly centred around the lucrative Ajah Motor Park, had left dozens dead on both sides. That month, one of Fatai's lackeys received a call from a screened number warning there would be bloodshed if he did not vacate his Ajah palace immediately. He called his boys out of the bus park to defend it, but by the time they got to the perimeter, they were surrounded. A battle ensued that left four of Fatai's fighters dead and one from the rival Ajah side. Later that day, Fatai realised with horror that his older brother Idowu, whom he'd installed to run the Ajah bus station as a 'union' member, had been killed in the fight. In mourning, he briefly wondered whether all the fighting was really worth it, but it definitely was: aside from the megacity vision, property prices were swelling right across the more desirable parts of Lagos, driven by a massive influx of stolen oil money. President Goodluck Jonathan's government, buoyed by years of record high oil prices, was turning out to be a bigger kleptocracy than even some of his military predecessors. The central bank governor, Lamido Sanusi, had just got the sack for pointing out that some $20 billion had disappeared from the state oil company's accounts. A sizeable chunk of the missing money was being squirrelled away in the classic money-washing destinations abroad—London, Dubai, New York. The rest was flooding into the property market in Lagos and Abuja, as oligarchs made vast cash purchases. If Fatai could secure his land, he could easily become as rich as the Elegushis, who by this time were one of the wealthiest families in the country, thanks to duplexes, hotels, malls and apartment blocks that had been built on their land. Even the scruffy, rubbish-strewn Royal Elegushi Beach, at which menacing 'area boys' collected outrageous fees for revellers to enter, was making him a killing without his having to lift a finger to develop it. The new ruler, Oba Saheed Elegushi, owned a custom-made, bulletproof Rolls-Royce. He was only in his thirties.

There was a knock at the Overlord's palace: the police were at his gate calling him in for questioning at the station about the fight. When he returned, Ajah residents were protesting, holding up placards accusing him of being a tyrant. It was all a long way from what he'd envisioned when he first set out to secure his birthright. As a servant closed the door behind him, he glanced out of the window past the black gates into the dimly lit street beyond, where motorbike taxis weaved through stalled traffic. As he often did in times of crisis, Fatai consulted his deities. He decided to appeal to Sango, the god of thunder and lightning. He ordered a consignment of kola nuts, schnapps, bitter kola and a live white ram be brought to the shrine behind the palace for sacrifice. The ram quivered as the red stain advanced across its white fleece, blood pumping rhythmically out of its throat onto the ground. *Please, Sango, bring me victory over these tiresome thugs or at least indicate a way to resolve this.*

Early the following year, some of Abija's gang were gathered once again near the Overlord's palace. One of them, Tunde, the one we met earlier, had been travelling back and forth between

Ajah and the bus terminus at Obalende, next to Lagos Island. He'd declined an offer to work under the Overlord's brother in the Ajah bus station because this wasn't really his home. He was a Lagos Island area boy, a dyed-in-the-wool son of the soil. How could he live anywhere else? He had smartly sold the plot of land he'd earned for his loyalty shortly after the announcement about the Chinese export processing zone started pushing up land prices in Ajah. His frequent trips to Ajah helped compensate for the loss of income he had suffered as first Tinubu and then his successor, Governor Fashola, cracked down on the unruly touts profiting from the chaos at the main Lagos bus stations. If they couldn't make a living by extorting money from bus drivers and holding up traffic, then at least good old-fashioned score-settling by a powerful politician could be relied on to refill the coffers. So he and Abija's other gang members took turns to guard Fatai's palace for weeks at a time while tensions were rising, then melted away when things calmed down.

In the ten years since Tunde first set foot there, the part of the Lekki Peninsula adjacent to Ajah had been transformed from a grassy swamp dotted with unfinished concrete buildings into a fine example of incongruous, postmodern, low-density urban sprawl: buildings with gaudy-coloured roofs sloping at multiple gradients with windows of various sizes distributed unevenly, tiny gardens and outsized car parks. It had shopping malls and events venues, including one called the Lamborghini. Then there was the Eleganza Gardens shopping and residential complex, whose front entrance was a mock neoclassical facade with arches and square Doric columns. Had it been less like something out of Disneyland, it might have brought some respite from the post-modern ugliness of much of Lekki, although the cheap, ill-proportioned houses inside bore the same jarring design, many of them empty because bought as an 'investment' while the investor waited for prices to go up. Eleganza was already starting to look shabby from the Lagosian humidity and the Lagosian lack of interest in maintenance. Every trip he made, Tunde marvelled at the pace of building along this sandbank.

* * *

At around five thirty on this particular rainy April morning, Tunde's tour of duty was over, so he and eight other gang members prepared to board a bus back to Obalende. They'd set off before first light so as to beat the rush-hour traffic between Lekki and Victoria Island. The bus park was a muddy mess, and flood waters were gathering in Ajah's perpetually blocked drains. As they were about to step onto the rusting yellow danfo, a man pulled a piece of wood studded with a nail from his jacket and lunged at Tunde. He ducked, and the weapon swung into Ade, a 20-year-old upstart gangster and the youngest of their crew. Ade let out an unhuman scream as blood poured from his face. His left eye was a burst jelly on the floor, the socket a bloody crater. Dark shapes emerged from the roundabout on the Lekki–Epe Expressway and ran into the bus park. Tunde realised it was an ambush.

'Scatter! Now!' he shouted at the other boys, and they scurried into the narrow alleyways of Ajah market towards the hotchpotch of cinder-block and coloured-glass buildings along the expressway. Gunfire chased them as they moved—and then Tunde heard more coming from the shores of the lagoon to the north of the motorway. They were surrounded. He pulled out his pump-action shotgun from one pocket, firing a salvo of bullets, while removing his phone from another. He was about to call for reinforcements when three Ajah Boys jumped out from behind a bus and attacked their group with cutlasses. 'Retreat,' Tunde shouted, and he sneaked out along with a group of fleeing civilians, ignoring the screams as the Ajah Boys pinned down and hacked two of his gang to death. By the time they had regrouped by the palace, five of the Olumegbon boys' bloodied corpses lay in the road, leaving only three of those who had been on the bus, including now eyeless Ade, alive.

Sitting on the concrete floor of the palace grounds, out of breath and disheartened, Tunde dreamed of revenge as he waited for one of the Overlord's assistants to meet them. After he'd explained what had happened, reinforcements were swift. Within hours, fifty Olumegbon boys gathered in the compound of his palace, including their leader. Abija addressed them.

'My warriors, we were victim of an unprovoked attack,' he said, standing next to his gleaming 4x4, inside the palace compound. 'Now is the time to retaliate,' and they cheered as they pulled cutlasses from their pockets—only seven of them had guns. Some kissed their fetishes and pewter amulets. Tunde thumbed his sacred talisman. It consisted of a disc of pewter with its outer edge cut into teeth. The centre had the skull of a small lizard glued to it.

'Today we have lost five of our people. So, we must take five of theirs,' Abija continued. 'It is a battle to the end. Do not fear death, my warriors: you are under the spiritual protection of the Overlord. Victory is what is important, and your victory will be had in blood.'

They pocketed their knives and pistols and fanned out into the area north of the expressway, towards the lagoon edge. Even this part of Ajah, once a marshy backwater, had changed immeasurably since Tunde and the gang first fought here in 2003. Gone was the tall elephant grass that used to inhabit this place. It had been replaced by red-roofed houses painted two tones of beige with lots of small windows, alongside unfinished ones with the scaffolding poking out of concrete. Some had been erected by land speculators told to 'use it or lose it' by Lagos State: they merely wanted to create the impression that work was in progress but had no intention of finishing it. Unused plots next to them had become makeshift rubbish tips, with piles of plastic bottles and sachets and tyres too worn to be recycled, besides the ash of other rubbish that someone had had the good manners to burn, with a few bits of elephant grass poking through it all to make a comeback. On the concrete perimeters of these Lekki estates, itinerant traders of the sort that spring up all over Lagos sat under parasols, waiting for customers for their wares as diverse as engine oil in jerrycans and readymade house windows: there was always a niche to be filled.

Tunde received call from one of the men who had stayed back as a rearguard: the Ajah Boys were south of them, on the expressway, cutting off their route back to the palace. Then he saw that there was another group advancing towards them from the lagoon side to the north. *Fuck*, he thought. *We're surrounded. It's a trap.* 'Turn back,' he shouted, and the few dozen men swung around and began marching south. At the expressway, they noticed Kazeem All-Rounder and at least a dozen of his thugs, so they ducked into a side street near the rundown, garishly coloured Ajah strip mall. From there, they saw that another group was moving towards them from the rear, in fast, urgent bursts of running and taking cover. Tunde's heartbeat became a sledgehammer. He pulled his shotgun from his pocket and started firing, triggering a smattering of return fire. 'Fire,' he shouted, and then a flurry of bullets whizzed from the five other people who were armed. They took cover behind a house. Two of them then swung around to fire at the group advancing from the north. 'Oh, this is bad, this is bad,' someone kept saying. A volley of bullets was fired by Kazeem's boys, taking up positions from near the exit onto the expressway. They looked better armed than the guys on the lagoon side. Tunde cast his eyes in both directions. Northwards was the lagoon shore, prime Ajah Boys territory. They'd never survive. Southwards, Kazeem's boys were blocking the road to the expressway. If they could just repulse them a little, they could hardly have an open gun battle on the motorway itself. That would surely attract the police. He decided to take one of the roads parallel to the expressway that would lead them to Addo Road and the palace, where they'd be safe. They fired at their enemies to the north, forcing them to take cover, then sent a few bullets south. And then they ran, attempting to ignore the gunshots and screams behind them. Gunfire followed them from both sides.

Tunde fell to the ground. Blood dripped from both of his legs and the side of his lower abdomen, as he realised he'd taken three bullets. 'Charge,' he shouted from the ground, as two of the gang grabbed each of his arms and hoisted him up, walking him back towards Ajah market and the lagoon. As he retreated, he saw two of the Olumegbon boys in hand combat with two of Kazeem's, but the latter were no match. As the bullets thinned out, the guys with blades unsheathed. In this, they were superior. One after the other, the Olumegbon boys wrestled their adversaries to the ground and stabbed them repeatedly until their quivering bodies went silent. Tunde smiled to himself. *Serves you right.* A group of Ajah Boys gave chase, but Tunde and his companions now knew these streets as well as they did, and they ducked and weaved through the alleyways until they had lost them. At this point Tunde began to lose consciousness. A few minutes later, the police arrived in vans and broke up the fight with batons. It was over until another day.

Back at the palace, two women washed down Tunde's bullet holes. All three were superficial wounds which had done little lasting damage but would still leave scars that would later testify to his machismo. All in all, not a bad result. As we've seen, his relatively light injuries were less miraculous than it seemed: these homemade weapons often didn't launch bullets with enough force to kill or seriously maim. But Tunde knew in his heart why he had come away with mere scratches: his juju magic had worked. Why else would all fifty of them have come back alive,

while at least two of the Ajah Boys, maybe more, had been con-
signed to the ancestral realm? He was especially pleased with his
egbe charm, the potion made from ground-up animal bones and
herbs. The egbe charm gives magical powers that enable you to
disappear from sight. That power had been in evidence when,
wounded and on the run, Tunde had melted into Ajah's sandy
alleyways with the Ajah Boys chasing him only yards away, he
would later conclude. It paid to invest in magic.

* * *

Early the following year, the guns in Ajah fell silent. The
Overlord and the two rival chieftaincy families quietly agreed to
a settlement and to try to resolve their dispute using legal means
and mediation, rather than by hiring thugs. Their agreement
lasted approximately four months, before they started to disagree
about what it said, and the dispute flared up anew. They took to
the local press, they took to the courts and they petitioned the
government—Lagos State and federal—to reopen this incredibly
resilient row. But they mostly stuck to their word in not bringing impoverished youths out onto the streets to die on their
behalf. They both agreed that was progress and, indeed, so did
everyone else caught up in this unceasing quarrel.

* * *

On 24 March 2019, Chief Fatai Olumegbon, the Olumegbon of
Lagos, head of the Lagos aristocracy and (nominal) Overlord of
Ajah, died at the age of 59. He had suffered a brief illness during
a trip to Dubai, the favourite haunt of the Lagos elite. The
Overlord departed this Earth, having never achieved his goal of
being crowned an Oba or taking full control of the piece of the
Lekki Peninsula he saw as his birthright.

Three days after his death, two rival cultist gangs—criminal
groups who combine mafia-style mob killings, armed robbery

and kidnappings with black magic rituals—rushed in to stake a claim to the Ajah Motor Park. This was the bus station the Overlord had set up all those years ago as a base for his foot soldiers. For the bus touts it was still the most lucrative racket in Ajah. After his death, it stood empty, as the touts like Tunde who had fought for him for so long paid their respects. Gunfire once again lit up Ajah as the rival Aye and Eiye 'confraternities'—believe it or not, Nigeria's murderous cultist gangs were once university secret societies—fought to seize this piece of prime real estate. The Overlord's body had barely cooled before Lagos mobs were rushing in to fill the power vacuum.

Six days after his death—which was somewhat bending the rules of the Muslim faith he professed alongside his Yoruba polytheism—Fatai was buried. They interred him at his palace in Ajah, so that he might join the deities who watched over it. His body lay in a dark wooden coffin padded with white satin, and he wore a white cap and kaftan. The body was draped in a sea-green blanket embroidered in the black leaf motif, the official cloth of the Olumegbon family. His wide-brimmed hat and staff for the masquerades, cut in the same colours, lay on top of him. Strung around his neck were thick orange coral beads, the jewellery that in olden times was used to signal divine powers.

The Overlord is dead, but the battle for supremacy over Lagos land will doubtless rise again in future reincarnations.

15

A BOTTLE OF SPIRITS FOR HIS DEITIES

Market behind Oba Oniru's Palace, Victoria Island, 2015

Today I must appease the gods. Apparently, they're not very happy with me. Chief Fatai Olumegbon's deities in particular are miffed that I failed to bring gifts the first time I went to interview him a week ago. Not just any gifts, but the specific ones required for a first audience with a man of such royal distinction. Fatai openly berated me for coming empty-handed. I did manage to get a short interview with him, so it wasn't an entirely wasted visit, but he was definitely grumpy about it. The standard gifts, dear reader, should you ever get a rendezvous with an Oba or other Yoruba noble, are these: kola nuts, 'bitter kola' seeds, and a 750 ml bottle of the finest schnapps. I'd better get the most expensive schnapps I can, especially since I'm rowing back on my earlier faux pas. Few things irk divine beings as much as bad manners. When a guest sets foot in such a hallowed house without bringing offerings, this can ruffle feathers in the spirit world. Best play it safe.

We've just stopped en route to the Overlord's Ajah palace at one of the less salubrious bits of Victoria Island, at a market near a grassy, rubbish-strewn wasteland. The market lies behind the prestigious Oniru estate. It is named after Oba Oniru, the local chief who has made a killing from developing the part of Lekki nearest to Victoria Island. His palace is just in front, and the exterior of his compound is covered with an elaborate wall sculpture depicting calabashes and other fetish objects, spear heads, a man blowing a horn, and abstract figures with elongated limbs. Beside his forbidding black gate is the gold sculpture of a lion: it's the kind of ostentation that the Overlord is aiming for, once he's managed to cash in his Ajah chips. I am with Segun Alabi, who is chauffeuring me and says he can help me find the correct offerings. The market consists of a small row of stalls, but they have all the things you expect in Lagos: sacks of fiery red bonnet peppers, cabbages, bitter leaf, the smell of fresh blood from dismembered animals hanging off meat hooks, the even more pungent perfume of dried fish. Segun eventually finds the stall of the lady selling gifts for a king.

These gifts are not for the Overlord himself (as he laboured to explain to me during my last visit). They are for his deities, so that he can make a ritual sacrifice to them in his role as high priest of the Ifa oracle. I might have been tempted to conclude this was bullshit in the case of the rather tasty-looking bottle of schnapps, but I know the Overlord doesn't drink. Fatai's deities include some real hotheads, like the notoriously bad-tempered Sango, who shoots lightning bolts out of his double-headed axe. Lagos's second rainy season will be starting soon. That always sets the sparks flying off Sango's axe. And then there's Oya, Sango's wife and sister. She's a sort of divine Lady Macbeth, constantly whispering poisonous suggestions in Sango's ear. If you recall, she's the goddess of winds, storms, death, destruction and rebirth. Quite a portfolio! It is said most of the terrible things Sango has done were her idea, a very familiar sexist formula. Behind every bad man, there's a woman to blame for his worst excesses! When Sango was a mortal king, so the story goes, he pitted his top two rival generals against each other, that they both might be destroyed. It was Oya's idea, naturally. The generals fought, but the victor survived, and then drove Sango out of his kingdom. In shame, he hanged himself from a tree and upon his death ascended to Heaven to become an orisha. Unfortunately, becoming immortal did little to change his bad-tempered capriciousness, and so he must be continually appeased. The fragrant and quite drinkable spirit I am about to purchase is not going in anyone's mouth. It is going to be poured on the ground of a sacred shrine in the Overlord's palace. From there, it will cross worlds to act like a kind of celestial tranquilliser dart, cooling passions in the pantheon above our heads.

'That will be 4,000 naira,' the market woman says in Yoruba, referring to the Seaman's Schnapps, in the bright-green square bottle with navy-and-purple label. What? Seems a bit expensive, so I ask Segun if he can negotiate the price down. They chat for a few minutes. The woman is wearing a bright dress in the colours of the All Progressives Congress (APC), the new coalition of ex-governor Bola Tinubu, formed in 2013 by merging his already merged AC with other parties. Tinubu's face is emblazoned on it, as usual looking icily through those round glasses of his. Earlier this year, the APC took the presidency, when Muhammadu Buhari kicked out incumbent Goodluck Jonathan—the first time the ruling PDP (People's Democratic Party) has lost the federal government since it took over after the death of military dictator Sani Abacha. Now the APC controls Lagos and Abuja. Tinubu has never been so powerful. The woman's stall sells bundles of herbs, kola nuts, the prized Seaman's Schnapps, a variety of potions, and one or two few fetish objects—some kind of small animal bones—as well as, incongruously, ordinary bars of soap and buckets of fresh tomatoes.

'She can't drop the price,' Segun says, and I glance at her. She casts her eyes down. 'She knows you're going to see a big chief with these things,' Segun continues, 'so you're going to receive a lot of money.' I'm going to receive nothing of the sort, but trying to explain that to her will keep me here all afternoon. When you visit a man of such wealth and power in Nigeria, like the Overlord, you expect to be offered inappropriate (from a journalist's point of view, anyway) gifts. Envelopes of crisp greenbacks or watches. There's then that shocked embarrassment when you explain why you can't accept it. But the Overlord never tried to give me anything.

'Fine,' I say. 'Tell her it's her lucky day. I can't see many other oyinbos (Europeans) around here likely to buy her goods at such inflated prices.' Segun translates and she giggles. I guess she must be about 60. Her hair is falling out from a lifetime of having used too much hair-straightener. Let me see, now, what else do I need? I already have six bitter kola seeds in my pocket that I just carry around anyway to feed my recently acquired semi-addiction. Well, five, if I remove the one that's damp from being half chewed. Segun advises I get a few more. Bitter kola seeds come from the *Garcinia kola* (Guttiferae) tree. They are light brown with a white flesh and about the size of an unshelled walnut. They contain caffeine and other strongish stimulants that seem to mimic the effects of nicotine, packing a punch not far off a cup of superstrong coffee combined with three or four cigarettes. They taste like a mouthful of garden soil, only bitterer, but once you get used to them, they really fire you up. In traditional West African medicine, they've been used for everything from flu and laryngitis to liver diseases and diabetes. In the end, I buy ten bitter kola seeds and six kola nuts, at equally inflated prices, and we head back to the motor.

We turn onto the main road at one of the Lekki–Epe Expressway's outsized roundabouts. Their gargantuan size doesn't seem to have prevented them from being clogged by traffic; if anything, it seems to encourage more of it. A blind old man in a

Muslim skullcap, guided by a child of indeterminable age, makes a desperate wailing sound, which I can't ignore. I wind down my window and stuff a bunch of naira into his hand. Another man is selling passport covers but is nearly knocked over by a keke napep rickshaw. For a place that's supposed to be laying the foundations for the Lagos megacity dream, Lekki is, if anything, a bigger eyesore than the rest of Lagos. The buildings of all shapes and sizes, with garish colours and windows in all different places, are certainly no more incongruous than those in old Lagos. But in the old city, the incongruity is stitched together in a kind of mad collage whose sheer vastness gives it a sort of sublime inverse beauty. By contrast, Lekki's 'anything goes' building designs each have a large plot to themselves, giving full rein to their specific variety of ugliness. There is the Wind Lounge, the Elegushi 'ultra-modern market', and the grey-blue Landmark Building, behind which the turrets of a mosque, with bronze crescent moons, poke out into the skyline.

If the gods really are trying to make my life more difficult because of some minor transgression, they're not doing a bad job. On the way here, we had three run-ins with the police, who, as I'm sure you've realised by now, are more predatory than most criminals. Every time a policeman stops a Lagosian for some pointlessly minor traffic violation in order to extort a bribe, the pressure cooker of anger can explode. Segun realises we've taken the wrong road and does a U-turn. There is no other traffic on the road, and no sign to show the U-turn is forbidden. A whistle blows, and out jumps a Lagos traffic cop with a belly bulging under his yellow shirt and maroon trousers—they call this a 'government belly' in some African countries.

'Your particulars, please,' he says, and Segun hands him his driver's licence and the papers for the car. 'That was an illegal U-turn. I'm going to impound this car.'

Before I have time to start cursing inwardly and dispatching involuntary flushes of blood to my whiteboy cheeks, Segun jumps out of the front seat as if he had just got an electric shock. Suddenly, he's squared up to the policeman, staring wildly into his face, which is now only a few inches away. He clenches his fist, and it sends a ripple of clenching through every visible muscle in his body.

'Comot! Or I go give you gbosa for head!' Segun shouts at the man in blind fury. *Get out, or I'll punch you in the head.*

Fuck, Segun, what is your endgame, here? At least, being a Lagos traffic cop, the man thankfully has no weapon except a whip. He pulls a radio from his belt clip. Lifting it to his mouth, he points to a detachment of about six other cops up the road about a kilometre away and informs Segun that he's going to summon them over to arrest him.

'You'll be knocked out before they get here,' Segun says, his eyes still possessed with pathological rage. The cop loses the staring contest, briefly weighs the situation, then makes a forward-waving hand gesture. In this game of chicken: Segun 1, Policeman 0.

* * *

At the palace gates, Segun suddenly looks scared, which seems like an odd emotion in a man who has just threatened to knock out a policeman.

'Sir, if they give you anything to eat, don't eat it,' he says. 'They have some powerful fetish, some real magic. They could poison you.'

'Segun, I seriously doubt it. Why would they do that?'

'They don't need "why". They can do it. Be careful.'

At a reception room in the Overlord's palace, we are welcomed by one of Abija's touts, who guard the palace on a 24/7 rotation. The Overlord's empty Louis XVI-style throne sits in judgement, and I tuck my shirt in. The walls are adorned with pictures of Fatai in full traditional regalia, or semi-naked with

the blue embroidered pork-pie hat of the Olumegbon masquerades, his chest wrapped in various amulets and fetish objects.
We stand as Fatai enters. He is wearing a radiant white lace
robe, fire-engine-red shoes with a gold crown printed on them,
a matching red 'fila' hat, the soft hat traditionally worn by the
Yoruba, two low-hanging blood-orange coral necklaces, and a
third silver necklace with a pendant in the shape of an anchor.
After the appropriate formalities—he seems happy with the
gifts I brought this time—we settle into a conversation about
the Ajah conflict. I ask him about his estate.

'I have the largest,' he says, not trying to conceal his pride.
'Much bigger than anyone else in Lagos State: 1,400 hectares, is
it not a lot?' I nod, asking him how much he's developed, and he
tells me only sixty-eight hectares. Much of the rest is still swamp
or slum. 'We are not rushing,' he says. Why are you not rushing?
'Because the land belongs to the dead, the living, and the incoming ones, the not-yet born, for they exist too. This land I inherited from my predecessor. It will pass to my successor. If I develop
all the land now, what will be left for my future descendants?'

'What entitles you to this land?' I ask him.

'My deities'—he looks slightly annoyed at the question—'entitle
me. I mediate through the deities. There is only one God. That is
God Almighty, the Omnipotent, the Omnipresent. Huh? Isn't it?
But there are millions of lesser gods, small-letter "g" gods that
people worship. All these small-letter "g" gods are a means to
God. Our deities are our ancestors, and we send messages to them.
We have special people in the palace who are in charge of that.
Because of this ancestral link, this territory is mine.'

'But in order to protect it, you have to use street thugs. How
do you feel about that?'

He sighs. 'It's everywhere in Africa. You can't stay in the palace without boys. They are part of you, members of the family.
You don't have a choice. You have to have boys around. The

police can betray you, but the boys can never betray you, because the property belongs to them too, spiritually. They are omo onile [sons of the soil].'

We discuss the Baale of Ajah's rival claim, and I present to him everything Chief Ojupon told me. He dismisses the lot. 'They gave you oral history, but did they give you written?' he says. 'If they own this land, you must bring proof. You must have a document.'

They gave me pages of documents, but I decide not to annoy him by showing them to him. I'm not really here to get to the bottom of their dispute.

'It will be resolved,' he says. 'Have you ever seen two rams fighting? Eventually they wear themselves out.'

We leave the palace just in time for rush hour. The Ajah roundabout is clogged with stationary vehicles full of angry, frustrated humans. We have another few to go before we can make the turning to the new bridge over the lagoon to Ikoyi. Hawkers weave through cars, balancing their various culinary offerings on their heads. As the traffic lurches forward, Segun narrowly misses running over a disabled beggar on a makeshift wooden skateboard. In anger, the man bashes the side of the car with his fist. 'Are you the owner of this roundabout?' he shouts, as Segun nervously checks that the doors are locked. Even beggars can be quite fiercely protective of their small spaces in the megacity. 'You are not the owner, so you can't just do anyhow.'

The logical implication only hits me later: it is just the *owners* of Lagos who can do whatever they want, even running over the disabled. Only the owners.

PART VI

NOAH'S LAGOON

Misery is when you heard on the radio that the neighborhood you live in is a slum but you always thought it was home.

Langston Hughes, *Black Misery*

Zangbeto, "Man of the Night", is a traditional masked cult among the Ogu (Egun) of south-western Nigeria and Benin Republic, which has evolved from local vigilantism to ... community policing, conflict mediation and justice delivery. Zangbeto exposes the inadequacies of the formal control systems (that) ... are estranged and alienated from the people whose interest they were meant to serve.

Dominic Okure, 'Symbolism and Social Control of Zangbeto among the Ogu (Egun) of Southwestern Nigeria'

16

NOAH

Makoko, 1993

Makoko is the first sight to strike visitors crossing the Third Mainland Bridge from Nigeria's main international airport in Ikeja towards the three islands of Lagos, where moneyed elites live and big businesses transact. Perched on stilts, this vast cluster of huts inside the lagoon is forever shrouded in mist emanating from thousands of fires smoking freshly caught fish. Canoes carrying fishermen ripple outwards onto the lagoon at dawn, then gravitate back inwards at dusk with nets holding enough seafood to feed this vast community—and sell an excess for profit.

Makoko residents' homes and vehicles could scarcely have been better adapted to humanity's flooded future: wooden boats flit through the brown waters, along the narrow gaps between huts next to patches of swaying water hyacinth. Most children know how to row before the age of five. The boats carry not only fishing gear, but also groceries, fried food, trash. Water-borne traders punt through the labyrinth of huts on boats laden with all kinds of goods. Some contain batteries, torches, radios, wires and other small electrical goods. On others, there are tomatoes, onions, garlic, bamboo for construction, jerrycans, mobile phone credit. Charcoal smoke from thousands of cooking pots lends the air a dreamy haze. For Makokoites, the lagoon is a transport network, a food source, a swimming area, a toilet, a rubbish dump. The lagoon's odour is often described by outsiders as that of sewage, but it's actually more subtle than that, almost more of a softer, meaty smell: salty, pungent, raw.

Its peculiar perfumes aside, Makoko is probably the most picturesque slum in Africa. That may not sound like much of a distinction, but few visitors fail to be entranced by it. Cityscapes reflected in water always have a serene quality. And Makoko, despite being all one-storey wooden shacks arranged unevenly instead of skyscrapers or grand cathedrals, is no exception. The floating slum is all the more striking for its proximity to the tall office and apartment blocks in the commercial district on the other side of a channel bordering it to the east. Lagos often seems to consist of separate cities so atomised as to have almost nothing to do with each other. For residents of Makoko, the whole notion of living on land is as alien as their riverine way of life is to everyone else.

So it was something of a shock to Noah Shemede when, at the age of six, this small boy stepped onto land for the first time. Imagine how he must have felt. The most solid surface Noah had ever graced until then was the huts his family slept in, held up by poles sunk into the lagoon's muddy marshes. And even those had the lilting feeling of motion, as the salt waters lapped beneath them. Other than in his family's huts, he'd spent his years on Planet Earth floating on the Lagos lagoon inside hollowed-out pieces of wood. But on this day he was going somewhere that virtually no Makoko kids ever went. Noah was about to start school.

The boy was the last-born of his father Moses's twenty-two children from three different wives, arriving in 1988. In very traditional West African societies, the number of a man's children is a measure of his power and virility, a display of the wealth he must have acquired to feed them. There are few surer signs of a man having 'made it' than a double-digit figure of offspring. But none of Moses's other kids had gone to school by the time Noah himself reached school age. What would be the point, Moses had reasoned, of forking out good money to teach children skills that would be of no use to them as fishermen? Everything they needed to know—how to mend and cast nets, how to judge the ferocity of an ocean storm—could be taught here, in the swirling waters of the lagoon and the adjacent Gulf of Guinea. Learning to swim would surely enable them to survive life in Makoko better than memorising those strange markings that the white people had always used to enforce their cryptic rules.

But his mother, Comfort, wanted to try educating at least one of their kids. Noah once overheard his parents discussing it. He had not the faintest idea what 'school' meant. And yet, casting his eyes over the lapping waters towards the Third Mainland Bridge—the strange strip of concrete forever crawling with restless metal ants—this small boy found himself agreeing with his father. What did a Makoko boy need to know about this school place existing on the land? Over time, though, Noah's mother went to work on his father and, as she often did, began to gently persuade Moses. Maybe, just maybe, she suggested, it would benefit Noah, the family and the community.

It is a day that the formally educated will never forget, when they are prised from their mother's arms and led into a classroom. For many, it is the first experience of a boundary between themselves and their home life. For Noah, that boundary was literally at the water's edge. Because there were no schools in Makoko's waterways, any kid seeking an education needed to go on land.

Most African children from poor areas are only too willing to start school, acutely conscious of how lucky they are to escape the domestic servitude of home, but Noah was in no mood to leave his beloved lagoon. His older brother Peter, the second-born of his siblings, was readying a canoe to take him.

'Come on, little bro, you've got a big day ahead,' he said, sensing Noah's reticence.

'I don't want to go to school,' Noah whined.

'I know,' Peter said, nodding towards the front of the boat to make it clear there would be no argument. Noah languidly slid off the house planks.

Early morning is Makoko's best hour, when clouded light bathes the waters in bashed silver, before the lagoon's cloying humidity starts steaming at full strength. The water city was already a swirl of activity. Young children filled jerrycans from a tap attached to a pipe leading to a borehole at the water's edge and loaded them onto boats. Traders selling sodas and cheap biscuits bumped past each other's boats. They sailed past the ubiquitous rubbish bobbing along, the universal effluents of our industrial age: plastic spoons, polythene bags, biscuit packets, cardboard boxes.

The boys' boat knocked against the jetty at Makoko Road. Peter held his hand to help Noah off. The first thing Noah noticed about the land city was the noise. In Makoko, the only sounds are the rippling of paddles, children's voices echoing across water, perhaps punctuated by the occasional rumble of a big man's generator. As Noah stepped off the jetty onto the dirt track, the din of motorbike taxis and traders shouting from their kiosks drilled in his ears. On a road strewn with plastic bags and drinks cans, an orgy of clamour battered his senses, ripping through his nerves like sharpened steel through fish guts. Motorbike taxis wove through precarious gaps between cars belching black fumes. Men shouted and fussed. Walking on solid ground made Noah dizzy: deprived of the gentle swaying of water, he felt unsteady.

NOAH

The brothers turned off into the main thoroughfare in the district of Yaba, one of Lagos's oldest and most impressively run-down neighbourhoods, but also one of the few where the colonial-era buildings have been spared demolition. They walked down Herbert Macaulay Road, named after the early-twentieth-century Lagos architect and grandfather of short-lived Nigerian nationalism, which all but died when the country got its independence and ethnic infighting unravelled its dreams in the 1960s. The noise from traffic was terrifying: angry drivers honked horns impatiently, engines roared. From there, he made his way towards his school in Ebute Metta, 'the Three Jetties', one of the oldest parts of Lagos, with ornate houses built by freed Brazilian slaves in the 1800s.

Noah felt the other kids stare as he quietly entered and sat down at his desk, saying nothing. The teacher opened the class in French, a language many Makokoites speak better than English, because most of them are ethnic Egun peoples, originally from neighbouring Benin, a former French colony. Noah spoke enough French to follow the class, but in every other way he just felt lost.

The next day, when Peter prepared to accompany Noah to school, he was nowhere to be seen. Peter eventually found him on a neighbour's jetty.

'This is for your own good. You will keep going to school,' Peter said as he held Noah down and issued four or five lashes of a cane to high-pitched howling. Noah's mother told her whimpering son that evening, 'Your brother is doing you a favour. If we take you to school, you will be successful. You will get a car, you will get a house, you will get a fine wife too.'

After weeks sitting by himself, too timid to even start a conversation, he met a boy called Joel, also from Makoko, but from the 'land part' of the slum, along the Makoko Road (Makoko is a combination of six villages, four on water and two on land). Joel made Noah feel more at ease. He gave him two notebooks and two pencils—Noah still didn't have any of his own. He helped him out with instructions he'd not understood. Noah hated school, hated being away from Makoko, but he was smart and keen to learn, practising French words, doing arithmetic, and learning about nature and parts of the body. As he grew more confident, he no longer needed to be dragged to school by his big brother.

* * *

By the time Noah graduated from a grammar school, at 18, he was about as adapted to land as is possible for a Makoko boy. The shy smolt who could barely communicate with his schoolmates was now a true polyglot: fluent in Yoruba, as well as English and his native Egun and a bit of French. He had also discovered a taste for late-night bar crawls with a crowd that included his best friend from the grammar school, Joseph Igboke. He would spend days at a time with friends, often only coming back to Makoko to earn some extra cash by fishing. Moses and Comfort weren't exactly overjoyed by his long absences, but they liked this socially fluent, articulate young man that Noah's schooling had fashioned.

It was late in the rainy season of 2007, and a rush of optimism was coursing through Lagos's clotted veins. The new governor, Babatunde Fashola, had just been sworn in and was promising to bring order to this notoriously irrational city, after eight years of patchy progress by his predecessor, Tinubu. And yet, residents of Makoko somehow knew little help would come to their haphazard settlement, which according to the government did not even exist (or rather, its existence was against the law). A city housing tens of thousands of people, yet with no electricity, no sanitation. Everyone shat into the same water, and its stink was a constant reminder of that fact, while the few clinics it had were run by charities. Had Noah grown up entirely on water, he might not have noticed these privations, but school life on land had given him a taste for what money could buy. His favourite course in school had been economics, something Noah, like many Lagosian hustlers, felt he understood intuitively. His best friend, Igboke, had gone into a business selling jewellery and had soon saved enough cash to pay for a decent diploma in architecture. He later landed a steady job. Joseph had been leaning on Noah to continue his education.

'The world is changing. You can't rely on a secondary school certificate anymore,' he told him over a beer in one of the many shack-bars full of shouting drunks on Makoko Road. 'Noah, there are so many opportunities out there.'

The allure of Lagos-on-land was impossible to ignore: money. Noah decided he would be a fool not to try and become the first of his father's twenty-two kids to succeed outside their watery enclave. He would get a degree and a high-powered job. Noah had visions of himself as an economist of some kind, maybe in a bank, armed with his degree, discussing the latest unemployment figures from the top of a corporate high-rise, like the ones that shimmered across the lagoon.

His plan was about to be inadvertently killed by another society located on the lagoon—one about as different from Makoko as it was possible to get.

* * *

The Lagos Yacht Club was founded in the 1930s by rich Europeans who ruled over Lagos with a cigarette holder in one hand and a pink gin in the other. It was located on Lagos Island, just across the channel from Victoria Island. Unlike the exclusive clubs of Ikoyi—that part of Lagos that the British colonial masters had reserved for whites and a few top African civil servants—the Yacht Club had never needed to keep out Blacks explicitly with a rude sign on the door. The extravagant cost of owning a yacht was enough to keep all but a handful of locals from attempting to join. While most of Lagos's playgrounds for the rich would later become the preserve of wealthy, oil-fattened Nigerian elites, the Lagos Yacht Club had always retained its air of expat aloofness. It still felt much more like the stuffy white settler clubs of Kenya—that fusty air of a British boarding school—than the loud, lively places in which Nigeria's many millionaires liked to spend their money. That was probably why cash-flush Nigerians were mostly to be found at the rival Lagos Motorboat Club, with its blingier, racier feel. The Yacht Club was a wonderful place to drink draught beer while watching sailing boats race each other against the industrial backdrop of the port on the opposite side. It was also a repository for a lingering residue of Africa's nasty colonial history: white guilt. The club was forever holding charity events, usually in order to build schools in poor areas (the classic escape valve for post-colonial guilt). In 2007, the year Noah graduated from school, the club had raised money for a river-based project, which made sense, given their obsession with boats and water. It didn't take long to hit on the idea of a project in Makoko.

It was around that time that a few wealthy tourists had begun to take an interest in the slum. Noah, being one of the few educated, swiftly fell into position as a tour guide. Noah has high but well-fleshed-out cheekbones, deep-set eyes, a warm smile and soft, almost teddy-bear-like features. One of the four Makoko villages that lie on water, Adogbo, was ruled by Noah's brother, Chief Emmanuel Shemede, the Baale (paramount chief). Shemede, who looks like a thinner, more wistful version of Noah, with shallower-set eyes that have a lost look about them, had been crowned three years earlier, after their father retired. The brothers were more than happy to charge rich people for a tour of the 'Venice of Africa'. Only later would Noah realise how valuable Makoko was as a potential source of tourist revenue, especially from photographers enchanted by its serene views.

The Yacht Club members arrived in a canoe on one such tour of Makoko's stilted huts. They stared wide-eyed at the half-naked children paddling boats between huts. There was certainly plenty for tourists to photograph: from the elevated decks of the huts, women stirred cauldrons of fish stew, while men paddled stacks of timber and piles of sand artisanally mined from the bottom of the lagoon and destined for markets throughout Lagos-on-land. Among them was Robin Campbell, a Canadian expatriate with blond hair and a gentle smile. She'd been in Lagos for decades, and she had toured Makoko a few years earlier. But she had a more serious purpose this time. She and her colleagues arrived at Noah's brother's house, its two storeys rising out of the water on stilts. After exchanging pleasantries, the group asked the chief what the community needed. Emmanuel glanced at his younger brother.

'A school,' Noah said, and the white visitors nodded. 'An English-speaking school. All these children we have here, but no school. They have to go to the mainland, and most of them cannot. We are water people. Why can we not have a school on water?'

It was true: Makoko did have English-speaking schools on parts that were on land, but here on the water there was nothing. Emmanuel and Noah sat watching the visitors take the canoe back to jetty to get back in their cars. Having seen the benefits that had accrued to Noah from his schooling, Emmanuel was just as keen as his brother to offer the chance to other kids. At first they doubted whether the charitable whites would come back, but they did. And, as promised, they'd secured money to build a school.

They did it in a more complicated, white-man way than a simple hut on stilts. They filled in the water with boatloads of sand to make a solid base—the sand wasn't hard to find, since one of Makoko's main sources of income is artisanal sand-mining, in which divers dive to the bottom of the lagoon to dig it up and bring back boats full of the stuff. This also meant that, unlike most Makoko huts, there would be an outside space for children to play. A month later, around April 2008, they built the two-storey frame from planks of wood, making it one of Makoko's tallest buildings. They installed a roof made of corrugated aluminium sheets, painted deep blue. The following month, the walls made of water-resistant timber were put up. Within a year of the Yacht Club visit, Makoko had its first ever school, and Noah and Emmanuel were proud to be able to bring education to the fishermen's kids without them having to trundle onto land the way Noah had had to. They called the school Whanyinna, or 'Love' in Egun. They got a Makoko elder, Theodore Affia, to be its chairman. As a community leader, Theodore understood the power of education through the lack of it: he wasn't literate himself. They also had the blessing of one of the most senior ethnic Egun chiefs of Makoko, Francis Agoyon Alashe.

There was, however, a problem. In a community where more than half the adult population was illiterate, and many of the rest didn't graduate from secondary school, where would they find teachers?

* * *

Night had fallen, black as the underside of a cooking pot. Apart from the few vehicle lights on the Third Mainland Bridge twinkling—red, white, red, white—all was darkness. A light breeze blew over the southern part of Makoko facing the Apapa port, almost chilly in the cool, rain-cleared evening. It foretold of the spirits' coming. Frightened children paddled their canoes extra hard to be at home before they arrived. For it was well known that they could do terrible things, the Zangbeto, with their occult powers of Voodoo and merciless defiance of law. As water spirits, these 'nightwatchmen' spent most of eternity on the lagoon, only visiting Makoko when called—which was only ever for a funeral of an elder or if someone had broken tribal law. Everyone knew the nightwatchmen wouldn't stand for even the smallest transgression. In legend, they had supernatural powers: swallowing glass, making objects disappear and reappear, identifying and scaring off witches. And when wrongdoing provokes the visitation of spirits with such prescience and other superhuman abilities, frankly, who needs police?

There was a bumping against jetties as their boats clanged to a halt one by one, and off they stepped. Terrible creatures they were, all wrapped in straw, for no one could be permitted to see the harrowing faces of these night spirits. Outwardly, they looked like cone-shaped haystacks with a blank sheet of cloth where their faces should be. No one knew what lay behind the cloth, which represented the nothingness before time. The leader heaved his grotesque, conical body of multi-coloured straw, twirling in mesmerising cycles, driven by an incessant, increasingly frantic drumbeat. The others also spun furiously.

Tonight, they had come for Stevie, who had committed the egregious sin of sleeping with his neighbour Agosu's wife, Albertine. Relatives of Agosu had seen them sneaking off together once, and since then Agosu had noticed Albertine was always taking a boat to shore in the evenings and not coming back until late. It didn't take them long to track down the motel on land where the two of them were meeting to engage in their salacious act. They had brought them back to see the Baale, Noah's brother, Chief Emmanuel Shemede.

'Why did you commit adultery?' the Baale had asked Stevie, in front of a crowd.

'I'm sorry, I couldn't control myself,' Stevie replied.

That very night the Zangbeto came to Stevie's hut. Drums beat progressively louder as they danced and swirled around.

Women and children in the adjacent hut hid under blankets. Eventually one of the swirling haystacks knocked on the wood of Stevie's hut.

'Where is Stevie, the weak man, the sordid adulterer who cannot control his prick?' the head Zangbeto said, his voice as gravelly as lagoon sand. Out Stevie came alone, his own wife and children cowering in the corner of his hut.

'Stevie, you have committed adultery,' the nightwatchman said, and drums restarted as all the Zangbeto repeated what he said in song. 'We are bound by Egun law to banish you from this community, and from the waters of the lagoon, for a minimum of five years,' the chief nightwatchman continued. 'Do you have anything to say?'

Stevie shook his head. The drums began again, beating ever more furiously. And the Zangbeto danced and began making fun of Stevie, in song. 'Oh, Stevie, his head is too big for his body,' they sang. 'Oh, Stevie, his nyash [arse] is too big for his bubu [robe]. Oh, Stevie, whose prick is too big. Oh, Stevie, you have such a big prick, but you cannot control it,' they sang, and the chiefs who had gathered on the jetty sang along and laughed. Noah couldn't help but burst out laughing himself. That night, Agosu also divorced his wife, and she, too, was forced to leave the community for a period. After the Zangbeto departed over the waters, everyone relaxed. Justice had been done.

The Zangbeto were what Makoko had always had instead of police. Bereft of the bureaucratic entanglements of modern life, they kept order with the power of Voodoo. The Egun people are said to have originally migrated from Ouidah, in what is now Benin Republic, to escape the insatiable slavers of the nineteenth-century Dahomey empire. Ouidah remains the world's capital of Voodoo, where priests in the Temple of Pythons still to this day drape snakes around their devotees (and nervous tourists). Closely related to the Yoruba, the dominant ethnic group in southwest Nigeria making up three-quarters of Lagos's population, the Egun had gradually rowed along the narrow creeks that southern Benin and Nigeria share, until they reached Badagry, now the city before the 'border' between the two countries, drawn up by Britain and France in the Scramble for Africa. Unfortunately for them, Badagry would turn out to be a slave-trading station nearly as prolific as Ouidah and Cotonou in Dahomey. A freed Yoruba slave called Seriki Faremi Williams had made a Faustian bargain with his former captors, agreeing to supply slaves to the Portuguese in exchange for his freedom. They went cheap: Williams once sold forty slaves for an umbrella, twenty for a mirror, ten for a single coral bead.

So the Egun fishermen continued east until they hit Lagos, at a place where the creek suddenly widened into a vast lagoon teeming with fish. Over decades, they were joined there by Yoruba fishing peoples such as the Ilaje and Ijebu.

For the two centuries during which the Egun had been dominant in Makoko, any crime, from murder to petty theft, was policed and punished by the Zangbeto, the ghostly guardians of their traditional Voodoo religion. They could do a lot worse than banish you. For stealing, you got beaten with a whip made out of knotted fishtails. Wife-beating also got you the fish whip, while any abuse of children or the elderly provoked a lashing with a wooden cane.

Of course, the whole community knew exactly whose job it was to enact the role of nightwatchmen. The Egun paramount chief of Makoko, Francis Agoyon Alashe, was one. But legend had it that their bodies disappeared as soon as they stepped inside the haystack, to be replaced by spirits. No one ever questioned their judgements. Despite an almost total lack of police presence, Makoko is still thought to have one of the lowest crime rates in all of Lagos, a fact which perhaps says as much about Nigerian policing as it does about these spectral apparitions.

The Zangbeto were a reminder of the powerful spiritual bonds tying this community together and linking them back to the times of the ancestors. Like many Makokoites, Noah was a Christian as well as a traditionalist. The missionaries had tried to outlaw 'heathen' practices like Voodoo, but they'd never succeeded. Most people saw no contradiction between their Christian faith and ancestral spirit worship. Noah mostly prayed to Jesus at home, and he fasted rigorously every Easter, but he respected the Zangbeto to the same degree.

The Zangbeto were also the most striking example of just how far outside the orbit of the state Makoko was. Aside from a couple of water pipes connected to boreholes, the state had provided nothing. The few that could afford it supplied their own electricity from generators; they had their own traditional doctors, apart from the clinics brought by charities; they taught their own children the skills and wisdom they needed to live.

Only now they had a school. A school, but no teachers. The Yacht Club had blown their budget on building the thing, leaving no money for teachers' salaries. Since the chances were slim of getting Lagos State to provide teachers to a community it did not recognise, the school risked becoming one of those rural African white elephant charity projects, destined for disuse and decay. Then one night, while Noah was still pursuing his dreams of making a financial success of himself on land, he was at his parents' house eating kokoro, a crunchy snack made from a paste of maize flour mixed with a little sugar and cassava or sometimes yam flour, and then deep-fried in red palm oil, and sometimes spiced up with fiery peppers.

'Noah, there's something I need you to do for me,' his mother said. Noah dabbed the last drop of red oil off his plate with his kokoro. His mother began talking about how much hope the new school had brought the community, and there was no one to teach, so all those efforts risked going to waste. Eventually she got to the point: she wanted Noah to take on the role of teacher. It was going to be hard to attract teachers to come and teach in a part of Lagos that was so strange and alien that many regarded it with horror. 'Now I know you're doing well on land, but ...'

'I can't do it.' Noah decided to nip this idea in bud. 'Things are going well for me outside, mother.'

'Look what education has done for you,' she spoke with the calm of someone who knows they have already won the argument. 'Think of how many children in the community could benefit, just like you did, with your help. Isn't this more important than your business plans?'

Noah protested, but he could see his defiance was testing her patience, so he promised to think about it. The next evening, he was back on land at Joseph's table, munching on grilled cows' kidneys. When he told Joseph of his dilemma, he was surprised by his friend's answer. Joseph had always encouraged Noah to make something of himself outside Makoko, but now he struck a different tone. Noah's mother was the one who had brought him into the world, who had looked after and nurtured him. It was to her he owed his education. 'You have to do what she wants,' he said.

That was how Noah found himself back in the schoolroom, only this time as the teacher. He would do it for a year, then go back on land to pursue his plans of making it big. Just a year, that's all. He looked around the newly built facility. There seemed little to distinguish the building as a school: no desks, no blackboard, no pencils, no books. A boat precariously piled with children rammed the side of the jetty. Then another. Then another. For a community supposedly aloof from the pressures of the modern world that European colonial powers had shaped, there was clearly a demand for education. Sixty-eight kids arrived on the first day. He lined them up as best he could and sat them down on the ground, since there were no desks. He remembered his first day at school: A, B, C; 1, 2, 3. And so he began like that, running through the English alphabet and counting to ten with the boys and girls, chanting by rote. He would later recall feeling almost tearful at the sea of innocence before him, mimicking his every sound.

For weeks, Noah taught all the classes himself. Some of the parents shared food with him as a way of thanks. It was a far cry from his dream of making it big on land, but he was the pride of his community. Like many Lagosians, Noah was a hustler at heart. He started aggressively plugging the contacts he had made, showing rich tourists around for contributions, and, piecemeal, they came forth with donations.

In the evenings, Noah would often stay out until very late on his night fishing trips, heaving a full net behind him on the way back with all the lagoon's bounty: croakers, barracudas, red snappers, crabs, crayfish. He would sell his excess to the Makoko–Asejere market, one of the most flourishing seafood markets in the city. That, plus the money that was coming in from wealthy benefactors, had made him more liquid than he'd been since leaving school. Yet seeing Lagos-on-land had also made him acutely aware of the poverty in which he'd grown up. Every time he paddled his boat through Makoko, he saw destitution, which made him sad: children without shoes paddling boats with cracks that had to be bailed out. Had he never been to school, he would have seen these children as contented with their lot in life and living peacefully. Now, all he saw were children with no education, with no future.

That was what made him realise, about a year after he started teaching, that he could never leave Makoko. It was early in the school day, and he was writing school reports on all his children for eager parents—many of whom, being illiterate, would have to have them read to them by someone else. Lagoon waves were lapping against the wood of the school building in a hypnotic cadence. The water was catching the morning sun and fracturing it into crystals of pale light. And Noah realised teaching was bringing him far more joy than any land-based business venture could have done. He saw that it was God's plan, his destiny, that he stay on water.

In any case, the noise and haste of Lagos-on-land were stressful. There were bank accounts to think about, forms to fill in, police extortion, traffic, expensive food. In Makoko, the only thing to worry about was the tide—and keeping the school going. Both meant a daily struggle for survival, but there was a gentler pace here, softened by the lilting motion of the lagoon. Terrestrial Lagos was a seething cauldron of hustle and hostility, one he could never change. Makoko was somewhere he could make a difference—not to mention boosting his standing in a community that was still more important to him than anywhere on land.

17

ACTS OF GOD AND MEN

Makoko, 2010

There was a moment Noah realised Makoko might be in trouble. One morning, he switched on the radio to hear a Lagos State government official talking about his home. It sounded so different from Noah's own experience that he hardly recognised it; he almost doubted for a second whether the bureaucrat was referring to the same place. The official called it a health hazard and a blight on the waterfront, which could otherwise be developed into prime real estate. He described its residents' homes as 'unplanned' and 'illegal', and he spoke of them as 'encroaching' on the lagoon. At some point, he said, the 'squatters' would need to be relocated. That was what burned the most. Squatters? Nearly two centuries they'd been here, and yet they were squatters? How was that possible? And what did it mean that the government regarded a whole community as illegitimate? Could they come with bulldozers (or whatever the amphibious equivalent was for knocking down buildings on water) and just level the place?

Noah didn't yet know enough to answer any of these questions. But in fact, five years earlier, while he was in his last years of school, Makoko had had its most recent taste of what could happen when a rich man decides he can think of something better to do with this conveniently located stretch of prime waterfront. In April 2005, armed police had escorted bulldozers to a section of Makoko on the lagoon shore. They'd proceeded to demolish scores of houses—and some clinics and churches for good measure—while delivering a sound beating to anyone who objected. It was impressively efficient. It took them just three days to make 3,000 people homeless. There'd been no warning, nor explanation. A court had ruled the land belonged to a private landowner. They were illegal settlers. Why would anyone need to consult them?

Governor Fashola was showing a degree of determination to impose order on the monster megacity that few had thought possible. Elite and middle-class Lagosians were amazed at the way Fashola had set about doing what he'd promised, collecting rubbish, easing traffic, tackling crime. In Makoko, he'd become popular by cracking down on extortionate rents. Next in his sights was curbing the gargantuan growth of slums, which had seen the city multiply beyond any capacity to provide for it. And there lay the problem: unfortunately, places like Makoko really didn't fit into Fashola's vision. And there was the double irritation that the slum was on the water in such a fine location in between the airport and the islands. Just think what luxury hotels, resorts, golf courses, office buildings and pleasure parks could be built here!

Noah went straight to the elders after hearing the radio message, paddling his boat with such speed that he churned up rubbish bobbing in the lagoon waters. After being welcomed into Chief Aji's house on stilts, he said, 'Chief, I heard on the radio this morning that the government doesn't recognise our community. They think it should be taken down.' He was still out of breath from his manic paddle. 'Are you sure?' the chief asked, while he and another of the chiefs, Baale Stephen, raised their eyebrows. Noah said, 'I'm sure. It was on the radio. They were very clear about it.' But Aji and Stephen let out a mutual chuckle. 'Don't worry about it, Noah. They can't just come here without consulting the chiefs. How can government just come here and destroy us, without a legal document?' Stephen said.

What Noah appreciated, but what the chiefs couldn't yet, was that it was in fact Makoko that needed a legal document. You could be a thriving community of hundreds of thousands of happy, productive people. Without a sheet of paper saying you owned where you lived, you were nothing. In 1990 a slum near the millionaires' sanctum of Victoria Island had been demolished, in the biggest eviction in Lagos's history, to make more space for the millionaires. Three families behind the demolition had a legal document saying they owned the slum. None of the 300,000 people turfed out of their homes had a legal document saying they could stay.

* * *

There was something on which Governor Fashola and Noah, if they'd ever had a conversation, might have agreed on: the importance of school. For education was what the governor was banking on, perhaps more than anything, to drag Lagos into the twenty-first century. 'I have children of my own and I do not believe that they are entitled to anything better than you are entitled to,' he'd told Lagosians in a speech. 'As long as I remain ... governor, I will give you as much as I give my own children.' No one believed it, but everyone appreciated the sentiment. He'd ordered schools to be made free and was doing his best to provide them. But as with everything else, Makoko, being illegal, would miss out on free schooling. Not only that, but its grey status was proving an impediment to getting private funds for Whanyinna. Robin Campbell, mindful of the risk of the Yacht Club's pet project atrophying, had been calling around, trying to get charities to stump up for monthly costs. An American NGO, which had built quite a few schools, agreed to help pay salaries—and then swiftly backed down when it figured out this was an 'informal community'. Nobody wanted to upset the government.

And yet, hustler that he was, Noah was finding plenty of ways to get cash. By now it had well and truly dawned on him that Makoko's mystique was drawing in all manner of curious visitors: journalists, photographers, architects, the whole cognoscenti of urban visionaries and urbane intellectuals. They came here to see what they wanted to see in the slum: a vibrant, colourful community, an African shithole, a beautiful ugliness, the dark side of our ruthlessly globalised economy. Whatever their take, they all brought the same advantage as the Yacht Club folks: tug on their heart strings hard enough and money fell out. Noah would charge the tourists 4,000 naira ($30) for a tour of his slum. He'd show them the school and they'd go all weepy and misty-eyed at the cute kids in their matching blue-and-yellow uniforms on a school jetty that frequently flooded. They'd offer money, and he'd tell them to pay cash or make out a cheque—to him, of course, although promising it was for the school, which it mostly was.

The donations to the school—money from multiple charitable sources, few of which were asking him to account for it—were almost becoming a successful business venture in their own right. Community members noticed him with better clothes and nicer sunglasses, a better boat, some improvements to his home, and plenty to spend on food from the grilling houses. Some began to raise eyebrows, and tongues started to wag. Noah was fashioning himself into an oga, like his brother Emmanuel, they said. Most didn't mind, though: that was how Lagos worked everywhere. If you wanted to do something for the community, you had to amass resources. You could talk about changing

Nigeria for the better and doing things right, combatting corruption and setting an example, but without playing the game you'd get nowhere, because no one would give you access. And only the ogas had access. Without it, you'd just be sitting at the back shouting your mouth off alongside tens of millions of other powerless Nigerians. In an African patronage system turbocharged by oil money, the ogas were the fountainheads trickling down to water the needs of everyone else. And the school's needs were limitless.

One thing the school needed was more teachers. People like Noah: originally from Makoko but having gone through school on land and come back with worldliness and book learning. People like Yewande Akinwe. Yewande was from the other side of what sometimes seemed like a cultural chasm in the community: Makoko-on-land. Her parents were ethnic Yoruba from the interior who had migrated to Lagos for work and settled around Makoko Road. Her father traded spare car parts and her mother was a nurse who had trained at Nigeria's most prestigious university, Ibadan. Yewande's home life was poor by Western standards but, by the standards of most Makokoites, extremely comfortable. While many chewed small smoked fish and padded them out with cheap noodles or pounded yam, Yewande's family had the pick of Makoko's net-caught bounty: fresh catfish, grilled or made into a broth with peppers and bitter leaf, fried crayfish and crabs, served with mountains of rice and bean cakes. She had the rare privilege of being one of very few going to university. There, she majored in teaching and banking, but, despite writing to several banks, no jobs were forthcoming. One morning, when the last of the fishermen were paddling their boats out into the lagoon and singing songs, she quietly came up to Noah at the school and asked him for a job. She was still studying for her degree at the weekends but was renting a place on the water with some friends. Noah hired her.

'Just teach them what you know, like you were taught yourself. You'll do fine,' Noah told Yewande. Everything about teaching the 200 students, about twenty-five in each class, was hard: the lack of books and pens, the fact that at least a few of them were evidently hungry, and the initially insurmountable language barrier. Most of the kids spoke only Egun, which was related to Yewande's native Yoruba tongue but not closely enough to be understood. A small handful of more recent arrivals from Benin spoke a little French, and all the material was in English. And the school, like all of Makoko-on-water, was filthy. Like those of most land dwellers, her nose was not accustomed to the mixture of sewage and diesel fumes wafting off the lagoon—she was shocked at how readily the children splashed and swam in the water. She was too repulsed to eat at the school in her first week.

Yet every time she paddled through the rubbish-strewn waterways, past huts connected by wooden planks, where naked infants squealed and mothers hitched up their colourful dresses to enter canoes full of the milk powder, bubblegum and soft drinks they needed to sell in order to feed them, she was reminded of why she was doing this. She saw people not wearing shoes, children working around the creeks. Some barely out of infancy were hawking sweets and fish, while others transported these items. They knew no languages beyond their ethnic dialect. Without the school, all of these children would have the same fate: the boys would become fishermen; the women, housewives or petty traders. No choice. In fact, choice was exactly the thing her own parents had given her by schooling her. She was in Makoko, but if she wanted to, she could leave. If at least some of these kids ended up with that choice, she and Noah would have achieved their mission.

Besides teachers, the school desperately needed to expand. There was already a long waiting list. They needed another building, and more money to maintain the existing one. The school often flooded when it rained, which it did a lot. Around the time Noah was pondering this problem, he got a richer, more famous tourist than anyone in this slum had ever seen. The tourist was a man Noah had never heard of: Hollywood star Ben Stiller. He was in Nigeria to research a comedy film about 419s, those infamous Nigerian email scammers who con the gullible and greedy out of money on the promise of fictional untold riches. The scam was named after the number in the Nigerian penal code for such offences. The film never got made, but while he was in Lagos, Stiller toured Makoko.

Noah told Stiller to get in touch with his friend Isi Etomi. Isi was a young Nigerian architect who'd studied in Britain and done her Nigerian youth service—the great leveller, which all Nigerians are required to undergo, regardless of class, at least in theory—by teaching at his school. Isi was Makoko's most reliable defender in the world outside. Sensing that this Ben guy was someone more important than the usual red-eared expats he showed around, he called Isi. 'This guy Ben says he wants to build a school for us,' he said, and, sure enough, later she received a call from the Ben Stiller Foundation. She explained to them the project would be highly contentious, given Makoko's non-existent legal status. They paid for a nice shelter over one of the jetties used by canoe taxis while she drew up a plan.

The following year, 2011, Makoko was getting even more attention. Journalists were practically queuing up to tour the slum, film it, snap it, write about it. But Noah noticed a lot of them, especially local journalists, were going away and writing bad things about his home: calling it unclean and overcrowded and unhealthy. He resolved to start charging them more for their tours. *Fine, write whatever rubbish you like, but you can give something back*, he thought. In March that year, a Baptist missionary from America moved into Makoko. Missionary Dave Douglas was a well-fed, bald white man with a well-fed brunette wife, Jeannie.

They came with plenty of cash. Emmanuel rented out his two-storey house on the water to him. 'Jeannie saw her upstairs living room and kitchen for the first time and she cried!' Dave wrote in his blog, next to a picture of the empty room. 'I remodelled it and she loves it now. Happy wife, Happy life! Oh yeah!' he wrote, next to a picture of the room transformed beyond recognition by a kitchen table, chairs and a sink. Dave and Jeannie were an endless curiosity, although Makoko was by now probably more habituated to white foreigners than any other slum dwellers were.

Another mover-and-shaker to pay a visit was Kunlé Adeyemi, a Nigerian architect with sharp, angular features and an even sharper dress sense. He was living in the Netherlands. After seeing the school on tour, Kunle asked Noah what the school's biggest challenge was. Expansion, Noah told him. They needed another school building to keep up with all the demand. Like Ben before him, Kunle promised them a new school building. But when he came back with a plan, it was for a 'floating school'. Shaped like a pyramid and resting on empty barrels, this revolutionary school, which he proposed be paid for by Stiller's foundation, would make a powerful statement about marginalised communities. He said things to drum up excitement among fellow architects, words like 'ecological', 'self-sustaining' and 'indigenous'. Noah and Isi were both sceptical: why not just do something like the existing building, which would be cheaper and more practical? Though the Stiller Foundation eventually backed out, Kunle found funding elsewhere for his floating school, which began to cause quite a stir in visionary architects' circles. Noah said any school would be fine. He just needed more space for more kids.

* * *

On the morning of 12 July 2012, Makoko awoke to find eviction notices posted on about 400 of its houses furthest into the lagoon. Noah pulled one off a neighbour's house to read—something which many of the occupants of these houses were not literate enough to do.

'You have continued to occupy and develop shanties and unwholesome structures on the waterfront without authority, thereby constituting an environmental nuisance ... [and] impediments to economic and gainful utilisation of the waterfront,' it said. Worry throbbed through Noah's skull. 'Notice is hereby given to you to vacate and remove all illegal developments along the Makoko/Iwaya Waterfront within 72 hours.'

Four days later, a hotchpotch of police, private security men and area boys arrived in speedboats armed with Kalashnikovs, machetes, axes and chainsaws. They shouted through a megaphone to the people to vacate their premises. Swiftly, the area boys began hacking down the huts furthest into the lagoon, as young children screamed and men shouted at them to stop. As Noah was teaching maths on the blackboard, some boats belonging to parents of the children arrived, panic on their faces. After finishing a prayer with a mother who'd stayed behind, he jumped into his canoe to head home. The demolitions went on for four days, during which Makoko's waters churned with panic. Boats paddled along laden with whatever their occupants could salvage from their now ruined huts. In one house, Noah's friend Hunge and his wife broke down in frenzied wailing and sobbing. In their rush to grab their belongings from the house before it was destroyed, their newborn child, Jacob, had drowned in the water down a gap between their hut and the next one, round at the back of the house. Noah saw a mob of area boys armed with knives coming and jumped into the water, swimming off in the direction of a meeting place for the elders hidden deep inside the slum.

Yewande, the junior teacher, had also rushed home when the demolitions began. Her parents' house was among those marked for demolition. When she got there, it was too late: the house was a ruin of planks. Her mother had tried to act strong but couldn't hold back her tears. They had invested a lot in that house over the years: buying a gas cooker, getting armchairs with soft foam cushions and covers. Now it was all trashed. A white-haired old man looked panicked as he paddled past. 'Need a lift?' he asked Yewande. She made a 'thanks but no thanks' wave of the hand. Instead, she couldn't resist the urge to take her boat in the other direction, towards the mayhem. Police in boats had surrounded rows of houses furthest into the lagoon and were shouting in pidgin through megaphones—many in Makoko don't speak it. She saw more policemen coming in boats. As they began hacking down the wooden structures with axes and chain-saws, a local newscaster was there on the scene filming. *Why do they always film but they never do anything to stop it?* she thought. Some people jumped off the sides of their houses into the water to escape the mobs. Those made homeless were sitting in their boats laden with whatever they could salvage. Some were eating stocks of dried fish—the food they would normally take out with them for a day's fishing. They had nowhere else to go.

On the fifth day, a fracas developed which ended in the police shooting dead one of Makoko's most revered elders, Timothy Hunpoyanwha. The outcry was enough to halt the destruction, but by then some 3,000 people were homeless. That evening, Noah prayed. Only divine intervention, Noah thought, could save Makoko.

* * *

According to Egun myth, near the beginning of time Ajaka, the god of thunder and brother of the Yoruba thunder god, Sango, had an insatiable sexual appetite that no amount of fornication was ever enough to quench. Ajaka always liked hanging out around the water, and he frequently wandered through the creeks connecting the Lagos and Cotonou lagoons, hovering above them with the power of spirit. He would often scour the edges of the lagoon in search of a hearty wench to make his latest conquest. One night he appeared to a woman as she walked by the sliver of lagoon that runs through Badagry. Thunder roared and she joined Ajaka at his side. They had many children together before he disappeared into the steamy, sunless skies. Those descendants called themselves the Bada, and their children eventually made up the most prominent families of the Egun people in Badagry—including Noah's ancestors. It was his favourite myth about the founding of his people.

When the British seized control of Lagos in 1861, they more or less ignored Makoko. It wasn't close enough to the harbour to be much of a nuisance to maritime trade, let alone a strategic threat. And while British missionaries were schooling a tiny elite in Nigeria's south, none were bothering to do so in this opaque collection of smoky huts on stilts. No surprise then that Noah's father, Moses, never went to school. What he did manage to do instead was join the Boy Scouts, an obnoxiously imperial youth organisation with an urgent mission to civilise the natives. Moses quickly showed himself to be bright and adept, learning Yoruba and English, how to navigate from a map from its most rudimentary symbols, how to read a compass, and, that time-honoured badge of honour in elite circles, how to ride a horse. He became a boxing champion, winning several titles. His newly acquired polyglot skills soon became of use in resolving disputes in Makoko, between Egun and Ilaje, Yoruba-speaking fishing peoples from upland Ogun state, or between either of them and the Ijaws, who had come up the eastern creeks from the Niger Delta. Moses found himself arbitrating between factions and in no time became youth leader of the community. He married his first wife in his early thirties, late for a man from a poor rural community. His manhood signed and sealed, he became a Baale (chief) of Makoko, shortly after Nigeria's independence from Britain. From then on, the standing of Noah's family in the community was assured.

* * *

The attack on Makoko backfired on the Lagos State government. That was thanks partly to Noah. As he'd been showing around journalists for years, he had all their numbers, and had the presence of mind to call them up with details of the onslaught that was going on. Some arrived to film, photograph or otherwise report on the demolition. It made front-page local news and featured prominently in foreign outlets like the BBC. The state government defended itself somewhat touchily, saying it only ever planned to destroy a handful of houses that had encroached on the lagoon too close to some electricity pylons, not the whole community. Still, it was negative attention of the sort it could do without, and the bulldozers and chainsaws were temporarily silenced.

All this did wonders for Adeyemi's proposed 'Floating School', which was now not just a school but a beacon of hope for a community in the crosshairs of developers looking to sweep away its inhabitants. In early 2013, about a year after the demolition of those Makoko houses, the school was finished: a three-storey blue triangle floating on barrels. It had a bottom level of more than ninety square metres. Noah thought it was silly, but he had learned by now that anything that brought positive publicity to Makoko was a good thing. As part of the launch, Makokoites had held a fishing-boat race on one of its channels. Beautiful, iconic photos of the slum and the Floating School were published in newspapers around the world.

That year was a turbulent year for Noah. His father died in September—they buried him in the Egun ancestral homeland of Badagry, a place of palm-fringed creeks, white beaches with straw-roofed shelters, and weather-beaten old colonial buildings, mostly former slave houses. The Zangbeto came out in force for his funeral, as they did for all big men of the community. The ghostly haystacks whirled like dervishes and drove the congregation in wild, passionate mourning for the loss of this man who had done so much to enable the Egun to be taken seriously by Lagos's more powerful ethnic groups. Three months later, Noah's mother died, heartbroken by the loss of her husband. After interring her in Badagry, his heart heavy with grief, Noah suddenly felt the burden of everything he was trying to do to rescue Makoko. His parents had been his mentors and spiritual guides on this path, and now they were gone. Noah had long since stopped going to church every Sunday—much to his pious mother's consternation—but he always felt his life had been guided by the Divine Plan. Seeing the Zangbeto dance wildly, the human forms inside them momentarily dissolved to make way for beings of pure spirit, always reminded him of his deep connection with the spirit world. Noah was a Christian who didn't exactly believe in traditional spirits. He always felt close to Jesus Christ when he fasted at Easter, trying to imagine what it was like to die for the sins of every human being. But the Zangbeto were a connection that had always shown the people of Makoko what to do and how to prosper long before the missionaries came along. His ancestors had migrated from Badagry nearly two centuries previously because they saw that this was a place where they could thrive and live in peace.

* * *

The 2012 demolition had kicked up such a stink that the Nigeria Human Rights Commission was investigating it, and a lawyer-activist called Felix Morka, who had been defending the slum for years, was preparing a lawsuit against the government. A group of Lagos State officials and rights commission appointees in suits turned up at the jetty on Makoko Road in a dozen jeeps. They'd arrived to survey the damage that had been done during the demolitions. It was already November of the following year, but still many of the evicted had not found anywhere to live, and many lacked the means to erect new shelters. Guided by Noah's brother Emmanuel and Chief Affia, the officials were treated to scenes of people made homeless, sleeping under bridges. Like all tourists to Makoko, they came to visit Noah's school—the actual, functioning one, not the fantasy floating one. Before their boats came into view, Noah hit on the idea of getting all his kids to come out in their yellow-and-blue school uniforms onto the school's jetty and sing the national anthem, which they did. 'Oh God of Creation,' they sang, as the officials paused to savour the moment. It was so moving, one official looked as if he was shedding a tear.

A year later, thanks to the savvy publicity of its architect, the Floating School had become one of the most famous buildings in Lagos. Journalists relentlessly arrived to snap photos and take film of it, and Noah, as the school manager, made sure he charged them a hefty contribution to his educational endeavours—in the form of cash which, as usual, passed into the communal tub via his own pockets. It was an irresistible story: it involved education of African children, a marginalised community threatened with demolition, a way of life most people in rich countries could scarcely imagine; it was about humanity's urban future, about climate change adaptation, about how visionary architects can bring hope to a world tarnished by inequality and blight. The Floating School was so many themes rolled into one: just thinking about it could leave you suffused with a balmy intellectual glow.

Noah still wondered why the school had to float: Makokoites had been living on water for centuries, but had never seen the need for a building that floated. The lagoon was only a few metres deep. Why not just do what they'd been doing success-fully for generations: get four guys to wade into the water up to their armpits holding long poles, plunge them into the silt and then nail them as deep as they'd go, then build the thing on planks around this four-pole suspension. What could be simpler? Even filling the lagoon with sand to make another school like Whanyinna would have been more straightforward.

But Noah was smart enough to see that the young architect wasn't just trying to make something practical. He was trying to make a statement, in that hoo-ha fancy way that contemporary architects liked, a statement that was getting news coverage. And that was putting Makoko on the map as never before, a fact which might—though, of course, this could also backfire—make it harder to destroy. There was a problem, though: because it seemed so unsafe and wobbly, Noah feared a decent gust of wind might topple it over, and he dared not use it. He and Yewande kept on teaching classes in the old school, which was so over-flowing that there was a weeks-long waiting list. To keep up the pretence, he moved his kids into the Floating School every time a journalist showed up to report on it—then swiftly moved them out again before anyone got panicky.

In the tropical heat, the Floating School—which after a year still hadn't been used—began to undergo rot. Some of its beams ruptured, and thieves stole copper wiring from it. Noah didn't have any money to repair it. By the following year, 2015, the state government had realised there was such a buzz around the school that they were including it in a plan to regenerate the slum. It had won awards and been featured in many maga-zines. But nobody had any money for repairs, which were the sort of boring thing that never got you any publicity. Nigerians were always better at erecting structures than keeping them upstanding. The chains holding the Floating School to its mooring became detached, and it drifted off free-floating on

LAGOS

the lagoon, crashing into some huts. Noah resolved not to risk putting the kids in there anymore, not even for photo shoots. It was just too dangerous.

The final blow came from the weather. A tempest—the sort that most Makoko houses withstand just fine—gathered on 7 June 2016. It whipped through the slum, peppering houses and boats with rain. There was a crashing sound. From his vantage point on the jetty of the real school, wet to the bone from the driving rain, Noah peered out across the lagoon. The Floating School, which had once lit up the horizon and attracted incessant boatloads of paparazzi, was gone. It had collapsed in the storm.

246

18

THE HAYSTACK GHOST KING

Makoko, 2016

'If there's a strong storm, that building's going to come down,' Noah tells me of the Floating School, as we paddle away from the dilapidated structure on one of my many visits to Makoko. (This, my last visit, happened about three months before the school finally did collapse.) 'Even now, if there's a storm, it shakes,' Noah continues. 'I'm just not going to use it anymore, not even for the media.' He grudgingly acknowledges that the Floating School was a great opportunity to shame the state government into finally recognising Makoko, if indeed that's what they've done. He also knows that it helped him raise his profile, so much so that he's thinking of going into politics. Noah comes from a long line of Shemedes who know how to seize an opportunity. 'My dad's nickname was "Sea Never Dry",' he says, smiling that wistful half-smile of his.

As we enter one of the many channels between Makoko's maze of huts, a trader passes us in a boat laden with boxes of Gala sausage rolls, a luminously red-orange species of cheap beef frankfurter enveloped in pastry, very popular in Lagos's poor parts. In one of the huts, there is a shop. It sells instant coffee, sachets of water, Coca-Cola (of course), and powdered milk. In an adjacent hut, loud traditional Egun music blasts out of speakers hooked up to a smoking diesel generator. It is ear-splitting, yet still only just loud enough to drown out the terrible grumble of the generator. A group of half-naked children of mixed sizes are dancing in pure joy. An angry cock chases an impertinent young chick around in circles. Children fill a jerry-can from a hose connected to a water tank that springs a leak, spraying precious clean water into the black lagoon. Noah and I are on our way to see Francis Agoyon Alashe, one of the most senior chiefs in the community (at least according to some), and one of the main interlocutors with the land of the dead. In his other guise, Francis is one of the Zangbeto, the scary hay-stack ghosts that come out to maintain order and justice and preside over funerals.

'It's not human being inside, it's spirit,' Noah explains, when I ask him about Francis's role as one of the beings. 'He disappears when he enters them. If you open up [the haystack], you will not see anybody inside. You will be fearful. People that don't belong to them are very afraid. The spirit is very dangerous. They can float over water. They will shout your name, and you will know you are in trouble.' I ask him how he reconciles this belief with his Catholic faith. 'If you become a Christian, you aren't supposed to have something [anything] to do with them, but you do. I have faith in Christ, but they still come out to me. I still come out to see them.' When the fishermen go out on the water, they often pray to both Christ and the Zangbeto for protection. Fishing is a dangerous enterprise, especially out on the sea. Everyone knows someone who has lost a loved one on a fishing trip, usually after a series of waves overturns their boat. We pass under a bridge where a woman is selling juicy prawns off the side of her boat. On another, a woman is scaling a spiny fish with a large knife. Noah bows his head in greeting to an ancient woman with a hunchback and no teeth, who effortlessly paddles past us.

We arrive at the jetty of Chief Francis Agoyon, a partially grey-haired man in his fifties and one of the most revered spiritual leaders of the Egun. There are three boats outside his house: the one, evidently, that he uses, then another filled with a fishing net, and a third one filled with clam shells. Beside one, a crab is struggling to free itself from a whirlpool of thin plastic in the brackish water. Noah has things to do, so heads off on his boat, promising to come back later. Chief Francis is wearing a flowing agbada in a psychedelic yellow-blue pattern. He welcomes me with a warm smile accompanied by only brief eye contact. He invites me to sit on the wooden bench at right angles to his, which I do. Francis has two wives and many children, but none of them are in this home, which is where Francis receives visiting dignitaries and strangers. I want him to tell me some stories about the origins of the Egun.

'It all starts with Te Agbani,' he tells me, beginning a monologue that flits between English and French, a language with which he is more familiar on account of his Beninoise origins. 'Te Agbani was a great sorcerer and king who founded the Egun nation and began the Zangbeto,' he continues, before pausing, deep in thought or recollection. 'Back in those days the Egun lived all over Ghana, Togo and Benin. Dahomey was a mighty slaving empire, so the Egun—they didn't call themselves that yet—left to flee the slavers, under the leadership of Te Agbani. He had had a misunderstanding with his brothers, and so he left, with his followers. They went to Porto Novo [the capital of neighbouring Benin Republic]. There were no traces of [human] life yet in Porto Novo. There were wild animals in the forest, leopards, lion, snakes, hyena. Te Agbani killed a large antelope, and before butchering it, he removed its horn. He made a small hole in the narrow end, then from the other end he scraped the horn empty. And then he blew it, and out came the most terrible sound, loud as anything on earth. All the wild animals were terrified. They fled the place, running in every direction to escape. Te Agbani cleared some of the thick forest, and they settled there, where he ruled as king over the Egun people. That's how he established the kingdom, and how he became the one who instructs the Zangbeto. Even now, he is the one they originate from. Whether or not they will answer the call from the elders, it is up to him.'

This naturally leads to a discussion about the Zangbeto, the haystack ghosts that make up, for me, one of the most fascinating aspects of Egun culture.

'The Zangbeto are something really powerful,' he tells me, and his face gets that slightly lost, thoughtful expression again. 'Any witchcraft that any has ever tried to use to spoil our community, they have beaten it back with their own powers. In the 1960s, there was a terrible epidemic of chickenpox in Makoko. It killed many, especially children. But then the elders called the Zangbeto. I was there. One night, they came out to our community. The next week, the epidemic was over. They killed it with spiritual power.'

'What's it like, when they come?'

'People will hear the voice first. Their voices blow over with the wind. They usually appear at night. They can come in daylight, but that's mostly for the festival. The original Zangbeto had antelope horns, but not so much anymore. In the past, if the king wanted to do something, he called the Zangbeto. Everyone had to obey them. To defy the Zangbeto, that is a malediction. They are water spirits. You can call them from over the sea. But I have seen them take the form of fire.' Now I'm really intrigued. 'One day, deep in the night, there was darkness all along Makoko. Then I saw fire in the night. I approached and the fire took the form of a human being. You can't run from them: you're finished.'

'These Zangbeto are very old. They are from the days when we didn't need all these things.' He waves his hand vaguely in the direction of the modern world. 'We didn't need things like school.'

'But now you do?' I ask.

'Yes. The school, it has really helped us. Lagos today, you can't live and not be educated. It's also'—he shuts his eye while he thinks about how to express himself—'for our legitimacy. That's why we want you here, Mister Tim Cocks. I want you to tell the Lagos State government on our behalf: we belong here. We can't leave. We are like the fishes. We must live on water,' he tells me. Now he's making eye contact, almost for the first time since that initial glance when we started speaking. 'Makoko, that school has helped us a lot. Maybe they can't remove us now.'

I ask him about the Floating School, and he quickly expels through his lips, reverting to angry French. 'We never wanted it,' he says. 'We just wanted another school, like the one we have. More space. If you want to do something for us, you must think about it. Will it work? Will it last? They've wasted their money.' Then he spends a few minutes complaining about how they could have used the plastic drums on which the school sits for something better. The sticky heat is gathering now. I can feel it under my shirt. The stink of the lagoon is really assaulting my nostrils.

'Are you a father?' he asks. 'No, I'm not a father yet,' I reply, which inevitably triggers the question 'How old are you?' and I tell him I'm 39. 'Thirty-nine years without a child? Serious?' This, he decides, is the most tragic thing he's heard in ages. Francis himself has eighteen children. 'I'm going to pray for you,' he says, and before I get a chance to say, 'Really, there's no need', he's already grabbed my hand between his two, and is bowed in silence. My eyes are starting to sting from all the smoke coming off nearby woodfires. He coughs, then clears his throat. He quits alternating with French and delivers the whole prayer in English.

'Our Father in Heaven, the source of life. We pray for you, Tim Cooks. You are moving tomorrow, back home. We pray that God should guide you, Mister Tim Cooks, since you are taking flight home soonest. We pray that God should guide you to the right place. We pray you arrive safely to your destination, and that you bring with you the joy you have seen here and carry it to your people. So, everything is clear.' He starts to lose his thread a bit, then he pours himself and me a shot from a bottle of local moonshine that he's had by his side since I arrived. Well, I wasn't expecting that! Then he brings a kola nut from his pocket. 'This kola, I want to use it to pray for you,' he says, removing the shell and pulling out the segments. He mutters something silent over them, then drops them on the floor. Then he removes some alligator pepper and scatters the seeds on the floor. I have no idea if this is some ancient ritual or if he's just making it up, but I'm enjoying it nonetheless.

'So, Mister Tim Cooks—Cocks, sorry,' he corrects himself, 'take this to finish our prayer.' We clink our shot glasses. I'm about to down mine but I see that, from his seated position, he just pours his on the wood of his front jetty, next to the kola nut and alligator pepper. He explains to me that all these things are an offering to the ancestors. I do the same with my shot, and he nods, to indicate that I've done it correctly. Two of the kola nut pieces have fallen 'open', concave down. 'This is good luck,' he tells me. 'Very good luck.' He squints a bit, scrutinising the mess we've made on his balcony. 'The kola nut is saying a close friend will soon give you advice. You should listen to it.' He pours me another shot. 'That one is for you,' he says. We clink our glasses and down them: a noxious fire ignites in my throat. 'Wow,' I say, and he pours me another one. After three glasses, plus the humidity and the fact I've been running around all day, I'm starting to feel light-headed.

Noah arrives, sparing me a fourth shot of the firewater. I thank Francis profusely, and promise to write as much of what he told me as I can. Noah takes me back to the jetty at Makoko Road on his boat. I tell him some of what I discussed with Chief Francis, and he nods, as if he's heard a lot of it before. Noah says, 'A lot of journalists, they don't write truth about Makoko. They say bad things. We are unhealthy, backwards.' I say I've no interest in promoting that idea. I want people to see Makoko how he sees it, I tell him. They already know how outsiders see it. He nods, but he doesn't look massively convinced. A duck-like wild bird wades through a floating pile of discarded polythene whose colours have long since seeped into the water.

'You must tell people the real story of Makoko,' he says. 'They call it a shanty. We don't call it that. We live here. We can't go anywhere else. We are water people.' And with that, he turns his boat around and disappears into Makoko's rolling smoke-fog.

PART VII

THE AJAH WOMAN AND THE
RIVER GODDESS

Her cooling waters heal, the Mother of Mothers.
She removes infertility. That which was barren will swell from her waters.
That which was poor can become wealthy ... The whole world will always be in
search of her.

Ose Meji saying (odu), recited by Yoruba priests in praise of Osun,
the goddess of love, fertility, sensuality and fresh water

No women may see the 'bullroarer' (Oro) and live, and all women are obliged,
under pain of death, to say that they believe Oro to be a powerful Orisha, and
act up on that belief ... Oro himself, in a long robe hung with shells, and a
wooden mask painted white, with lips smeared with blood, parades the town
with a numerous following.

A.B. Ellis, *Yoruba Shamanism*

Wherever the river current runs through, there you will find the Ilaje.

A saying of the Ilaje, a Yoruba-speaking traditional fishing people who
have settled all along the coast of the Lagos lagoon from the interior

19

KEMI

Ajah, Lekki Peninsula, 2006

It was when her Ajah neighbourhood erupted into gunfire at the hands of warring men that Kemi decided to seek protection from the river goddess. On that day, she awoke at five, as usual, ready for the day's hustle at the sand-mining sites at the edge of the lagoon. Outside was darkness—like most Lagosians, she had to start early if she wanted to earn her daily pounded yam. Sleep was still in her eyes. During her slumbers, Kemi's spirit often travelled to the ancestral plane, to places where gods make mischief and goddesses tempt it. Kemi was a devoted follower of Osun, goddess of love and sensuality, of all fresh water, and especially of a river of the same name that flows from dwindling forests upcountry into the salty Lagos lagoon, not far from Ajah. Kemi liked to say she was a water spirit. She'd always felt that her soul had come into this world across water, and that it would leave the same way. It seemed fitting, then, that she made her livelihood from extracting sand lying deep beneath the waters of Lagos.

On this humid morning, she said goodbye to her mother, Moriliatu, who was lying on the couch in wistful contemplation, as usual. Then she scraped open the ill-fitting rusty iron sheet she used as a front door to her unpainted concrete bungalow and headed out to work. Her path to the lagoon sauntered alongside a sewage stream meandering through trash obstacles beside the sandy streets of her ramshackle Ajah neighbourhood. Streets were pocked with ditches that could sink a saloon car in the rainy season. Herons picked crumbs of food from puddles of toxic sludge, lizards scuttled, and chickens and bleating goats fed on morsels lodged inside plastic takeaway bags. She arrived at the lagoon edge, a shoreline undulating with vast piles of sand that had been deposited there, waiting for the dump trucks to pick them up and take them to building sites. The miners were already out on the lagoon to dive for sand and bring it back to traders like her.

From a distance, the Lagos sand miners are indistinguishable from the lagoon fishermen. They travel in the same traditional wood-carved boats—a few of the more fortunate ones powered by motors instead of muscle or wind—out into the middle of the lagoon. They represent the same mix of indigenous Yoruba with ethnicities from further afield, the great majority of whom ended up in Lagos simply because they had nowhere else to go. They wear the same often-tattered T-shirts and loose trousers tied at the waist with rope. They sport the same wiry, herculean constitution that comes from gruelling manual labour using the full range of one's muscles—and eating only the calories needed to keep one moving. But when they reach the lagoon's centre, instead of casting out nets, they move to the boat's edge and pinch their noses. Holding their breath with that hand, while the other holds a bucket, they plunge to the bottom of the lagoon—usually about four metres deep—to fill the bucket with sand.

When they surface, they dump the sand into the boat, and dive in again. Their eyes will fill with stinging liquid because of all the salt and pollution. This action they repeat until the boat starts to sink under the weight of the sand. Their burdensome cargo reaching its limit, they row back to shore where the sand traders who run the operation collect the yellow-brown sludge and bring it to market. And, in a city changing as fast as Lagos on the back of a massive construction boom requiring 40 million cubic metres of sand a year, there is *always* a market. Kemi wasn't exactly passionate about the sand trade, but she was a business-woman before anything else. She liked the thrill of the hustle, the cat-and-mouse game of haggling. When she started trading in basic goods like soap and pasta under her mother's tutelage, shortly after leaving school, she knew she'd be good at it. While the miners dived for sand out on the lagoon, she boiled herself some tea over a charcoal fire and fished some plain white bread and margarine from a plastic bag.

Not long after that, the gunfire started. It didn't take Kemi long to figure out the reason: the Overlord of Ajah, Fatai Olumegbon, and the Baale of Ajah, Amida Kareem, had been waging war in the streets over who owned this up-and-coming territory for the past two years. But this wasn't the usual light scuffle: the *pop-pop-pop* of shotguns was relentless, and it went on for several hours. She could hear the shouting and commo-tion, the sounds of women screaming and bullets ricocheting. There was the faint smell of burning from houses that had been set on fire. Some of the Ajah Boys, the gang controlled by the Baale, were shouting, 'Olumegbon is a thief!' That worried her. Centuries ago, Kemi's Abereoje clan had aligned themselves with the Olumegbon family in their land dispute with the two power-ful Ajah chieftaincy families that produced the Baale of Ajah. Kemi's family head, Muka Abereoje, was a cousin of Fatai, the current Overlord of Ajah. Her whole family was therefore a tar-get of the Ajah Boys, who controlled the area towards the lagoon where she lived, yet as a long-time Ajah resident she was equally a target of the Overlord's gang, because they were clearing whole

Ajah neighbourhoods on his behalf so they could be demolished and sold to developers.

The gunfire was all coming from the direction of her house, which meant she was trapped. At least she had no dependants to worry about. Funmilola, her only child—apart from the boy that polio had claimed in his infancy—had been taken away from her by her husband when they divorced many years ago. But she worried about her mother trapped at home with no phone to call her on. Unsure what to do, Kemi closed her eyes and prayed to Allah. While she was praying, Osun, the goddess who so often haunted Kemi's dreams, came to her mind. So she prayed to Osun to make the threat pass: to bring a powerful gust of wind or to flood the lagoon and sweep all these rough boys away. Then she phoned her cousin Ahmed.

'We can get on a boat to take us to Ijebu,' he said. 'We'll be safe there.' He arrived at the shore looking almost as panicked as she was, and they hugged briefly. After what seemed like an hour, with the gun battle still raging, a medium-sized ferry arrived crammed full of refugees. By now, dozens more had gathered on the shore to try to squeeze on the boat. Forming an orderly queue is not something that happens in Lagos even in tranquil times: everyone pushed and shoved, shouting and arguing. Kemi didn't even recognise half of them: they must have come from more distant parts of Ajah. Eventually, she and Ahmed made it onto the boat.

As it pulled away, with the lagoon waters gently lapping against the hull, the water goddess Osun returned to Kemi's mind again. Osun's seat was in the sacred grove of Osogbo, two hundred kilometres northeast of Lagos. There was a giant clay statue in homage to her there, featuring the goddess's small breasts and outstretched arms like Christ on the cross, but she was also present in all fresh water and in the lagoon where her waters ended up. The image Kemi had of her was so clear now:

the goddess in pink and white, smiling gently. That was when she knew that, whatever happened, Osun would decide whether she lived or died. Osun would protect her—or perhaps kill her—but, either way, her life would be dictated by her whims. As soon as this latest Ajah battle blew over, she would visit her shrine and make a sacrifice. Then she would devote herself to the goddess.

* * *

Kemi Wahab nearly wasn't born. Her parents, Wahab and Moriliatu, had been trying to conceive for years without success. Kemi's mother, Moriliatu, had lived in Ajah all her life. She was from the Abereoje clan, the powerful local Ajah family that was allied to the Olumegbon family in their dispute with the co-ruling Ajah chieftaincies. Moriliatu, like other members of the clan, was related by blood to both sides. The Ojupon noble favoured to be the next Baale of Ajah was her nephew, although, like most residents of this marginal fishing village, Moriliatu had grown up poor. She never went to school and from her early teens had scraped by in the Ajah market selling meals of cooked rice—a staple she never herself ate, except at festivals, because rice was habitually eaten only by those of higher social status.

She'd met Kemi's father, Wahab, in the late 1950s, just as the British colonisers were preparing to leave Nigeria. He was a fisherman from a respectable Ajah family, the sort the Abereoje clan could do business with. They swiftly had a son, Jamil, but after that she'd suffered inexplicable barrenness (traditionally always the woman's 'fault' in West Africa, until proven otherwise). She prayed hard in the mosque, although she refused to consult the Ifa oracle to seek answers from Orunmila, the Yoruba god of knowledge, wisdom and prophecy. She was a pure Muslim who always chose the mosque over the shrine. Then one day, about a week after she had prayed long hours at Ajah's Kajola Mosque—a modest, domeless building with a rusty tin roof and peeling mint-green paint—she missed her period. It had been nearly a decade since she'd started trying to get pregnant. When Kemi was born, the whole village was so stunned at her mother's miraculous second wind of fertility that the elders gave the new daughter the Yoruba name 'Oluwatoyin' at her naming ceremony. It meant 'God is worthy to be praised'.

But Moriliatu's elation at her new issue didn't last long. When Kemi was less than two months old, Wahab died suddenly. Moriliatu was heartbroken and angry, but she resisted the temptation to blame his death on the black magic of some mischievous neighbour or other. 'It was his time, as Allah willed it,' was all she had to say on the matter. This admirable stoicism was hardly going to help her bring up two kids. Wahab had been her second husband, and she had no desire to marry again. Her work selling street food would hardly pay the bills, so she took up the lucrative trade in a commodity that was ready money to many in Ajah: sand. And so began a business that would bring her and her daughter more wealth and prestige than many poor slum dwellers could have hoped for. Moriliatu was reasonably well connected, and she swiftly managed to establish herself as a tough sand trader. It paid for both Jamil and Kemi to complete school.

After graduating from school, aged 19, Kemi enrolled in a fashion school with the dream of becoming a dressmaker, but, as so often happens in Lagos's more deprived neighbourhoods, pregnancy curtailed her dreams. The father was a local welder a few years older than Kemi called Musibah, one of the ones you often see by the roadside staring intently at sheets of metal as white sparks fly up at their eyes, which are protected only by cheap sunglasses. After a hasty marriage, Kemi gave birth to her first daughter, Funmilola, meaning 'give me wealth'. While she brought Kemi more joy than anything she could have imagined, the man who helped beget her did the opposite. He was one of those husbands who are controlling in a way she found utterly stifling. He always jealously questioned where she was going and complained about her work down at the market selling basic goods, even though he knew they couldn't live off his meagre earnings as a welder. They argued constantly. She got an opportunity to work as a flower gardener at the Chevron compound— the largest complex to have been built on the ruins of Maroko— and he refused to allow it, because he didn't trust her not to meet another man there. Then, within a year of being born, their second child, Soni, died of polio. Musibah, after a blistering row with Kemi, had sneaked Soni onto his family farm, where he'd contracted the virus. Utterly heartbroken, Kemi travelled to their farm for a last glimpse of her son before he was buried. When she got there, Musibah's family refused to allow her to even see his body. Never again would she experience the pain she felt on that day. The same year, Musibah left her, taking their daughter, Funmilola, with him. So, family life for Kemi ended almost as soon as it had begun, and her experience with Musibah would colour her perception of men for some time.

*　*　*

After that particularly vicious gun battle in Ajah, Kemi and Ahmed spent three days at Ijebu. She was worried to the point of nausea about her mother, after hearing no news, but there was little she could do to contact her. When they finally returned, to find Moriliatu at home and in good health, Kemi did as she promised: she went to offer a sacrifice to Osun. She passed the usual Ajah scenes of domesticity and sleepy commerce: wiry youths pushing wheelbarrows full of outsized tubers to the market, phone credit stalls, women tossing dirty washing water out of their front porches onto sandy streets. The Osun shrine was on the shores of the lagoon, not far from where the river bearing her name empties into it. Moriliatu didn't exactly approve, purist

Muslim that she was, but neither did she object: Osun was a deity that had been in the Abereoje family for generations. On the way, Kemi bought the appropriate sacrifices for the goddess: a jar of honey—Osun loves honey more than anything else—mangoes, oranges and other light-coloured local fruits, two bottles of beer, a single hen as a blood offering, coconuts, and some cheap boiled sweets.

Osun wasn't an obvious choice of deity to turn to over a land war, but Kemi couldn't help but feel that a dose of femininity was what was needed. Men in Lagos were always so covetous and aggressive, shouting and arguing, posturing. Osun represented the opposite qualities: the power of feminine persuasion. According to one legend, Osun had protected the Yoruba town of Osogbo—where the sacred grove devoted to her has since become one of Nigeria's main tourist destinations—from the jihad of Usman dan Fodio. Osogbo was one of the very few Yoruba towns that were never captured by Usman's Fulani warriors. The story goes that when they swept down into southwest Nigeria in the mid-1800s, Osun appeared in the form of a camp follower, and presented the hungry jihadists with a spicy dish of cooked vegetables. The scorching, fibrous meal acted as a strong laxative, loosening their bowels so that it was impossible for them to storm Osogbo without soiling themselves. In their embarrassingly unfit state, the Fulanis were defeated by the Yoruba armies sweeping up north from Ibadan. That was the feminine touch: women could win wars with cooking. Kemi gathered her sacrifices in a plastic bag and lifted up the hen by its legs as she disembarked from the ferry.

There was another reason she'd decided to turn to Osun. Kemi's elder brother, Jamil, was a high priest and custodian of the cult of Oro, the most important deity in their Ajah neighbourhood. For most of the past year, he'd been praying to Oro to end the conflict in Ajah. He would leave the compound in his elegant white priestly robes to visit the shrine—just an unassuming patch of land accessed by a hole in the wall of a building that had never been finished—carrying offerings of kola nut, bitter kola and a live chicken to slaughter on site, along with some schnapps and a handful of alligator pepper. She never saw him: women were forbidden to ever lay eyes on the Oro priests. Oro is the Yoruba deity of justice and punishment, bringing peace and harmony to the community by ensuring that no transgression goes unpunished or at least uncompensated; just like the Zangbeto, those twirling haystacks of the Voodoo religion. Oro, the 'bullroarer', whose name means ferociousness, rage, storm or provocation, was power personified. He was celebrated every four years at a festival in Ajah, the last one having been held a few months previously. Oro strutted through town in white robes and a wooden mask holding a wand that made a dreaded whirring noise. At the feast in his honour, they sacrificed a white ram, spraying his blood across the sand. In olden times, Oro would visit the houses of those who had committed offences and mete out justice, the masked figures who represented him often handling any executions themselves on the nights of their appearance. Though they could no longer kill at will, the fear they instilled remained strong, and Kemi would always be relieved at the drop in robberies for a few weeks after the procession had passed through town.

No woman must ever see Oro. Kemi was forbidden to venture out when the masked figure was walking the streets. On the night he came out for the festival, only initiates of the cult—all men, of course—and other males who were from the area were permitted to move freely. Any woman who ever laid eyes on Oro could be killed there and then. This had happened to a Hausa woman who was murdered by a mob in the town of Sagamu, just outside Lagos, in 1999. Nigeria had thousands of cults, processions and festivals, but none had ever managed to be quite so uncompromisingly sexist as Oro. Kemi didn't mind the old boys' networks associated with the cult, and the unfair advantages they conferred on men, but her experience with Musibah had given her a taste of how powerless women could be in Nigerian society. That was one of the things that had made her, gradually, inexorably, gravitate towards Osun. Here was a power the sisterhood could claim as their own.

* * *

Bar Beach, Victoria Island, 2009

Three years later, Kemi was at a ceremony to Olokun, the goddess of the deep sea, on Bar Beach, just off Victoria Island's Ahmadu Bello Way. Her devotees, including Kemi, were all dressed in robes of white to symbolise ritual purity. There must have been twenty of the women, including her cousin Ahmed's wife, Bose. Everyone was shrouded in loose cloth that gleamed in the violent sun. Only the five elders, all men, could wear coloured cloth for the ritual. They included Dialu, their community's spiritual leader, and Kemi's family head, Chief Muka. Two of the elders carried instruments, a talking drum and a goje—the traditional two-string fiddle with a lizard-skin body. They were covered in spots of white pigment from head to toe.

Before it was fenced off for the construction of the Eko Atlantic city, Bar Beach was probably the most popular seaside spot in Lagos. It was a riot of stalls under parasols selling beer and ice creams beyond a thick wall of dolosse—reinforced concrete blocks shaped like anvils to prevent the shore from being swallowed up by rising sea levels. The beach was littered with stinky wet garbage. It was also a favourite among the pious, a place where church congregations in white garments beat drums and said outlandish prayers. Earlier, in the military era, Bar Beach had been a site of public executions by firing squad.

KEMI

The worshippers stood on a spit of sand facing the Atlantic Ocean. Waves crashed and churned. They called out to Olokun, using the regular prayer, 'Olokun, the orisha that lives in water, she spreads herself across Earth, she uses her power to sweep you off your feet, we beg you, do not make us fall. The ocean is the most powerful of all waters. Help us achieve our desires. Olokun, Queen of Water, fill our houses with riches as you have those from distant shores.'

'She is ready for the sacrifice,' said the priestess, in front of the waters lapping the shore. The worshippers brought out a female white fowl, black-eyed bean cakes—called akara—and kola nuts. Kemi removed the knife from her pouch and handed it to the priestess. A rip of blood spattered the sand. They placed the dead fowl and the other offerings at the shore's edge. And then they waited. As the priestess had foretold, a large wave then washed up onto the shore, scattering the party as its faithful hitched up their robes to avoid getting soaked. 'Olokun has accepted our prayer,' Dialu, the Ajah elder and one of the few men at the ceremony, said, after the sacrifice had been washed back into the Atlantic.

After the ceremony, Dialu beckoned Kemi over. She had been devoting herself to the goddess Osun with regular sacrifices and rites for three years, since vowing to take her into her heart, and the elders said the goddess was well pleased with her fidelity. Dialu said, 'Next week, the elders will consult the oracle to choose the new priestess to Osun. Your name is among those that have been put forward.'

A week later, the fetish priest put the question to Osun with a kola nut, divided into its four segments, which they threw onto the ground before interpreting the answer. 'The oracle has chosen you. Now pray to Osun for the whole of Ajah, pray for everybody. Pray for peace, most of all,' the priest said outside the shrine. Utterly stunned, Kemi bowed her head in prayer. At the ceremony for her investiture, the other women curtsied to her.

Her goddess was the one that brought fertility, after all, so it was well worth having her earthly representatives onside. Kemi wore robes as white as the dry season's clouds and a long chunky necklace of blood-orange coral, chains and cowrie shells.

Soon couples with fertility problems were knocking on Kemi's door, asking for prayers to Osun. She prepared concoctions for fertility in Osun's blessed name: chalky-white Miss Paris perfume ground up into powder and sprinkled in a glass of water, mixed with bitter leaves and herbs. She would chant magic incantations over the mixture. 'Osun, the goddess of the river, the queen of the river, the provider, the lady most high who can give life,' she sang. 'We beseech you to bring a child to this man and his dear lady.' She began convening a weekly service of worship of Osun at the shrine, every Thursday. Sometimes she would go into a trance and speak in strange tongues.

'So things are going well for you,' her mother, Moriliatu, said one evening, while they were eating eba, a thick ball of cassava dough, with efo riro, a rich spinach stew with locust beans, crayfish, smoked fish, scotch bonnet peppers and cow stomach. 'I hope you haven't forgotten your duties to God, to Allah,' she added later, while she was sweeping out the unpaved floor of her house with a hard-bristle brush.

Moriliatu had a point: it had been a while since Kemi had been to the mosque, although she still tried to pray five times a day. But in truth, all her energies were now devoted to the goddess, and though Osun could be kind and compassionate and generous, she had one hell of a temper if you failed to appease her correctly. She continued to beg Osun to bring peace to Ajah, hoping that the feminine touch would rub off on her troubled hometown. Meanwhile, women and men from all over continued to come to her, seeking to harness Osun's powers, and Kemi became renowned as a great sorceress.

Then one morning Kemi woke up feeling feverish and weak. She cancelled her planned visit to Osun's shrine and lay in bed.

KEMI

The sickness seemed to come in waves, which made her think it was malaria. By the second day, it was clear it was something far worse. Her body was heavy as lead and her bones ached as if they'd been shattered. Her bed was drenched in sweat.

When the illness seemed to be subsiding, she went to the witchdoctor, Shino, to find out what was wrong. 'God, the supreme being, no longer wants you to worship at the shrine or consult the oracle,' he said, after casting the kola nut pieces into the chalky-white powder. 'The spirit is telling you to concentrate on being a Muslim. You can't practise here anymore.' Her mother was right: she'd been neglecting her Islamic faith. She said her last prayer to Osun and resolved to abandon being a priestess. 'You can tell my followers it's finished,' she told the elder, Dialu.

She went back to bed, depressed at her necessary decision to abandon Osun, after years of devotion. Her mother brought her some tea and herbs, and paracetamol, and for a while she felt better. But the next day, the pain was so indescribable she could barely move. Moriliatu considered consulting a doctor, but it seemed to her daughter that this was a spiritual matter. The outcome would be decided in a realm far beyond this one—that was what the oracle had told the witchdoctor. They called the elders, and Dialu said he would consult the imam at the mosque and the other elders who knew the Koran. Every night the elders prayed to Allah, pleading with Him to spare the former priestess's life. On the fourth day, she was delirious with fever, barely able to get up and go to the toilet, and there was no place on her body without pain. She asked her mother to contact her daughter, Funmilola, in case these crushing breaths turned out to be her last. Moriliatu nodded. 'Keep fighting,' was all she said, but Kemi's illness only got worse.

* * *

Death stalked Kemi in her bed, hovering like a shadow. After seven days of sickness, weak with body aches, drenched in sweat and feverish to the point of hallucination, she pressed her head against her pillow and begged God to revive her or just let her die. Somewhere in the room, her mother was weeping. Moriliatu had called Kemi's ex-husband to try to track down Funmilola, and she'd arrived too. Kemi had missed her a lot, and it gave her courage seeing her there, mopping her mother's scorching brow. In too much pain to even groan, she said her final prayers to Allah silently.

Then she waited to die.

20

SHIFTING SANDS

Maroko, 1990

When Moriliatu had first started selling sand in the 1980s, she moved herself and her daughter to Maroko, a riotous slum of fishermen, sand traders, street hawkers, hustlers, hookers, artisans and con men. In Maroko, opportunities for a fast buck were many times those in the sleepy village she'd grown up in. It was right next to the millionaires' financial district of Victoria Island, and a short hop by boat to Lagos Island. The people here were poor, but there was a dynamism that excited Moriliatu, a sense of possibility. The then president, Ibrahim Babangida, once described it as a 'mini-Nigeria'—just before he had it demolished—because it drew in every one of Nigeria's hundreds of ethnic groups: a third of a million people crammed into 150 streets. As in much of Lagos, most were inventing marginal forms of employment to get by, but a lot of those people had managed to position themselves doing odd jobs for the wealthy in Victoria Island. It was a bit like standing ten feet from someone having a shower in the hope of catching a few drops on your own skin.

Some residents had skills the rich needed, of course: mechanics and plumbers and carpenters and stonemasons. Others did things like shine their shoes or even wash their feet. Both Kemi and her mother would nonetheless later remember it as being one of the happiest places they'd ever lived in. Moriliatu raised Kemi to be a tough trader and a devout Muslim—which in southern Nigeria doesn't exclude drinking the odd bottle of Guinness. She also advised her to avoid foolish quarrels between the menfolk, regardless of the cause. Let their big male egos fight it out between themselves. When the rumours started that the military government was going to destroy Maroko, Moriliatu didn't wait for the soldiers to move in: she just packed up what they could carry and put them and her teenage daughter on a boat back to Ajah. So, after more than a decade amid the bustle, fumes and dirt of Lagos's most vivacious slum, they returned to their ancestral land with the money they'd saved. As the ferry pulled in from crossing the lagoon—much quicker and with less hassle than trying to navigate the clogged-up roads—Moriliatu realised how much she'd missed it. Ajah was so much quieter than frenetic, diesel-choked Maroko; it still had the rhythms of peaceful village life. Kemi continued going to the government school in Maroko, from where she successfully graduated.

In July 1990 the bulldozers arrived to level the 'mini-Nigeria' that she and her daughter had grown to love. Many of the 300,000 evicted fled to Ajah, swelling its already booming population. When Kemi returned a week later, in place of the house where they had lived and the school she'd attended lay piles of cinder blocks and wooden planks, festering in Maroko's ubiquitous mud. She salvaged their iron roofing so that her mother could use it for the new house they'd almost finished building in Ajah. She paused for a moment to cast her eyes over the wreckage: some powerful people were going to make a lot of money when this place was sand-filled and rebuilt. Whoever came to live here next, she knew it wouldn't be the same people who'd been turfed out to make way for the developments. It would be the well-heeled in their Toyota Land Cruisers paying top dollar for the prime location next to Victoria Island. She hopped on the ferry home.

Although Kemi had no idea at the time, the destruction of Maroko to make way for luxury housing was the start of a building spree that would transform the entire Lekki Peninsula all the way up to Ajah and beyond. In doing so, it would heat up a contest for land that would break out into street battles, like the one that sent her fleeing by boat to Ijebu in 2006. But it would also bring a boom for the one commodity that Kemi's family could get their hands on in abundance: sand.

Ajah, Lekki Peninsula, 2012

Kemi survived her mystery illness, by the grace of a God she later decided she'd been neglecting. But it took a lot out of her: for almost a year, she could barely leave her house, so weak she was. She never visited a doctor, never found out what it was that had made her so ill. But on some level she knew it was something to do with the dark arts she'd been practising, and the conclusion was evident: she must stop all this fetish stuff. All that dancing and calling up the spirit of Osun and the other deities had distracted her from her true Muslim faith. At least that was how she later interpreted the sickness. She'd never felt any contradiction between her Muslim and traditional West African faiths before. In her Ajah community, both were seen as important and respected. Yet after that week of pain and fever, and the weakness she felt after, she was surer than ever that she needed to choose the God of the Koran over anything. Moriliatu said nothing, but she was secretly relieved that her daughter had chosen the pure Muslim path.

As the second decade of the twenty-first century wore on, Kemi's material preoccupations were growing at least as important as her spiritual ones. The sand trade was exploding, and so was the competition for this precious commodity all around the lagoon. As we have seen, Lagos had been undergoing a phenomenal construction spree on top of swamps filled in with sand. Builders had been literally conjuring land out of water. As with the elite in so much of Africa, the model that Lagos's leaders sought to emulate most was Dubai. Never mind that the Emirate's gargantuan growth had been fuelled by virtual slave labour, that it was so energy-intensive that it managed to consume seven times as much electricity as the entire country of Nigeria produced, or that underneath those garish skyscrapers lay a totalitarian state. Nigerian elites came back from their luxury shopping trips to Dubai's gilded malls and kitsch faux-baroque hotel lobbies dreaming of doing the same in Lagos. And nothing set them dreaming quite like Dubai's ostentatious Palm Islands, where billions of cubic feet of sand had been poured into the sea to complete one of the world's most impressive engineering feats.

Building on the soggy marshes around the Lagos lagoon also required filling them in with colossal quantities of the yellow stuff. Sand-filling machines were everywhere along the Lekki Peninsula, turning soggy marshes into the foundations of buildings. Great big pumps with vast, ugly pipes running off them were feeding gallons of sandy sludge into the sea and the lagoon between which Ajah was sandwiched. And on that new land, luxury waterside housing was popping up—the Eko Atlantic city, Lagos's own answer to the Palm Islands, being the most ostentatious example. To Ajah's long-established peoples, many of whom traditionally dealt with Lagos's waterlogged spaces by building huts on stilts, it all looked somewhat bizarre: huge, incomprehensible hunks of metal pumping sand back into the very lagoon from which it had been mined, building cities on land where once there was water.

* * *

Kemi's Abereoje clan controlled an area down by the lagoon from where the miners launched their boats, an area in which, mercifully, there was no conflict with the Baale's people. They were able to share the sand-dredging sites amicably. There was a reason for this unspoken truce: both were in competition with a clan of Yoruba-speaking settlers called the Ilaje, who had first come as fishermen and had then swiftly been wooed by the far bigger sums of money in the sand trade. The Ilaje were originally from the Yoruba hinterlands, but many had settled in Maroko, before the military government demolished it. Like many Maroko residents, after fleeing the onslaught, they'd arrived en masse in Ajah. The Ilaje had a couple of boats mining sand in the lagoon. It was a small stretch of swampy slum, and their mining operation was modest. Still, both sides in the Ajah conflict—those allied to the Baale of Ajah, Chief Murisiku Ojupon, and those allied to the Overlord, Fatai Olumegbon, like Kemi's family—regarded the Ilaje with suspicion and shared an interest in keeping them contained.

Kemi's business was flourishing more than ever. She was sending out several crews at a time into the middle of the lagoon to pull out sand by the boatload. She was pilling it up into dunes and sending it on weather-beaten old trucks to various construction sites all over Lagos. She was often doing six boatloads of sand a day or about sixty tonnes of the yellow stuff, enough to pull in 12,000 naira in profit in a single day, more than she'd ever managed before. The money was enough to buy her a lunch of gbegiri, a bean soup flavoured with spinach and dried fish with amala, gritty yam-flour dough balls, or spicy tomato 'native stew' with chunks of cow stomach and palm fruit, cooked in the deepest, reddest palm oil, pretty much whenever she wanted. She could afford nice sequined fabrics or even the occasional imitation Dutch wax or African prints from which to make clothes for herself instead of just for her better-off customers. Her daughter's school fees no longer required begging from more affluent branches of the Abereoje family. And her main source of pride: she'd bought a plot of land and built a house out of cement and cinder block. She felt safer, happier and richer than she'd ever been.

* * *

On one sweltering late afternoon in early November 2012, she was dealing with her last boat. The miners she had hired to dive for the sand docked the boat at the lagoon edge and wiped away some of the sand caked on their faces from multiple dives to the bottom. Then they began using shovels to transfer it onto a pile on the shore, their wiry, mud-flecked biceps glistening in the cloud-white Lagos light. After they'd finished, a separate group of loaders started shovelling the sand onto the truck that would take it away. She paid the loaders and her sand miners their share—in total, a little under half of the total that the consignment of sand would make. She put aside another third to give to the boat's owner, who in true capitalist spirit got the biggest cut just by possessing the vehicle in which the sand was transported. She also completed the sale to the truck driver, who paid her 20,000 naira—a good haul.

The truck driver made it as far as the first turning when he was stopped by a gang of young men in the traditional Yoruba 'up-down' dress of kaftans and matching loose trousers. This looked ominous: could it be some of the Ajah Boys returning to stir up trouble against the Overlord? Surely they wouldn't target the sand trucks. There was supposed to be a truce. One of the youths said to the truck driver, 'This is our territory, and you must pay us our dues if you want to leave here.' The driver immediately started shouting at them, but they stood firm. Only then did Kemi recognise who they were: it was the Ilaje.

'What is this? We've already paid our taxes,' exclaimed the driver, using that favourite quaint euphemism for extortion. 'You boys move along,' he said, before resignedly agreeing to the 500-naira fee.

'Tell all the other truck drivers, from now on, they will pay for passing through our territory,' the leader said. 'This road belongs to the Ilaje.'

That evening, at a council of elders, Chief Muka Abereoje was furious. Muka's house was unremarkable for a man of his stature, made of cheap cinder block like the neighbourhood's other shacks. One of the few things to mark out his higher status was his old Toyota saloon car. Muka poured himself a shot of bitter spirit, packed with herbs, from the local witchdoctor. It was in a reused litre spirit bottle, stuffed full of roots, which had marinated to make the liquid the colour of dirt. He swore it did wonders for his back pain, although whether because of the herbs or just the sheer quantity of undistilled booze in it was never clear. He always winced ever so slightly when he downed a glass. It seemed to do nothing to calm his nerves.

These Ilaje people were his tenants, living in Ajah only by the grace of his goodwill, he thundered. How dare they try to extort truck drivers passing through with their sand deliveries? That was for the rightful owners of the public road—the Abereoje family—to do. Kemi prayed Muka wasn't going to launch straight into a street battle: the last thing Ajah needed was more violence. But after much deliberation, he said, 'We shall try to talk to them. If their boys are collecting tolls, they must give us our share.'

The following week, as the Ilaje were lining their pockets from every sand truck that drove out and even those that brought sand in for filling the lagoon, some elders, led by Muka and guarded by wiry members of the Ajah Boys, on loan from the Baale himself, approached the Ilaje roadblock to negotiate. The Ilaje moved all their muscle into the dirt road, and there was an almost visceral tension rising in the air. Unsmiling, Muka presented his proposal: the Ilaje could continue to collect these tolls, but they must surrender half to the Abereojes, who would in turn pay a portion in tribute to the Overlord and to the Baale of Ajah. At this, the Ilaje chief, Oluwale Adejuni, delivered a long, rambling speech in which he ran through the Ilaje's history as settlers in Ajah, which he dated to long before the recent expulsions from Maroko. Their people had been plying these shores for fish and settling here from upcountry for generations, rowing from the creeks and jungle streams of Ondo State to set up fishing camps all around the lagoon. They claimed five generations of heritage in Ajah, almost as much as the first settlers. They pointed out that land was becoming more expensive, as the construction boom swept eastwards from Lekki Phase 1, so they couldn't give up their rightful land just like that. Everyone could see Ajah land was hot property—the dreadful Lagos traffic, which had always spared this neighbourhood, had at last arrived. At that point, Kemi realised the Ilaje had much bigger designs on Ajah than merely taxing a few sand trucks: they wanted to stake their claim to the land on the outer fringes of Ajah, so they could cash in on the next phase of the boom that would surely transform this scruffy swamp into neatly laid-out waterside housing. Chief Muka shook his head, before indicating to the other elders to turn round and head home. Kemi shuddered. As if the conflict between the Overlord and the Baale weren't enough, her family was now embroiled in a whole new scuffle over turf with the Ilaje.

Although she wasn't to know, Muka wasn't exactly a wholly innocent party: he had his eyes on some of the Ilaje settlements around the lagoon, which he planned to seize as his own; in his mind, it was his ancestral land so he had the right to do so. He'd also ordered the demolition of some Ilaje huts that the Abereoje clan claimed as property, to ready the land for the splendid condos that were bound to sweep across this stretch of the lagoon shore as the money flooded in. During one heated exchange between the Ilaje and some of the sand traders allied to Kemi's family, the Ilaje chief pulled out signed title deeds which he claimed showed that the Ilaje had bought the land from Muka's late father. The alleged title included all of the area along the road on which they'd started collecting tolls, and much of the area Muka was planning to sell to developers. Muka had always maintained the land was only ever leased to the Ilaje, all of whom had for decades been his clan's ancestral tenants. That was always the problem in Lagos: someone could always pull out a piece of paper to show he owned a bit of land, but how to tell if it was genuine or not? There were so many undetectable forgeries, so many rival claims.

As prices shot up, land ownership in the Lekki corridor, and across Lagos, had never been more contentious. Apart from the lofty megacity vision of the town planners, billions of dollars of stolen oil money was sloshing through newly built houses and apartments, the perfect onshore washing machines for loot. People would buy a house or flat—on the exclusive Banana Island, which had Africa's most expensive property anywhere, if they had managed to steal a lot, or Lekki if they'd stolen a more modest amount—and, hey presto, dubious suitcases of cash were converted into a clean, sellable asset. No one knew how much it was pushing up prices, but the knock-on effect had clearly contributed to some Ajah plots now going for 180 million naira, an absurd amount for people in this poor neighbourhood.

By late November, Muka was starting to lose patience. He wrote to the Ilaje chief to tell him he had applied to the council to rename the main street where the Ilaje had settled 'Odugbese Abereoje', after his late father. He repeated his demand for a share of the money from the sand trucks coming in and out of the area by the shores of the lagoon, and reminded him they were his tenants, occupying Ajah at his pleasure. The Ilaje chief appealed to the Baale of Ajah, Chief Ojupon. Ojupon was normally not a great friend of Muka's, but Muka figured that Ojupon had as much of an interest in resolving this as he did. Ojupon suggested they take up Muka's offer of a compromise on the sand tolls: the Ilaje would collect tolls on some days, and the Abereoje family could collect them on others. The Ilaje refused: as far as they were concerned, this was *their* land.

* * *

By late November, even Chief Ojupon was realising that doing deals with the Ilaje was going nowhere. He had gone down to their roadblock, only to be stoned by a gang of angry youths. The Ilaje had their claim on the Ajah waterfront, and they wanted to hold on to it until the big developers arrived with their millions. So, on 26 November, a large contingent of a few dozen Ajah Boys, by now allied to their erstwhile enemy, Muka Abereoje, gathered to apply the only alternative that was left: force. On that day, Kemi had woken up, as usual, at five and was at work an hour later. She broke for tea and bread at seven. By ten, she'd sold a twenty-tonne truckload of sand.

Shortly after her sale, the Ajah Boys arrived at the Ilaje road-blocks, where they warned them to stop collecting the tolls and leave that to the Ajah 'indigenes'—themselves. Kemi was too far away to witness anything of the scuffle, but what she missed was the classic Lagos street fight: the Ajah Boys pulled out their guns, combat knives and some broken bottles. Some were carrying jerrycans of petrol. The Ilaje, meanwhile, were threatening their enemies with magic charms, including a koboko whip,

made from animal skins. It was believed an incantation pronounced on it turned it into a lethal weapon. While rubbing it
with the sacred ogbo leaf, you had to say, 'You are as tall as a tree
and white as a cloud,' and when you used it, the whip would
cause its victim's heart to stop or his tongue to fall out. Kemi
realised, at around one when there were no more sand trucks
coming in, that something must be wrong.

At a hand signal from the leader, the Ajah Boys sprang their
attack, firing shots into the air and lunging wildly at the Ilaje
gang, who scattered into the streets towards the lagoon, gunshots following them. They returned fire, and a gun battle
ensued. Kemi ducked underneath the dump truck onto which
her sand was being loaded. She still couldn't see anything. The
Ajah Boys started going from house to house, including all the
ones that had been marked by Muka for demolition, and told the
Ilaje they must leave. They began sloshing petrol on some
houses, which whooshed into flames as the attackers flicked
matches onto them. Smoke coiled above the Ajah skyline. Ilaje
women and children fled along the sand roads with as many
belongings as they could carry. They looked like refugees fleeing
a war zone. Two Ilaje youths died in that battle, and several were
wounded on both sides. The Ajah Boys rampaged through the
contested street, demolishing houses, looting shops and destroy-
ing an electrical transformer (which would have plunged the
whole community into darkness if the power company were actually providing them with any electricity). After hours of gunfire,
the police showed up, and both gangs of youths melted into the
side streets. As Kemi headed up the road towards her house, two
Ilaje youths stopped her in the street.

'You have killed some of us, and now you will die,' one said,
holding up a knife.

'Please, I'm just a sand seller. I'm unarmed,' she said, before
the flashing lights of the police rounded the corner in a pick-up

truck, and the Ilaje fighters dissolved into the distance. In what seemed like the blink of an eye, the neighbourhood was empty. She stole back to her house, where her mother was lying outstretched on the couch. The following day, police arrested Muka, Chief Ojupon and several Ajah Boys, denying them bail and remanding them in Ikoyi prison. In court, they were accused of negligence as community leaders, of inciting violence, and of failing to control their mobs. A judge gave them three months in prison for instigating violence.

Loyal to her family, Kemi was convinced it was the Ilaje's fault, for their obstinate refusal to be reasonable about the sand tolls. But she also rolled her eyes at the renewed violence once again perpetrated by her menfolk. Why did Lagosians always have to fight over land? Did this happen in other countries? It was infuriating. She thought briefly about returning to Osun, the deity she had always felt closest to before her dreadful illness. Would Osun protect her? That illness had brought her closer to death than she'd ever been in the presence of a gun or a knife. She meandered through Ajah's scruffy streets the day after the fighting, avoiding the Ilaje street that had become a war zone. She thought about what she could do and realised that, as always, she was powerless. It was always the men talking at the council meetings: no woman could contribute anything. She plodded down towards the mosque, where she prayed once more for peace in her community.

* * *

Ajah, Lekki Peninsula, 2016

Kemi and I are at the stretch of lagoon shore that has been her place of work for nearly two decades. Today she has an important gathering: the Sand Traders Association are meeting to discuss the latest scourge, the gravest threat yet to their livelihood. Not the conflict between the Overlord and the Baale of Ajah over land. Not the conflict between Kemi's clan and the Ilaje over who controls the sand trucks coming in and out. No, something far worse: the machine sand dredgers.

These machines, some operated by Chinese and Lebanese businessmen, have been suctioning the sand directly out of the water, hoovering up huge quantities of the stuff, eroding the shoreline and, some say, worsening the inevitable flooding that blights Lagos every rainy season. Fishermen complain the sediment they have stirred up is killing fish. But there's an altogether more Luddite reason why the sand traders are up in arms about them: these machines are putting their muscle-powered sand-mining operations out of business. The machines operate on the edge of the lagoon, so in that sense there is no direct competition with the artisanal sand miners, who gather sand far away from the shore. But, as always when mechanisation competes with muscle power, the machine dredgers have flooded the market and depressed prices.

When Governor Babatunde Fashola took office in 2007, much of the machine dredging was made illegal—which in Lagos hardly stops anything, though it adds a lot of costs in terms of bribing the authorities, so it was severely curtailed. But the new governor who came to power after Fashola, Akinwunmi Ambode, lifted the restrictions on the machine dredgers. And they then let rip, flooding the market with cheaply mined sand. The commodity is now going for about 10,000 naira a tonne, half of what it was. And it's worse than it sounds, because the naira, too, is falling.

Kemi is attending the meeting as vice chairlady of the Sand Traders Association, Eti-Osa division, a huge area which covers Victoria Island and the Lekki Peninsula. It's the typical Lagos 'union' racket: she gets a cut from the earnings of other sand traders lower down the chain—they pay a registration fee equal to about five boatloads of sand before they even get started, and then another 200-naira loading fee per lorry that they fill up. But the association also does sometimes act like a proper union: standing up for the rights of sand traders, who now face an existential threat from their mechanised competitors.

They are meeting under a marquee a few hundred metres from the lagoon, with the obligatory rows of white plastic chairs. The skyline is a mess of man-made sand dunes, cranes, half-finished concrete buildings and wooden shacks close to being engulfed by the encroaching lagoon waters. Right there, in front of us, is one of these monstrous sand-dredging contraptions, sucking sand out of the water and depositing the yellow sludge onto the shore. The association says there are at least fifteen of them operating in Ajah alone.

'What those guys take out in a week, we couldn't even get that much sand in five years with these boats,' says Korede Shittu, vice chairman of the association, with typical Lagosian hyperbole. He has noticed a white man holding a notebook in the presence of their meeting and has figured, correctly, that this might be an opportunity to publicise their plight. Shittu has a round face, a broad build and a warm smile. He wears a dark-blue kaftan. 'Unlike us, who are obliged by the regulation to go far out into the lagoon, the dredgers are right onshore, and this causes a lot of problems,' he adds. These include erosion of the coastline, which, he says, is putting Ajah's structures at risk of collapse. He later shows me a road that looks metres away from being swallowed by the advancing lagoon. By all accounts—and this seems to be the case across Lagos—machine dredging has become a scourge: polluting borehole water, killing fish, shaking the foundations of buildings too close to the shore. Mindful of these issues, the Lagos State government told the machine dredgers to halt their operations in Ajah while they assess complaints about the impact. They don't appear to be paying attention. One by one, the sand traders take turns with the microphone, which has become a tool for airing their grievances.

'The government needs to stop all these dredgers,' shouts a particularly angry member of the association. 'We don't have anywhere else to go. This is our home, this is our land. The dredgers come from outside, they come from foreign countries, and they destroy all our property. Can we go to their country and do such? Look at the road: the condition is not good. That's the dredgers.'

But the dredgers are in a much stronger position. They pay taxes to the money-hungry Lagos State government or, failing that, bribes. They have the ships, they have the men, they have the money, too, as the jingle goes. For all the conflict over who controls this lucrative trade, the winners won't be the ones with the most thugs, the sharpest knives or the loudest pump-action shotguns. They will be the ones with finance capital and state-of-the-art sand-mining equipment. And very few, if any, will be from this rundown Ajah neighbourhood.

* * *

Back at Kemi's house, we are drinking tea. Moriliatu is lying flat on the couch, reflecting on all the turmoil Ajah has seen in the past decade. She'd got used to the quarrel between the Overlord and the Baale: it was a sort of natural outgrowth of tensions that had been simmering across generations for centuries. But the dispute with the Ilaje really took her back.

'No one was greedy about sand until this fight between the Ilaje and Ajah. It all started then,' she says of the skirmishes in 2012, which still haven't ended. 'Suddenly we went from sharing the sand to trying to grab as much as we could. It is as if the Devil himself was using the sand to pit people against each other.'

After a while, they seem to tire of talking about the sand trade. Kemi reflects on her illness, and her decision to abandon Osun, the water goddess for whom she felt such an affinity. 'I still just pray to Allah,' she says. 'That sickness that happened to me was not a small thing; I nearly died. I don't know if it was

Allah or the oracle or Osun, but they wanted me to stop being a priestess, and concentrate on the thing I do best, on business. We've done well out of sand,' she says as she sips her tea.

'I still believe in Osun. And I still think Osun did protect me from the violence in Ajah, even from sickness.' She pauses, then stares at the peeling paint on her wall. 'Someone protected me, because I'm still alive,' she says, and her eyes mist up slightly. 'I just keep thanking God that I'm alive.'

EPILOGUE

GODS OF HUSTLE

Just as the constant increase of entropy is the basic law of the universe, so it is the basic law of life to be ever more highly structured and to struggle against entropy.

Václav Havel, 'Open Letter to Dr Gustáv Husák, Communist President' (of Czechoslovakia), 8 April 1975

The African Mind has a lot to contribute, not only to world understanding of the arts but to an understanding of spiritualism. That is the contribution Africa will make to the world of the future—an injection of sanity into the environment.

Fela Kuti, in an interview with the *Washington Post*, 1986

Lagos

'You'll make it, in Jesus' name. In His name you will succeed,' cried the preacher, triggering a zealous chorus of amens. The preacher, 'Bishop' David Oyedepo—who with four private jets had definitely 'made it'—had just turned 60. And he'd decided to celebrate in the style to which he is accustomed. It was a rare opportunity for me to meet Africa's richest Pentecostal pastor. Oyedepo's minions had installed a marquee on the immaculate lawns of his church's 10,500-acre 'Canaanland' estate, an oasis of neat, trimmed lawn in the rusting north Lagos suburb of Ota. When he was young, David Oyedepo was a church janitor in a poor town in southwest Nigeria. When I went to visit him in 2014, he was worth $150 million, according to a 2011 estimate by *Forbes*. Apart from his jets, which include a Gulfstream V and a Lear, he had a lucrative network of thousands of churches in Nigeria and hundreds in some sixty other countries. He owned luxury properties all over the world. It was exactly the kind of dream for which so many Lagosians strive against ludicrous odds. And the richer he got, the more people wanted to give him. A Lagosian friend once explained the logic like this: clearly God has rewarded this man with riches I could scarcely dream of, so if I do what he tells me to do, I could similarly be in line for unimaginable divine blessings. And what he tells me to do is give ten per cent of my income to his church.

'We see tithe as a way of securing our investment, so that the Devil will not bring down all that we have laboured for,' Oyedepo told me during an interview in his hardwood-panelled office. 'It is written: bring all your tithe to the storehouse and your cup will be full.' Still, *ten per cent*, in a city where most people struggle to pay their rent? Yet I have many Lagosian friends who dutifully give their tithe every month, whether they can afford it or not. Isaak Abrak, a TV journalist with whom I worked on many occasions, explained, 'The Church tells you that if you don't pay ten per cent, it's a waste of money, you won't get blessed. God demands ten per cent. Sometimes I have gone to church on Sunday and my money is finished, but I still pay my tithe.'

For a while I became a little obsessed with these wildly popular Pentecostal churches and how they manage to extract so much hard-earned dough from so many millions of people. They seemed to embody a connection between success—that is, money and power—and the invisible spirit world that is key to why Lagos is the way it is. Eventually, I realised they were merely the loudest—and no doubt the greediest—manifestation of a deeply ingrained spirituality. Without this spirituality, Lagos simply couldn't function. Or rather, no one would be able to tolerate its dysfunction.

* * *

About six months after spending that weekend at David Oyedepo's church, I had a glimpse of what Lagos might look like after the apocalypse. Streets deserted, not a car on the road, the odd rag-picker sifting through trash blanketed on a side street, smoke from distant fires, birds scanning the stillness for peckable morsels. I'd never known the Third Mainland Bridge to be so empty, nor the air above it so clean. It was Lagos State governorship election day in 2015, and there was a lockdown on all movement except by voters on foot. I happened to be on my way to watch the city's *numero uno* political godfather, former governor Bola Tinubu, vote in the Lagos gubernatorial election (and, naturally, doorstep him for an interview). He was backing his handpicked successor's successor, a civil servant called Akinwunmi Ambode (whom he later fell out with and had removed).

Tinubu, and those whom he installed after him, like his star pupil Babatunde Fashola, really *have* tried to clean up Lagos. And not just by the wanton destruction of slums and displacement of people (although there's been plenty of that), but by bringing order, an order that for its main beneficiaries—the elites and diminutive middle class—has felt like that merciful gust of wind that sometimes eases Lagos's oppressive humidity. Tinubu may have achieved this in his signature thuggish, mafioso style, using street gangs against those who opposed him. He may have made himself even more fabulously wealthy along the way—by, for instance, legislating that his own consultancy collect tax on behalf of the Lagos State government, creaming off a cut of all taxes paid: what a stroke of genius!—but at least he actually got Lagosians paying their taxes for the first time. He may have helped himself to an immodest stake in the companies building roads, rail projects and fancy hotels that he, as a politician, commissioned. But at least he got them built. Lagos traffic might still be hell, but it's sure better than it might have been if nothing had been done about it. And the streets, while hardly something you'd want to eat your dinner off, are cleaner than they've been for half a century, Lagosians say. In this way, the Lagos State government, which Tinubu's party has ruled since the end of military dictatorship in 1999, stands virtually unique among the thirty-six states of Nigeria. Most of the others have very little to show for the billions in oil money that they've squandered over the years.

'I inherited a mess,' Tinubu told me, outside one of his many residences on that day. He was wearing a sky-blue kaftan, burgundy beret folded down on one side, and his trademark thin spectacles, under which his eyes dart around like horseflies. Still quite handsome in his sixties, with defined cheekbones and a neat triangle of a nose, he exuded that unshakable confidence that is the birthright of the Nigerian big man. 'I don't care what anybody says. Today, Lagos State has improved. I inherited, Bola Tinubu, 400 million naira a month internally generated revenue [from tax]. Today it's 20 billion. That is financial engineering and accountability,' he continued, before being mobbed by a crowd of street urchins seeking to get their hands on the bills of naira the Big Man is expected to hand out everywhere he goes.

Yet even with the best will in the world, trying to keep up with a metropolis undergoing such monstrous growth is a losing battle. Many more subsistence farmers worldwide will soon abandon their farms this century, as the climate crisis slowly chokes rural life. They will have one place to go: the city. In 2018, researchers in the University of Ontario Institute of Technology predicted that Lagos, based on its current birth, death and urbanisation rates, will have 100 million people by the end of the century (making it by then the world's biggest metropolis). Even for those of us who are used to this bleakly futuristic dystopia, that is a shocking thought. But the trend is unassailable: half the planet currently lives in cities; by mid-century it will be two-thirds. If you think the sheer magnitude of Lagos is overwhelming now, try it in eighty years' time. And as numbers swell, the spiritual upheaval will only become more acute. The story of any large city is the toil of every citizen to avoid being totally consumed by it, to maintain an identity, a relevance, a role; to not be simply absorbed into that seething, striving, warring multitude; to not end up as that unclaimed body on the roadside.

Nearly a decade ago, Governor Fashola's state planning commissioner—a job I do not envy in the least—told me he thought 4,000 migrants were arriving in Lagos each day, way more than is normally estimated. It sounded on the high side, but I've often thought, *what if he's right?* That's a city the size of Stockholm rocking up every year. When I asked him how Lagos authorities cope with such unimaginably fast population growth, the commissioner, Ben Akabueze (who later became director of the national budget office), was succinct. 'We're running just to stand still,' he said.

Which is to say, it is going to take a lot more than faith to save Lagos from the forces that formed it.

* * *

The people in this book each had their own way of coping with what Fela Kuti called the 'impossibility-ism' of Lagos. Noah used his education and street sense to reach out beyond the shores of his watery home in search of wealthy benefactors—foreigners mostly—who would take pity on its plight and open their wallets. Becoming that link to the outside world and its capacious bank balances, positioning himself as that conduit for the charity that sometimes emanates from them, made him more powerful than almost anyone else in his marginal lagoon settlement. He now has a local council seat. Uju overcame her obvious gender disadvantage in the oil business by adopting the alpha female role, never taking no for an answer, not even from her husband, refusing to accept she'd lost even when it really looked as if her risky venture was about to fold, and aggressively networking with the city's most rich and powerful until she became one of them. Her company has expanded into Ghana.

The Overlord of Ajah, Chief Fatai Olumegbon, faced a challenge to his power and authority that the law couldn't make go away. He dealt with it by setting up his own parallel military force of fearless street thugs. Eric overcame his rotten lot on the rubbish dump with brash Lagosian over-confidence, and by relentlessly *living* his dream of being a singer, rather than simply chasing it, to the point where his obstinacy made it a reality. Maybe if the BBC film-makers hadn't turned up on the dump-site to find him singing, he'd still be there. Maybe. But I get the feeling he'd have found some other opportunity with which to pull himself up out of the garbage ditch by his bootstraps. He now runs several small charities, continues his singing and is opening a recording studio in Ajegunle. Kemi managed the ups and downs of Lagos by being always flexible, always adaptable, able to abandon a trade when it was no longer working for her or threatening her life, and focus on another means of making a living. Last year, she married for a third time with a man she hopes might finally make her happy. For Toyin, it was the willingness and ability to use her fists, control her fear and project her ego as big as the menfolk in her gang that enabled her to rise through the ranks of the gangs who control transport in Lagos. She carved out a niche for herself in a habitat defined by violence and intimidation, and when her conscience started to make her recoil from it, she was so well respected in that world that she was able to continue milking it without having to raise her fists much. Sadly, in October 2021, Toyin died from an unknown illness. Her children rushed her to four hospitals in desperation before she was pronounced dead. Her fellow gangsters at the Obalende Bus Terminus were equally devastated. For someone so tough, she touched a lot of people's hearts.

* * *

My quest to find Lagos's spiritual heart took me to far-flung corners of the Supernatural City. It brought me to the mega-churches like Oyedepo's, rising magnificently out of satellite slums; to 'mosques' in the middle of rubbish dumps, where men in their cleanest kaftans prayed on tattered carpets; to shrines for West African gods in jaded apartment blocks reeking of sacrificial blood.

The venues changed, but the underlying anxiety was always the same. The wheel of fortune is spun by forces no human has ever managed to control. Wouldn't *you* want to appease them, if you could?

A NOTE ON SOURCES

All descriptions of places are from my own observations. When they are the scene of action that takes place in the past, I have sometimes modified the description based on reports from my sources or interviewees as to what, if anything, is different about the place now. Occasionally, I have had access to pictures that show how they looked at the time. All events described in these places which I did not witness, including some peripheral 'scene-setting' actions, were told to me by those who did. The description of the Eyo Festival after the death of the King of Lagos, in Chapter 13, is cobbled together from interviews and multiple written sources. All currency conversions from naira into dollars are based on a historical chart giving the rate at that particular time.

A couple of scenes or descriptions in the characters' stories that do not advance the plot have been inserted into the past narrative, when in fact I witnessed them years later. This obviously runs up against the limits of creative interpretation when it comes to non-fiction; so just to be clear: the scenes made no difference to the development of the story, but they did set the scene or reveal character in a way that helps better understand it. They were also faithful to how I recorded them. They are:

The scene in Chapter 2 in which a bus tout jumps onto the side of a bus on Mobolaji Johnson Avenue to extort money off

A NOTE ON SOURCES

the driver. I witnessed that from inside the bus in October 2015. The description of the witchdoctor's shack in which Toyin is treated in Chapter 3 did not come from her, but is a generic one based on several that I have seen.

In Chapter 5, the conversation Eric has after his first day on the dumpsite with Maggy and his other Ajegunle music friends was actually one I overheard them having several years later, in 2014, in what may have been a different bar altogether (though Eric did indeed go with them to an Ajegunle bar on that day). The description of the goats arriving for sacrifice at the witch-doctor Usman Mudi's shrine, Chapter 6, and the description of the shrine itself are based on a visit I made there years later, in 2016. Similarly, the description of the Muslim prayer scene and the description of the Promise Land Café are from a 2016 trip I made with Eric to the dumpsite.

In Chapter 9, the material on Igbo history and Christianity comes from a variety of sources, but especially F. K. Ekechi's 'Colonialism and Christianity in West Africa: the Igbo case, 1900–1915', in *The Journal of African History*, 12:1 (1971); and *Christian Missions in Nigeria,1841–1891*, by J.F. Ade Ajayi (London: Longmans, 1965).

In Chapter 11, the material on Yoruba mythology comes from speaking to various custodians of Yoruba tradition. The story of the Golden Chain of the Sky is fleshed out with reference to *The Origin of Life on Earth: An African Creation Myth*, by David A. Anderson and Sankofa (Mt Airy, MD: Sights Productions, 1991); the subsequent Yoruba creation myth, which was also told to me by Yoruba custodians, draws many of its details from Philip John Neimark's *The Way of the Orisa*, Chapter 6 (New York: HarperOne, 1993). Neimark's book also furnished some of the material about the goddess Osun that appears in Chapter 19. I've spelled orisha (deity) the Caribbean way, rather than how Nigerians (and Neimark) spell it (orisa), because the Caribbean way is more phonetic. I have not done this with Osun (pro-nounced closer to Oshun) because this spelling of her name is so well established in Nigeria.

The history of Lagos told in Chapter 12 (as well as scattered throughout other chapters) likewise draws on several corrobo-rating sources, but most prominently, *History of the Peoples of Lagos State*, edited by Ade Adefuye, Babatunde Agiri and Jide Osuntokun (Ikeja: Lantern Books, 1987); *Lagos: The Development of an African City*, edited by A. B. Aderibigbe (Ikeja: Longmans, 1975); Kristin Mann's *Slavery and the Birth of an African City* (Bloomington, IN: Indiana University Press, 2007); Robert Smith's *The Lagos Consulate, 1851–1861* (London: Macmillan, 1978); Ellen Thorp's *Ladder of Bones: The Birth of Modern Nigeria from 1853 to Independence* (London: Jonathan Cape, 1956; Ibadan: Spectrum Books, 2000) and Pierre Verger's 'Les Côtes d'Afrique Occidentale entre Rio Volta et Rio Lagos (1515–1773)'—in Journal de la Société des Africanistes, tome 38, Paris—1968.

At the start of Chapter 13, the description of the ritual used to determine who shall be the Olumegbon of Lagos is mostly drawn from an interview with Chief Fatai Olumegbon himself, in April 2016. He presented some details as 'the kind of thing that is done' in these rituals in general, rather than as part of this specific one. When pressed, he wasn't keen to clarify, so it may be that not all of the details applied to this specific event. I ran with the description anyway.

In Chapters 16–18, my understanding of the Zangbeto and other aspects of traditional Egun culture mostly came from speaking to prominent Makoko residents, but it was also enriched by a conversation with a priest in the Voodoo 'Temple of Pythons' in Ouidah, Benin Republic (one made more memo-rable for my having had a python around my neck for some of it). It was further aided by reading Dominic Okure's 'Symbolism and social control of Zangbeto among the Ogu of Southwestern Nigeria' (PhD at the Institute of African Studies, University of Ibadan, 2016) and Alain Sinou and Bachir Oloude's *Porto Novo, Ville d'Afrique Noire* (Marseille: Parenthèses, 1988).

ACKNOWLEDGEMENTS

Thank you to all the Lagosians who shared their stories, dreams and visions with me. I hope I was accurate in portraying your lives (materially and spiritually).

To my wife, Monica, a fine journalist who, as a Nigerian, understands Lagos better than I ever will, thank you for reading some chapters and for believing in me—not to mention tolerating the huge amount of time that I had to spend sitting in front of a computer to finish this book. Thanks to my mother for correcting some grammar and removing inappropriate slang from several chapters, and to both my parents for showing the sort of enthusiasm only parents can about their offspring's pet projects. Thanks to Antony Goldman, a veritable Nigeria encyclopedia, for coming up with helpful suggestions for some chapters (and helping with a couple of fact-checks). Other people who gave helpful feedback on my initial proposal for this book: Nancy Campbell, Andy Rice, Jonathan Wald, and my agent, Andrew Lownie. To my editor, Russell Martin, thanks for helping me polish the draft while leaving it very much intact. Thanks to Akintunde Disu for some helpful (historical and cultural) suggestions on Part IV. And thank you to Stella Kasrils for some last-minute corrections of Yoruba words. Thank you also to fellow journo Matt Green for a career's worth of general help and advice, and being a good friend.

Lots of Nigerian friends helped shape my understanding of Lagos, but the two that stick most in my mind are Fola Fagbule and Akintunde Disu.